Sue Silberberg is a historian, curator and arts administrator. She was educated at the University of Melbourne, Monash University, Deakin University and the International Centre for the Conservation of Cultural Material (ICCROM). She holds a doctorate in History from the University of Melbourne, where she has been a research fellow at the eScholarship Research Centre. Previously Silberberg was a museum curator and director in London and Victoria, specialising in historic buildings. She held senior government positions within the arts and was the director of the Cultural Festival for the 2006 Melbourne Commonwealth Games.

A Networked Community

Jewish Melbourne in the Nineteenth Century

Sue Silberberg

MELBOURNE
UNIVERSITY
PRESS

To my sons Louis and Ben

MELBOURNE UNIVERSITY PRESS
An imprint of Melbourne University Publishing Limited
Level 1, 715 Swanston Street, Carlton, Victoria 3053, Australia
mup-contact@unimelb.edu.au
www.mup.com.au

Text design and typesetting by J&M Typesetting
Cover design by Philip Campbell Design
Printed in Australia by McPherson's Printing Group

 A catalogue record for this
book is available from the
National Library of Australia

9780522876345 (paperback)
9780522876338 (hardback)
9780522876352 (ebook)

Contents

Introduction

In 1860 Nathaniel Levi, head covered and swearing on an Old Testament, was the first Jewish parliamentarian to take his seat in Victoria.[1] Levi, a native of Liverpool, in many ways exemplified the typical settler of nineteenth-century Melbourne. Born to middle-class parents, originating from and educated in a regional English city, Levi had been first attracted to the Californian goldfields, but after parental intervention he postponed the journey in favour of a 'temporary' sojourn in Victoria.[2] Realising quickly that greater prosperity could be achieved through commerce than through mining, Levi established a number of manufacturing and commercial enterprises. As a parliamentarian, as founder, trustee and president of the Chamber of Manufacturers, and as president of the Melbourne Hebrew Congregation, he attests, like many of his generation, to the integrated position felt by Anglo-Jewry in the Australian colonies.[3]

Jews have been present from the outset of Australia's colonisation and members of the community have been at the forefront of settlement in many of the Australian colonies. In what was to become Victoria, Jews were sponsors of the Port Phillip Association, investors in land at the first land sales, and early settlers across the district. Although the Jewish community of Australia has always been small (throughout the nineteenth century it constituted approximately 0.5 per cent of the population), members have participated widely in public life, perhaps the most high profile being Sir Isaac Isaacs, appointed the first Australian-born governor-general in 1931, and Sir John Monash, commander of the Australian troops in the First World War, while architects such as Nahum Barnet and developers such as Benjamin Fink were instrumental in shaping the fabric of Melbourne.

The Melbourne of the 1840s in which the first Jewish settlers found themselves was a small town, a mixture of free settlers and those for whom immigration had been under sentence—convicts and ex-convicts—establishing an economy founded on the production of wool and supported by mercantile interests. Melbourne was established at a time of vast European migration, and the discovery of gold in 1851 stimulated a flow of new colonists, transforming the population and its economy. Included in this mass migration were several thousand primarily Anglo-Jews, settling on this new frontier in the burgeoning city of Melbourne, which quickly rose to be one of the wealthiest cities in the world.

These Jewish settlers fashioned a society that was at once integrated in the wider community and proudly Jewish, emphatically positioning themselves as equal citizens of the metropolis. They expressed the values of nineteenth-century Jewry—'distinct, rather than abnormal'—considering themselves a part of 'the ethnic heterogeneity' of the colony.[4] This identification was overlaid with that of an international perspective developed through their diasporic history. Jews are considered 'quintessential cosmopolitans—a transnational community that was at home everywhere (and nowhere)'.[5] For those arriving in Melbourne, their British birth provided a normalcy of settlement and a shared settlement experience, expressed through strong and repeated loyalty to Britain and her empire; yet their cosmopolitan values allowed an outlook and connections independent of those of other British settlers. These proved beneficial not only for personal and professional gain, but were also employed in the international positioning of this emergent society. A tiny community, these Jews influenced the development of the city intellectually and physically: as arbiters of public policy and public opinion, designers and builders, politicians, newspaper proprietors, international correspondents, businessmen and financiers. As with other Jewish communities in the large centres of the world, they responded to the freedoms of an emancipated society, maintaining their religious beliefs while manifesting contemporary social values and fashionable appearance.

As British settlers, or immigrants to a British colonial experiment, these settlers understood themselves to be part of the British Empire, but this very 'Britishness' was formed from a variety of global forces, which drew settlers from across the world to form a new British colony in the Antipodes and bringing with them a new sense of connectedness outside that of the wider society. Bearing these frameworks in mind, this book considers how an acculturated Jewish community, settling as equal citizens in a new society, created an identity and Jewish community reflective of their values and aspirations. As engaged citizens, this group used its considerable networks to influence the intellectual and physical fabric of the city. This book therefore pays critical attention to the ways in which this acculturated community came to a novel settler society without pre-existing communal institutions. It further considers how the institutions they created and their social interactions exhibited their values, how they assisted in the intellectual and physical formation of Melbourne by employing the networks of empire and of the Jewish diaspora, and how they ultimately became active participants in framing a new and wealthy society.

Urbanism for Jews has been a multifaceted beast. It has been structured as a space of confinement in ghettos and *mellah*, transforming in the nineteenth century into a place of promise and modernity. Yet it has also simultaneously been a threat to Jewish identity and a stimulation to the theological reimagining of culture and religion through the emergence of new pluralistic forms of Judaism. This dichotomy has led scholars to see an interdependence between urbanisation and secularisation.[6] For Jews and Christians, urbanisation impacted on their observation and connection to their religious practices. It has been argued that urbanisation changed not only social structures but also the idea of 'religion' itself, its perception and practice in the modern world.[7] While in the Christian world, from the mid eighteenth century expanding urbanism coincided with a decline in religious attendance in western Europe.[8]

Similarly, the emancipation of Jews in the two great urban centres of European Jewry, London and Amsterdam, allowed participation in the distractions of the modern world, without their Jewish communities abandoning their religious affiliation.[9] These were also cities with significant Sephardi populations, communities whose historic migrations had resulted in experience on the margins of two religions. For many scholars, Amsterdam and London are not central to the narrative of Jewish urbanism; rather, the central urban experience is Germany, with Berlin epitomising the model of urban Jewish modernity. This has been retrospectively perceived within the framework of the waves of anti-Semitism culminating in the Holocaust. This model equates urbanism with the abandonment of Judaism and Jewish values, negating the specific circumstances of time and place. The model often perceives the threats to the community, rather than appreciating issues of communal sustainability. Importantly, urban centres provided educational opportunities unavailable in small homogenous rural communities. The changes brought about by modernity need not be a threat, they could be central to new developments in reclaiming and expanding new territories for Judaism and the Jewish experience.[10]

In pre-emancipatory societies Jews were excluded from formal participation in political life as 'their political status was inseparable from their religious status. There was no Judaism outside the Judaism of the *kehillah*'[11] and the *kehillah* was structurally responsible for a number of legal, social and philanthropic activities. No community is static, as witnessed in the loosening of rabbinic authority, brought about through the power exerted by wealthy merchants and court Jews.[12] In Australia, South Africa, England, the Americas and other parts of the English-speaking world, religious affiliation was a private and personal affair, without a requirement for formal affiliation. In societies where Jews were not excluded, new opportunities for a variety of interactions and social involvement offered alternatives for members. If we accept Berkovitz's assertion that acculturation was a part of the diaspora experience, then we can consider the distinct responses by communities, without judging these as destructive of Jewish identity.[13]

Australian Jewry provides a unique illustration of the urban Jewish experience. As Jews flocked to the large cities of Europe in the nineteenth century, Melbourne became an alternative for those brave enough to sail vast distances into the relatively unknown. Unlike the settler society of America or the large cities of Europe, where the new arrivals came from small rural communities, Victoria was settled by predominantly urban English Jews. In contrast, for many European immigrants, England had been a stepping stone of forward migration to the colonies.[14] For some, this was an ongoing and peripatetic existence, moving between the English-speaking colonies, seeking economic improvement and familial connections.

The 'East European School of Jewish History' has been characterised as holding a negative view of modernity, and a belief that the survival of Judaism can only be achieved through a single identity model.[15] In contrast, this book argues that modernity and emancipation led to new conceptualisations of the civic role of Jewry and their influence in creating a new colonial society, and a religious community that reflected their engaged outlook.

Notes

1   L.E. Fredman, 'Nathaniel Levi,' *Australian Dictionary of Biography* (1974), http://adb. anu.edu.au/biography/levi-nathaniel-4015.

2   Hilary L. Rubinstein, *The Jews in Australia, a Thematic History* (William Heinemann Australia, Port Melbourne, 1991), 103.

3   Parliament of Victoria, 'Nathaniel Levi', accessed 3 May 2012, <http://www. parliament.vic.gov.au/re-member/bioregfull.cfm?mid=513>.

4   Derek Jonathan Penslar, *Shylock's Children: Economics and Jewish Identity in Modern Europe* (University of California Press, Berkeley, 2001), 134.

5   Michael L. Miller and Scott Ury, *Cosmopolitanism, Nationalism and the Jews of East Central Europe* (Routledge, Oxford, 2015), 8.

6   Tobias Metzler, 'Secularization and Pluralism: Urban Jewish Culture in Early Twentieth-Century Berlin', *Journal of Urban History* 37, no. 6 (2011), 872. Others have seen a growth in the construction of churches and synagogues throughout the nineteenth-century; see Anthony Steinhoff, 'Nineteenth-century Urbanisation as Sacred Process: Insights from German Strasbourg', ibid., 834–837.

7   Lucian Hölscher, 'Secularisation and Urbanisation in the Nineteenth Century: An Interpretive Model', in Hugh McLeod (ed.), *European Religion in the Age of Great Cities 1830–1930* (Routledge, London, 1995), 263.

8   Hugh McLeod, *Secularisation in Western Europe, 1848–1914* (St Martin's Press, New York, 2000); Owen Chadwick, *The Secularization of the European Mind in the Nineteenth Century* (Cambridge University Press, Cambridge, 1977).
9   Steven M. Lowenstein, 'Was Urbanization Harmful to Jewish Tradition and Identity in Germany?', in Ezra Mendelsohn (ed.), *People of the City: Jews and the Urban Challenge* (Oxford University Press, Oxford, 1999), 80–91.
10 Metzler, 'Secularization and Pluralism', 872.
11 Todd M. Endelman, 'Secularization and the Origins of Jewish Modernity—on the Impact of Urbanization and Social Transformation', *Simon-Dubnow Insitute Year Book* VI (2007), 161.
12 Jacob Katz, *Out of the Ghetto; the Social Background of Jewish Emancipation, 1770–1870* (Harvard University Press, Cambridge, Mass., 1973), 31.
13 Jay R. Berkovitz, 'Acculturation and Integration in Eighteenth-Century Metz', *Jewish History* 24, nos 3–4 (2010), 272.
14 Tobias Brinkman, '"German Jews?", Reassessing the History of Nineteenth-Century Jewish Immigrants in the United States', in Ava F. Kahn and Adam Mendelsohn (eds), *Transnational Traditions, New Perspectives on American Jewish History* (Wayne State University, Detroit, 2014), 149.
15 Michael Clark, *Albion and Jerusalem: The Anglo-Jewish Community in the Post-Emancipation Era* (Oxford University Press, Oxford, 2009), 12.

Chapter 1

Jewish Space and Place

To celebrate the Duke of Edinburgh's visit to Victoria in 1867, a grand (male only) levée was held in the Exhibition Building, 'such a one as has never been seen in the colony before. All who desired to honour the Prince as we have honoured none who have yet stood on Victorian shores, passed before him yesterday'.[1] Given equal entrée with the major dignitaries including senior parliamentarians, judges and the heads of the diverse Christian churches was 'the Head of the Hebrew Congregation'.[2] The formalities of the event included the presentation by religious and cultural organisations of forty-three addresses to the Prince, including those of the Melbourne and East Melbourne Hebrew Congregations, both of which expressed their loyalty and attachment to the Sovereign. The *Argus* published less than half of these, but significantly reported those of the two synagogues in third and fourth place in their list, behind the Anglicans and Presbyterians and before the Wesleyans and Congregational Churches (there was no listing of any Catholic address).

Included in the 'general presentations' at the levée were sixty or seventy members of the Melbourne Jewish community, including the rabbinical leaders of both Melbourne synagogues, five men who were or would become members of the Victorian Parliament and a cross-section of the Jewish community, from the sons of convicts to members of some of the wealthiest Jewish families in Britain. Two weeks later in Ballarat, Prussian-born Emanuel Steinfeld hosted the Prince in his capacity as mayor of East Ballarat. In return the Prince presented a silver claret jug to Steinfeld, commissioned from the Victorian goldsmith William Edwards and marked 'by appointment to His Royal Highness'. Those attending these events had been born in England, Scotland, Germany, Poland, Russia, the United States, Jamaica and Gibraltar.

Ashkenazi and Sephardi, they represented the social and cultural diversity of the local Jewish community. Social acceptance, both as Jews and as members of a 'respectable class', was markedly different from that which many of these individuals would have expected in their place of birth, but significantly reflects the sense of place that this small community had forged in Melbourne.

The mid nineteenth century saw the culmination of the assertion of rights and emancipatory processes concurrently taking place in many parts of the Jewish world. Those settling in Melbourne brought with them their knowledge of this struggle and their encounters or otherwise in emancipated societies. Jews in Melbourne did not suffer from formal exclusion or restriction and the community endured limited anti-Semitism. These conditions coalesced to create opportunities in a new colony, providing for engaged forms of intellectual, political and physical space.

No place has a fixed identity. Invasions, migration (both forced and voluntary), changes to national boundaries and other geopolitical upheavals influence and create identity and these are reinforced through evolving traditions, cultures and language. A consequence of the complex history of Jewish migration has been the formation of local identities shaped by the internal and external connections maintained across time and place.[3] Migration creates a reciprocal process. For minority communities, adaptation to their new home results in varying levels of assimilation and acculturation; while for the host society, national identity is subtly changed by the presence of resettled and minority communities.[4]

Jewish self-consciousness has centred on 'exile', both as a physical and a geopolitical identity. Exile created a diaspora, a spatial reality identified with a lack of space, a loss of space and a loss of control over space.[5] This was an exile in which Jews were politically and socially inferior, lacking sovereignty over land, disconnected in time and place. 'My heart is in the East [Jerusalem], my body in the extreme West [Spain].' Thus Judah Halevi described a 'space of the heart, a space of the body, and in between them a void'.[6]

This is not just a sociopolitical existence, but also a religious one. From a Christian perspective the Jewish lack of a homeland was closely connected to concepts of Christian redemption and the relationship to the divine.[7] A Jewish diaspora has existed for millennia and Jews have been characterised by their high degree of mobility and as a globalised community, reflecting the experience and settlement patterns encountered and adapted through this journey. This has also led to the loss of space, both through destruction and abandonment and from an intellectual perspective, compounded by a focus on 'anti-spatial' issues: religion, history and language.[8]

Current thinking challenges this perception, considering the peripatetic nature of the community as a more complex experience. This can be seen as a duality in the understanding of space, that of the physical location and that of spaces of reference, combining to create a Jewish spatial experience. Jews have traditionally not been constrained to the nation in which they resided; rather they responded (or were forced to respond) to the legal frameworks, expulsions, changes in economic conditions and at times riots and massacres that were encountered, hoping to find new opportunities in other areas.[9] This experience was transnational and multi-rooted, uninterested in the borders between political entities and identifying space through emotional, familial, cultural or economic constructs.[10] Thus, as Jews considered history outside the Christian linear progression towards Grace, so too was their connection to a particular location understood from a fundamentally different perspective.

Anglo and Australian Jewish history is that of communities epitomised by global and local connections. While their Jewish identity and communal affiliation have not followed a single format of observance or social and political interactions, these have been framed by emancipation, historical experience and determined by particular concepts of space and identification with place.

Intellectual Space, Religious Space

The land of Israel and Jerusalem in particular are the historical and metaphysical centre of Judaism. This is a perception of space that has fundamentally shaped Jewish practice and Jewish thinking, and provided an opportunity for a collective memory of shared 'thought and remembrance formed and maintained there through the ages'.[11] Space was of fundamental importance to ancient Jewish life, represented in the symbolism of the structure and layout of the Temple in Jerusalem and its hierarchy of religious significance.[12] This spatial imperative was transferred through the rabbinic interpretations of the Talmud into abstract and symbolic representations in religious practice and religious ritual. Space becomes a physical expression of religious practices, reflected in the built form in permanent structures such as synagogues, in theoretical forms such as the *eruv* or in the more ephemeral, in the *Sukkah*, built and demolished annually for the festival of Sukkot.

Whereas traditional notions of space focus on a specific location, ritual and religious spaces create a symbolic place of belonging. Synagogues are both emblematic and physical spaces, defined by their liturgical function, providing meaning and memory for the participant: 'religion is expressed in symbolic forms that unfold and cohere in space. This condition alone guarantees its continued existence.'[13] Synagogues and synagogue architecture have been public manifestations of Jewish identity. Prior to emancipation, synagogues were characteristically small places for Jews to gather, providing space for study and worship, to meet socially and to conduct community business. These tended to be discrete from the outside, but could contain lavish interiors. Post-emancipation, throughout Europe, Britain and the New World, synagogues reflected a confident public style. Presented as monuments to emancipation, a public articulation of the new 'spirit of Judaism', these buildings were designed to present the Jewish community as an integrated presence in the nation.

Places of remembrance also have a duality in Jewish thinking. Traditionally these have been considered places of destruction, while the core of Judaism itself forms a site of memory, delivered through the liturgical calendar and the Talmud, delivering 'the Mobius strip of the collective and the individual, the sacred and the profane'.[14] Places of remembrance and destruction are particularly poignant for Jewish communities, reinforcing the image of placelessness and the metaphor of the Wandering Jew. Places of memory exist as the real places are lost.[15] These are often spaces of postwar experience, death camps, Holocaust memorials and extinct ghettos.

Remembered space can pertain to Jewish themes that are superimposed and defined by non-Jewish agents, creating a nostalgic 'constructed cultural space' and a homogenous community identity.[16] Lost Jewish space can also become a major tourist attractor, as has happened in Prague, where the once thriving Jewish community has been reduced from a pre-war population of 96,000 to 1600, but where the Jewish quarter of Prague is now marketed as a major cultural attraction with synagogue tours, visits to cemeteries, museums and historic sites.

Jews have long been considered an urban people and literary descriptions of city life can be traced back to the biblical Babel and forward to modern Jewish literary writing, often 'preoccupied' by its urban setting.[17] Space conceptualised through text can reposition a community in a place, defining its identity through this relationship.[18] Text 'becomes a space in which collective identity can be formed without territory and consequently it can be a metaphor for exile and homelessness'.[19]

Text allows the imagining of Jewish place and space in many forms—from travelogues to sermons, novels, descriptions of place and rabbinical discourse, signifiers of an urban state of mind.[20] Religious text also provides an abstraction of space, 'neutralising space in the physical sense ... to live in metaphorical places'. As the Talmud and the Bible formed conceptualisations of the Jewish universe and Jewish history, so too were conceptualisation of space created in these writings—the Holy Land with its flora and fauna.[21] Landscape can also be imbued with meaning to create a 'Jewish space' and this is noticeably encountered in the legends of Jewish Poland, where the countryside becomes an element of the geography of the Jewish imagination, giving meaning to place through feelings and beliefs.

This is reinforced through the Judaisation of Slavic placenames providing biblical and homiletic meaning to the stories being told. Here, the importance of names and the meanings ascribed to them are linked to the Bible and rabbinic language of the Talmudic era, endowing a continuum of understandings to the stories and connecting 'sites of memory', preserving the collective memory of Polish Jewry from its settlement to its destruction in the Holocaust.[22] Contemporary textual space is also virtual space, providing a forum for Jewish identity and culture in online blogs and journals.

Lived Space

The models outlined above provide a summary of the theoretical framework of a Jewish conceptualisation of space. This philosophical context is important not merely to understand the intangible perceptions of space, which are at best a lack of interest in the physical manifestations of space, a hypothesis which asserts that we 'interact *through* space and only secondarily *in* space'.[23] This theoretical construct does not fully describe the experience of place of individuals, or how this impacts on community identity and community development. To realise this requires an investigation of the various urban models Jews have known over time.

The perception of Jewish space in the pre-emancipatory world is formed around confined space, that of the ghetto, the *mellah* and the rural *shtetl*. In the conclusion to his 1927 article 'The Ghetto', Louis Wirth describes the ghetto as a 'socio-psychological, as well an ecological phenomenon; for it is not merely a physical fact, but also a state of mind'.[24] Ghettos became the primary urban Jewish experience in much of central and western Europe from the sixteenth century. European Christian attitudes to Jews reflected the different and complex theological arguments concerning the nature of God held by the two religions. Christians believed that Jewish exile was inflicted by God as a punishment for the Jews' repudiation of Jesus as the Messiah and thus, the submission of Jews proved the truth of Christianity. Jews could be tolerated only to the extent that their conversion was to herald the second coming.[25] Over time this ideological propaganda was exploited as a means of excluding Jews from wider Christian society, both as religious dissenters and as economic competitors.[26]

Ghettos have a dual consciousness, that of forced cohabitation and that of a welcoming community in which group traditions are maintained.[27] Jews, like other groups in medieval society, chose to reside near family members and to live in close proximity to the synagogue and other community institutions. Often these places were identified as Jewish areas through placenames and localities: rue des Juifs, Judengasse, Judaeorum.[28] Ghettos initially established as cultural, linguistic or familial spatial groupings developed as an urban form controlled by the community. This voluntary urban structure enabled the subsequent formal segregation and restriction of Jewish residents. Ghettos came to represent a physical 'exile', displacement and exclusion from the wider city; a physical barrier, isolating inhabitants from the rest of the community.[29] The ghetto became a device that could be exploited to restrict economic activity, while ostensibly providing 'incentive' for Jews to convert to Christianity.[30]

In ghettos and in rural shtetls, Jews were considered by the ruling authorities not as individuals but as a 'community' and were governed as such. Marriage, divorce and inheritance became judicial communal matters, and collective responsibility was held for the community's actions. Although subject to civil laws, authority was undertaken under Talmudic law, a legal system employed for civil matters including litigation between individuals.[31]

Jews in ghetto environments were not entirely isolated from the world at large. Rather, they resided on the fringe of two worlds: the internal world of the ghetto and the external space of the majority society from which they were excluded. [32] This forced segregation of the community and provided a self-conscious identity that was at once warm and intimate and tied to an 'inner solidarity' by family life.[33] The ghetto formalised a separation of the economies of the two communities, with Jews engaged in occupations deemed permissible or useful to Christian society, often limited to moneylending or trade.

Initially ghettos were established with adequate areas for the community, but as populations expanded, the space was not increased and they became severely overcrowded and insanitary. Ghettos were also not entirely segregated from the outside world. Within this limited structure there was movement of people for education and business. Renowned religious academies (yeshivas) attracted youth from across Europe, while trade continued. Business connections were maintained at a basic level by pedlars moving goods across regions and throughout the more prosperous realms of upper-class bankers, court agents and purveyors.[34] The Enlightenment and subsequent Jewish emancipation led to the devolution of ghettos in Europe, as formal barriers were removed and increased communication throughout society was achieved.[35]

Throughout the history of the Jewish settlement of eastern Europe (and in Turkey), following the expulsions from Spain, Germany, Italy, France and the papal states in the fifteenth and sixteenth centuries, communities were established in Poland, Romania and Russia. Initially as immigrants from western Europe, these newcomers were culturally isolated from the local Jewish community, speaking Judaeo-German (Yiddish) rather than the vernacular of the region. The large number of people migrating in this period resulted in the dominance of these new communities, who imposed their cultural practices and language on the pre-existing Jewish communities.[36] Although strictly restrained in economic and social mobility, with more than 2000 regulations restricting their activity, as with the ghetto dwellers, these eastern European communities were largely self-governed within the constraints placed by the state.[37]

Shtetls were settlements with a Jewish 'centre', in which Jews were the majority of the population, 'a small settlement of less than 300 houses, which dealt mostly in agricultural produce, and at least 40 per cent of whose total urban population was Jewish', and like ghettos these were often overcrowded.[38] There is some debate over the date for the establishment of the first shtetls in a recognisable form, and they were certainly in existence by the eighteenth century if not a century earlier.[39]

Following the partition of Poland in 1772, Tsarina Catherine II further restricted Jewish occupation in her empire, in 1791 creating the Pale of Settlement and in so doing assembling a 1 million square kilometre–restricted zone for the Jewish population, further excluding Jews from civil life. This effectively froze Jewish conditions for the majority of Jews in eastern Europe, socially and physically isolating them from the rest of the population. Outside the Pale in Galicia, Hungary and Romania, shtetl life was less restricted but in all instances 'the shtetl fostered its own language—Yiddish, developed its own culture and took Judaism into new and exotic byways unknown in other parts of the world'.[40]

Education in the shtetl was limited, focused on Talmudic study. The impact of western education and acculturation of western European Jewry was viewed with concern by the orthodox shtetl dweller.[41] Voluntary associations were used to exert social control and maintain social equilibrium and the status quo, and structuring educational and charitable support at a communal level, rather than for the betterment of any one individual. Here, in order to maintain the community and its safety, the needs of the individual were secondary, and these communities did not develop 'aesthetic, athletic or economic' outlets or activities for 'the pleasure of the senses', which might have benefited individuals ahead of the community, creating values whereby the 'community is the brother and guardian of every other'.[42]

The experience of segregated life for the Jewish community was varied, and changes in the philosophical, religious and political expectations of states influenced their treatment. These pressures differed across Europe, reflecting the divergent philosophical and economic developments of east and west. Scholars have differing views on the seclusion that shtetl life imposed. It has been argued that the shtetl isolated Jews less from their neighbours, providing closer contact (although rarely intimate contact) between the two communities.[43] Western European Jewry was more likely to be urbanised and more intellectually integrated into the wider community than that of the east, reflecting ideas and social values of post-Renaissance thought. The Jewish communities of Russia, Poland and parts of Romania, however, existed in rural societies, isolated from the broad European intellectual ferment.

In the post-emancipation period and especially after a sharp rise in government-condoned anti-Semitism from the 1880s, eastern European migrants began fleeing their homes. Throughout England and particularly London and the manufacturing centres of the midlands, in France, Berlin and New York, these 'foreign Jews' crowded into the Jewish working-class areas of cities. In post-emancipation communities, these migrants were themselves seen as the 'other', uneducated, not speaking the language of their host country and espousing an ethnic solidarity to their place of birth, an attitude that was perceived as being disloyal to their new country.[44] These areas of voluntary association were themselves seen as ghettos, segregating communities by economics and poverty, language and customs as well as by occupation.

In many parts of the Muslim world, ancient Jewish communities existed that were established prior to the rise of Islam, with some dating back to the Babylonian exile in the fifth century BCE. As Islam spread across the Middle East and North Africa, Islamic theology imposed structural systems on society, informing the urban fabric of cities while manifesting local ethnic responses. The treatment of the Jewish community in Islamic countries varied greatly from Europe, based on the divergent theological views of Christianity and Islam in regards to Judaism.

Islamic law considered all non-Muslims (Jewish, Christian, Hindu or Zoroastrian) living in Muslim countries as *dhimmi*, protected yet inferior communities.[45] The status of *dhimmi* allows residence, non-forced conversions and protection in return for tax and other prohibitions (which were not constantly enforced), but could include prohibitions on the repair or rebuilding of houses of worship and the wearing of special attire.[46]

Morocco had the largest Jewish population in the Islamic world and much scholarship has been invested in understanding the particular urban response to the coexistence of the two populations. Morocco was the only North African nation outside Ottoman rule and 90 per cent of its large Jewish population lived in urban or semi-urban areas.[47] The Jewish community had a dual ethnicity initially established during the Phoenician era, comprising an indigenous Jewish community and later a significant Sephardi population, migrating (as did many Muslims) after the expulsions from the Iberian Peninsula in the fifteenth and sixteenth centuries. This Sephardi population itself was complex, with a transnational identity maintained for centuries. Further, elements of the Sephardi community were *Conversos*, who moved backwards and forwards between the two societies, before settling as either Jews (in Morocco) or Catholics (in Spain). This oscillation established a Portuguese or Spanish identity for generations.

Islamic cities are defined by their various 'quarters' and the overlapping nature of these areas.[48] Quarters could be based on economic, social or ethnic foundations, although these were generally ethnically and socially diverse. Moroccan cities developed a tripartite plan with the *kassbah* for the ruling class, the *medina* for the Muslim population and in some areas, the *mellah* for the Jews.[49] The *mellah* was traditionally a walled and gated area, located close to the royal compound of the city, regulated through Jewish intermediaries, rather than by Islamic officials.[50] The location was justified as protection for the inhabitants and to be convenient for the Sultan and his employees, many of whom lived in the space.[51]

The *mellah* was a unique response to this dual Jewish and Muslim population, developing a particular urban fabric for the cities in which it was imposed. *Mellahs* were not built consistently throughout the country and differed in urban form, depending on the demography, political and environmental situations of each place.[52] The first *mellah* was established in Fez in 1438, imposed, according to legend, after civil strife erupted when Jews were accused of putting wine in the lamps of the mosque. Similar stories of religious deviance justified the building of *mellahs* in other cities.[53]

While a more prosaic rationale for the establishment of *mellah* was as a response to local circumstances, particularly population pressures brought about by the integration of large numbers of Jews and Muslims from Spain (20,000 Jews were estimated to have arrived in Fez alone) into a society with a fragile ecology. This integration was hindered by communal conflict resulting from Catholic proselytisation, particularly on the Jewish community.[54] The creation of the *mellah* becomes a concrete expression of the theory of the *dhimma*, which defines the non-Muslim within the state, protecting yet humiliating a community. Thus segregation became a judicial response to maintaining the purity of the 'Islamic' space and assigning the role of the Jewish community as exceptional, rather than an integrated element in the wider society.[55]

International trading particularly by the Sephardi and Italian communities enabled the development of a new urban experience and a new perception for Jews of their place in the world. In the seventeenth and eighteenth centuries, these traders created thriving Jewish communities in non-Jewish cities of the Mediterranean, the Adriatic, along the Atlantic seaboards and later the Black Sea.[56] As a diaspora united through trade and familial ties they 'extended the boundaries of the Jewish world and imagined its contours'.[57] As post-expulsion Sephardic communities (including many *Conversos* and New

Christians), they had familiarity and interactions with the wider society prior to fleeing Spain, Portugal and the Inquisition and brought these experiences and expectations to their new homes.[58] These refugees from the Inquisition were permitted to settle as Spanish and Portuguese merchants in mercantile ports such as Salonika, Trieste, Amsterdam, Bordeaux and London, in the Dutch colonies of the New World and later in Odessa.[59] Here they were granted privileges and liberties, utilising their diasporic connections to enable international trade.

In an era before international banking, the large Sephardi diaspora allowed the communities to develop sophisticated transnational trade networks, connected through family and friends, enabling them to trade internationally with people they knew and trusted. In the New World, societies displayed greater flexibility in their rules than did their imperial homelands.[60] In the seventeenth century, Port Jews were influential in the establishment and mainte-nance of trade between Amsterdam and the Dutch colonies of South America.[61]

Whether *Conversos* or New Christian reconverts to Judaism, or Jews directly escaping the Inquisition, the experience, interactions and confidence of these communities provided opportunities for new ways to acculturate in wider societies while maintaining an independent Jewish identity.[62]

Developing Urbanism

The proliferation of Enlightenment ideas coincided with the spread of urbani-sation in western European cities resulting in changes to Jewish interaction in an urban environment. Gradually civil and political restrictions were lifted, including the removal of barriers to education, trade and place of residence. Communities strove to retain their Jewish identity, adapting and adjusting to the new conditions.[63] In Germany, the *Haskalah* endeavoured to merge Enlightenment views with self-awareness and Jewish intellectual study to develop an 'ideology of modernisation', while in England, Jews asserted their rights to participate in modern secular society while maintaining a Jewish identity.[64]

Acculturation within the fabric of western urban centres followed similar patterns, with local manifestations based on communal institutions, education, occupation and residential patterns. It has been posited that 'the degree to which Jews were involved in the early growth of a city and had achieved a notable and respected place in public and private life … directly influenced how later generations of Jews were received'.[65] Acceptance and acculturation acted as a 'pull' factor influencing the settlement choices of later immigrants.[66]

Newly found social mobility allowed Jews to move into the middle class and to the suburbs, distancing themselves from any identification with the 'ghetto'. The ghetto became identified as a place of fear and pressure that trau-matised its community. Reaction to the ghetto experience was expressed through 'antagonistic acculturation', defining identity and behaviours in contrast to previous modes of existence.[67] Overwhelmingly, urban Jewries felt that a certain communal vigilance was required to protect them from under-lying anti-Semitism. This intrinsic fear tempered outward behaviour, religious expression and notably as late nineteenth-century immigration from eastern Europe increased, was reflected in the concern for the 'otherness' of immi-grants' habits, appearances and values.[68]

Throughout the modern world, Catholics, Protestants and Jews brought their values to new urban environments and all engaged in debates, defining the role, function and place of religion in urbanised society.[69] Jews were at the vanguard of adopting modernity while also ensuring that their heritage was retained, 'developing new modalities of identity and community consistent with and unique to modernity'.[70] As with the wider community, urbanisation led to a decrease in the adherence to strict forms of religious observance.[71] Judaism was not abandoned, and like their Christian middle-class compatriots, Jews adhered to religious traditions, which adapted to reflect evolving values and cultural conditions.[72]

Communities developed new forms of Jewish solidarity: secular, ethnic and associational. Anglo-Jewry combined a pride in being English with a pride in their Jewishness, but in this lay a tacit agreement whereby Jews would be accepted in return for a level of cultural integration.[73] For many immi-grants, particularly for those in America and Europe, secular Judaism took the form of nationalism, Zionism, socialism and the labour movement.[74] Urbanism and high population density profoundly altered the way urban populations interacted, reducing connection to moral and cultural communities.

For European Jewish middle-class women, traditionally exempt from studying Jewish law, these new circumstances provided them with the oppor-tunities to speak and read in the vernacular, simultaneously learning social graces that would allow them to move in wider society.

Emancipation in England

Jewish settlers to Melbourne predominantly came from England, or were increasingly Australian-born children of English parents previously resident in other colonies. And for Anglo-Jewry, their settlement coincided with the final stages of political emancipation in Britain.

The readmission of the Jews to England in the 1650s happened without formal charter or decree, with the community petitioning for readmission as 'dwellers here with the same equalness and convenience which your inland born subjects do enjoy'.[75] These civil and legal rights were never formally clarified, nor were ancient and restrictive statutes such as the *Statutum de Judaismo* of 1275 ever revoked.[76] No charter or legislation regularising Jewish residence was established, leaving Jews in an ambivalent civil and social status in a statutory void in which some latitude was shown.

As early as 1667 Jews were first permitted to give evidence in a court of law, sworn on an Old Testament, and flexibility was provided to accommodate Jewish witnesses who were not required to appear on the Sabbath, and Jewish marital practices remained distinct from those of their Christian brethren. At the same time, Jews were excluded economically by guilds and trades. Non-British-born Jews were unable to purchase land and most importantly, until 1830, Jews were debarred as Freemen of the City of London, preventing them from operating there commercially. The Oath of Abjuration effectively disqualified Jews from several other civil roles including university study or teaching, as members of the judiciary or parliament.[77]

The motivations for Anglo-Jewish emancipation differed from those in other parts of Europe. Nineteenth-century England was a tolerant society of prevailing liberalism formed from centuries of religious turmoil following the Reformation. The assertion of authority by the Church of England, as the established Church, resulted in a variety of philosophical and theological debates. Of particular importance were John Locke's views on a separation of state and religion, while the Catholic and non-conformist churches similarly fought to gain greater civil and political rights. England was not philosophically isolated, and the ideas expressed in the American and French constitutions, the impact of the American War of Independence and the Declaration of the Rights of Man also played a part in changing values in British society. With the repeal of the Test and Corporations Act in 1828 and the introduction of the Roman Catholic Relief Act the following year, Jews remained the only segment of society excluded from political life due to their faith.

Many Protestants also considered the historic mistreatment of Jews by the Catholic Church as exemplifying un-Christian behaviour, which they wanted to prevent recurring.[78] Supported particularly by the Quakers and Unitarians, political agitation continued for full Jewish recognition.[79] As the population of British-born Jewry rose, there was a corresponding lessening of the rigid social constraints between Jews and Christians. New metropolitan diversions such as theatres, coffee houses, Masonic lodges and other social milieus presented opportunities for increased interaction. Although anti-Semitism existed, particularly in private among the upper class, in public Jews were treated as equal.[80] Civil restrictions took longer to be dismantled and gradual reform occurred in the period 1830–58, the final act of emancipation deemed to be the accession of Lionel de Rothschild to his seat in parliament, a seat that he had won eleven years earlier, but was unable to take due to the religiously restrictive nature of the oath.

A self-perception of 'exile' was particularly acute for Yiddish-speakers, who lacked access to the vernacular, whereas Anglo-Jewry's mastery of English provided a sense of intellectual and social connectedness. Proficiency in English helped Jewish philosophers engage with the intellectual debates of their day. Independent of the *Haskalah*, and in the wider English Enlightenment, English Jews fashioned their own philosophical and Anglo-centric views. Anglo-Jewish writers challenged conventional ways of thinking, creating and examining religious, philosophical, social and political issues.[81] Responding to religious reform and cultural redefinition shaped a new conceptualisation of religion, a concern for 'identity and definitions of Judaism', and a reassessment of rabbinic authority.[82] In engaging with notions of modernity, synagogue practices were amended and redesigned to address the externals of observance rather than liturgical ritual itself.[83] Unlike on the continent, the wealthiest (and by implication most acculturated) members of the community exerted change while remaining within Orthodoxy.[84]

Jews were validated 'not on the grounds of their Jewish identity but on the basis of their conformity to the values and manners of bourgeois English society', and in response Jews attempted to create a cohesiveness and compatibility between Englishness and Jewishness.[85] Britain was fundamentally a religious society, which provided the space and climate in which Jews could express their religious identity and 'justify adherence to Judaism'.[86] This was an expression of an ethnic identity compatible with participation in a secular world, while still remaining loyal to Judaism; tempering Judaism with a sense of middle-class propriety to create an orthodoxy with 'piety and dignity, modernity of method with strict adherence to traditions'.[87] This sometimes directed the community into an ambiguous position.[88]

To counter the anti-Semitic rhetoric that perceived Jewish culture as exclusive and insular, the community avoided conspicuous manifestations of 'Jewishness'. This included insecurity around overtly Jewish institutions and sometimes tempered the solving of communal issues.[89] A similar unease was expressed by British politicians, who, unlike their Australian counterparts, were careful to be identified as MPs first and of the Jewish persuasion second.[90] Nonetheless, English Jews maintained a strong attachment to institutions that epitomised Jewishness—synagogue, welfare agencies and family cohesion.[91]

The tenor of English–Jewish interactions had been established by the acculturated position of the Sephardi community that resettled from Holland, a community familiar with operating in a diverse environment. This fluency stemmed from the ethnic diversity of Iberian society, which had led to a cross-fertilisation of intellectual contact between the communities. The Jewish community's experience as *Conversos* and through the subsequent displacement resulting from their expulsion, further expanded intellectual contacts, and resulted in an education with a secular rather than a religious focus. This provided the new 'Spanish' and 'Portuguese' traders in British society with an outlook markedly in contrast to the culturally and socially isolated Jewish communities of central and eastern Europe.[92]

The early Sephardi community was comprised of merchants engaged in wholesale and international markets. Their business initially centred upon the exportation of English wool and the importation of bullion, later expanding to other products.[93] As merchants they traded with people they knew and trusted in the Sephardi communities of the Mediterranean, Turkey, the Caribbean and the Atlantic colonies. As with those who established themselves in the Caribbean, uncertainty of nationality worked to their advantage, opportunistically allowing circumvention of the restrictions on commerce with Spain and taxes due by British merchants on imported goods. The expertise that this international Sephardi trade brought afforded a complexity and sophistication of mercantile competence that was otherwise lacking in the English market. [94]

This initial foothold of Jewish immigration to England provided an opportunity for other Jewish communities to follow. From the seventeenth century Ashkenazi immigrants were drawn to the more favourable social and political conditions of England. The initial Ashkenazi community was founded by immigrants from central Europe, poor, unskilled, propertyless, Yiddish-speaking, with a religious rather than a secular education, immigrants escaping poverty and degradation. By 1720 this community had become numerically dominant. It has been estimated that six thousand mainly Ashkenazi immigrants settled in the first half of the eighteenth century and a further eight to ten thousand prior to the turmoil of the French Revolution and the Napoleonic Wars, at which point immigration virtually ceased.[95]

When immigration resumed in the post-Napoleonic period, it was marked by a significant demographic shift. These later immigrants echoed the economic, social and religious changes that were taking place in Germany, producing émigrés who had been educated outside a strict and limited Jewish education.[96] These later immigrants were arriving for economic reasons and to flee the cultural and religious hostility rapidly mounting in central Europe. The rapid urbanisation of the German-speaking areas provided a level of acculturation and education which resembled that of their earlier Sephardi counterparts. Unlike the previous generation, obliged to seek unskilled employment as hawkers and pedlars, the next generation arrived with trade experience and occasionally university or other professional training.[97]

Throughout the eighteenth century, Sephardim, particularly from Mediterranean countries, continued to migrate in small numbers, and their demographic makeup changed substantially.[98] Whereas the first waves had been prosperous merchants and those fleeing the Inquisition, the later Sephardim were from impoverished communities.[99] The two remained culturally and socially differentiated, referred to as 'German' and 'Portuguese', maintaining separate synagogues, schools and rarely intermarrying. Although the Sephardi community was numerically smaller, well into the nineteenth century they were disproportionately represented in Anglo-Jewry's elite.

Occupational exclusion, particularly from universities and professions, resulted in the slow evolution of a Jewish middle class. This exclusion was exacerbated by the community's concentration in London rather than in the developing centres of the north. By the early nineteenth century, Anglo-Jewry was divided between a small wealthy elite and a large lower class of pedlars, hawkers and small tradespeople.[100] The two groups not only inhabited differing worlds but also pursued alternate paths towards acculturation and integration. Most initially commenced on the lowest economic rung as hawkers, glaziers or other street traders, engaged in small-scale occupations, selling oranges, lemons, spectacles, costume jewellery, dried rhubarb, pencils, inexpensive framed pictures, as well as items such as slippers, cakes, glassware, sealing wax and buttons. In 1800, of an estimated Jewish population in London of 15,000, nearly 1500 were 'old clothes men', hoping that through street trade they could amass sufficient capital to establish themselves as shopkeepers.

Education was perceived as a formula for economic and social improvement. For the wealthier members of Anglo-Jewish society, this was a social concern tempered by self-interest, anxious that poverty-stricken Jews could potentially sully the community's reputation, stifling social advancement and political emancipation.[101] In England, where anti-Semitism was less overt, middle-class families educated their children in both newly established private Jewish schools (which taught secular subjects) as well as the non-Jewish boarding-school environments, with Jewish education provided by private tutors.[102] Here the middle class considered that providing a comprehensive Jewish education was a negative and backward ambition, believing that to achieve full emancipation and integration into English society required the removal of all barriers between the Jewish and non-Jewish communities.

This new focus on education aimed to provide occupational skills for the working class, equipping them for employment and ensuring that the community produced responsible and productive members of British society. In London, poor Jewish children were catered for in the Jews' Free School, whose population rapidly rose from its establishment in 1817 to be the largest school in Europe. By 1863 the school catered for 1800 students, with similar institutions created in Manchester and Birmingham. These schools provided only minimal Jewish education and most students graduated with an ability to read Hebrew and an elementary knowledge of the Torah but little other Jewish education.[103] This did not prevent an innovative Jewish life developing, or a sustained dialogue with the dominant culture. 'Jewish modernization was never inarticulate or non-reflective … [but] a constant negotiation and reciprocity between persons of variegated economic, social and intellectual standing.'[104] On the fringes of Anglo-Orthodoxy were a group of traditionalists, often immigrants or the children of immigrants from Poland, Germany or Holland who continued to maintain a scholarly life studying rabbinic texts, provided for by *hebrot*.[105]

London Jewry was concentrated in specific areas of the metropolis. Until the latter half of the nineteenth century, London was largely contained to the city and its immediate surroundings, initially expanding east. Although Jews were technically free to settle anywhere, their disbarment as Freemen of the City of London, and the religious requirements to be within walking distance of a synagogue, created a specific voluntary location in the east of the city.[106] The East End, as the area came to be known in the later-nineteenth century, became synonymous with poverty and crime. But this was initially not the case and change developed slowly, as the city itself depopulated and the fashionable and newly constructed West End became the desirable residential area. The areas of greatest Jewish residence were focused on Whitechapel, Finsbury Square and Houndsditch and analysis of mid-century census records finds whole streets containing only Jewish names.[107] Until the second half of the nineteenth century, the affluent and the impoverished continued primarily to live in these areas, with the wealthier inhabiting Goodman's Fields, Prescott, Mansell, Leman and Alie streets.[108] Mayhew gives prodigious contemporary detail of the London Jewish community, identifying Jewish occupations and their locations and this provides a detailed structural picture of the trades and occupations of mid-century East End Jewry.

> The trading-class in the capacity of shopkeepers, warehousemen or manufactures, are the thickest in Houndsditch, Aldgate and the Minories, more especially the 'swagshops' and the manufacture and sale of wearing apparel. The wholesale dealers in fruit are in Duke's-place and Pudding-lane (Thames Street), but the superior retail Jew fruiters—some of whose shops are remarkable for the beauty of their fruit—are in Cheapside, Oxford Street, Piccadilly, and most of all Covent Garden market. The inferior jewellers …

are also at the East-end, about Whitechapel, Bevis Marks and
Houndsditch; the wealthier goldsmiths and watchmakers having,
like other tradesmen of the class, their shops in superior thoroughfares ... The Hebrew dealers in second-hand garments and
second-hand wares generally are located in Petticoat-lane ... The
manufacturers of such things as cigars, pencils and sealing wax; the
wholesale importers of sponge, bristles and toys, the dealers in
quills and in 'looking glasses' reside in large private-looking houses, where display is needed for the purposes of business, in such
parts as Maunsell-street, Great Prescott-street, Great Ailie-street,
Leman-street and other parts of the eastern quarter known as
Goodman's-fields. The wholesale dealers in foreign birds and
shells, and the many foreign things as 'curiosities' reside in East
Smithfield, Ratcliffe-highway, High-street (Shadwell) or in some
parts adjacent to the Thames. In the long range of river-side
streets stretching from the Tower to Poplar and Blackwell, are
Jews, who fulfil the many capacities of slop sellers.[109]

In parallel with the decline in London's residential population, the second
quarter of the nineteenth century saw the upper and increasingly the middle
classes moving out of the East End. Throughout the century the outward
symbols of acculturation were witnessed in the change from what was characterised as 'foreign dress' with religiously prescribed beards, to fashionable dress
and a clean-shaven appearance.[110]

The class differences among the community tended to be by scale rather
than the nature of the operation. Jews engaged in the limited array of
commercial activities, principally the manufacture and distribution of
consumer products such as footwear, clothing, jewellery, furniture, trinkets as
well as luxury items and tobacco related products. As the general population
benefited from a rise in its standard of living, so too did those engaged in the
supply and manufacture of consumer goods. This was especially important in
the clothing sector, where Jewish firms fostered an industry of cheap ready-to-
wear clothes, supplanting the previous reliance of the working class on
second-hand garments.[111] Many of Melbourne's settlers were themselves or
the children of tailors, dressmakers, cap makers, or shoe and boot makers. As
early as the 1840s more than half the drapers in Melbourne were Jewish.

The Jewish community encouraged the acquisition of trade skills in
order to assist economic development. Throughout Europe, as a result of the
restrictions of Jewish ritual, apprenticeships and business partnerships were
more simply organised through other Jews.[112] A number of the children of the
Reverend Barnett Simmons, reader at the synagogue in Penzance, migrated to

Victoria. In 1851 three were living with their brother Moses in Penzance. Moses operated a carving and gilding workshop employing three men including his two brothers, Abraham, who subsequently became a reader in both Ballarat and St Kilda synagogues, and younger brother Levy as well as a Bristol-born apprentice, Barnett Levy. Simmons' sister Amelia, who also migrated to Melbourne, likewise lived in her married brother's household, and was employed as an embroiderer.[113]

The nineteenth century also saw the growth of a small Jewish professional class, particularly those professions that required practical rather than academic training, and a number of Jewish optometrists and dentists began to appear in England and the colonies. Melbourne had at least eight Jewish dentists, including the extended family of Louis Philip Eskell. Eskell was the son of Bristol-born dentist Louis Eskell and two of his uncles also followed this profession, including in Melbourne, Barris Meir. At least eight Jewish opticians also operated in Melbourne, all but one of whom had be born in England, although Dutch-born Moses Kasner had married in London in 1821, thirty years before he migrated to Melbourne, with his wife and daughter Anne.

Provincial Jewry

The differing economic foundations of provincial towns and cities in Britain created diverse patterns of acculturation for British Jews. Of those settling in Melbourne, just over one-quarter came from areas outside London. By the later eighteenth century the Jewish community had expanded outwards from London, with approximately twenty towns recording Jewish communities.[114] By the mid nineteenth century, the northern towns had the largest Jewish populations outside the metropole.[115] Many provincial towns had tiny Jewish populations and in a number of cases their emigration to Melbourne largely depopulated their Jewish communities. Such was the case for Sheerness, where a community was established in 1790, which at its peak in 1851 consisted of thirty-five members but three years later was only fifteen, with the majority having migrated to Melbourne.

The earliest significant Jewish presence outside London was Plymouth, where a synagogue was built in 1762 (the oldest Ashkenazi synagogue in Britain). Seaports were significant for the provincial Jewish economy, with eight of the initial eleven Jewish communities connected to the sea trade, including the naval ports of Portsmouth, Plymouth and Chatham.[116] These seaport communities owed their existence to trade with the navy, which expanded greatly in the period 1740–1820, providing commercial opportunities for Jewish businessmen utilising their skills in retail, clothing and money lending. As the trade with the navy diminished, a significant number of residents from these port towns migrated to Victoria.

With the expansion of the navy during the mid eighteenth century, opportunities arose to trade in a variety of consumer goods for this expanding market. Susser's analysis of Woolcombe's 'Picture of Plymouth' 1812, shows that eighteen of the forty-one small shop keepers advertised as slop sellers, merchants, jewellers, brokers, dealers in navel stores, stoles, silversmiths, umbrella and straw-hat makers were Jewish businesses and at least half of these were naval agents.[117] Two branches of Abraham Joseph's family settled in Melbourne. Joseph was a Plymouth-based mercer and wholesale slop seller, whose trade card proclaimed him as 'slopman to his Royal Highness Prince William Henry'.[118] This was obviously a profitable business; Joseph owned considerable property in Plymouth, as on his death in 1794 he left an estate of at least £7000.[119]

The navy considerably scaled back from 35,000 sailors in 1740 to just 19,000 in 1817.[120] As a consequence trade declined markedly. Jewish merchants left the port towns for other mercantile centres, with large numbers moving to London, while many took the opportunities that the colonies offered. Analysis of the social mobility of the navel port communities can be witnessed in the career of Charles Marks, father of Edward Isaac Marks, who arrived in Melbourne around 1860. Charles is first listed in 1841 as a naval agent, but five years later he became an assessor for Plymouth.[121] The Exeter-based Alexander Alexander, father of Melbourne residents Moses and Miriam Alexander, was an optician, a calling favoured by Jews. He moved to the top of this profession, writing a number of optometric treatises, including one dedicated to King William IV. He was optician-in-ordinary to their Royal Highnesses the Duchess of Kent and the Princess Victoria, and traded by appointment to Queen Victoria, one of only eight Jews given this honour in the first years of Victoria's reign.[122]

The Jewish presence in the industrial north of England took longer to develop. This area was initially settled by German Jews trading with the cotton industry in Manchester. Many German migrants arrived after serving apprenticeships in German companies, bringing with them skills and experience useful for large-scale commerce. These were middle class and secularly educated, able to read and write in German and in many instances other European languages as well. Young men, such as Moritz Michaelis, without capital but with connections, migrated intending to find employment as clerks or managers in the factories, offices and warehouses of their compatriots.[123]

Those migrating from the industrial north included former migrants from central and eastern Europe, those who had established themselves and those who were perhaps finding the conditions more difficult. Phillip Blashki, born Favel Wagczewski in Blashki near Kalish Poland, arrived in Manchester in 1855, fleeing the repression of eastern Europe and finding work as a tassel maker. In Manchester he met and married a young Polish widow, Hannah

Potash (nee Immergut). According to a family story, the couple were due to sail to America, and their possessions had been previously loaded on board another ship that had already sailed without them. The shipping agent errone-ously convinced them to sail to Australia that day, claiming that the difference in costs could be borne by the sale of their goods in America. Blashki's rise in economic prosperity followed a familiar pattern found both in England and Victoria. He initially established himself as a dealer on the goldfields before launching a jewellery business in Melbourne and subsequently in 1894 winning the tender to design and manufacture the Sheffield Shield.[124]

From the eighteenth century, with each wave of immigration, Anglo-Jewry experienced a constant and cyclical process of religious, cultural and economic acculturation. These conditions were also experienced by those seeking new economic opportunities as British emigrants to a new colony.

Towards Emancipation
Germany
The various factors influencing the formation of the Melbourne Jewish community resulted from the composite ethnic and social backgrounds of the settlers and residents of the town. The second-largest contingent of Jewish settlers was from German-speaking areas of central Europe, either immigrating directly or after previous residence in England. As German migrants they were products of the mass migration that Germany experienced during the political turmoil of the nineteenth century. As German Jewish migrants, they were seeking refuge from the economic and social restrictions imposed on their community. The first waves of Ashkenazi settlement to England was predomi-nantly from Germany. For those who had previously migrated to England, their onward migration to Victoria is an extension of the settlement patterns of Anglo-Jewry and Germans to the Australian colonies.

The literature on German Jewish history is immense, focusing on the various expulsions from cities and states throughout its nearly 2000-year history; the social and political outcomes of the Thirty Years' War; the expan-sion of German territories; the influence on the German and Jewish Enlightenments (*Haskalah*); the inconsistent and repressive restrictions placed on individuals and communities prior to emancipation in 1871; and finally the events leading to the Holocaust and the analysis of this catastrophe. The eman-cipatory experience of German Jewry was markedly different to that occurring concurrently in either England or France and resulted from differing political, social and philosophical transformations taking place in the German states.

This process was not completed until 1871, a generation later than had occurred in Britain and a generation after the political turmoil of

1848. Emancipation coincided with the changing economic foundations of German society, which transformed from the old economies of agriculture, guilds and mercantile interests into new industrial commercial markets.[125] German Jews had historically faced greater and more repressive restrictions over all aspects of their lives than those in England, and the removal of these restrictions was gradual and inconsistent. Eighteenth-century German absolutism considered loyalty as a significant political virtue, with Jewish integration dependent on individuals and communities demonstrating benefit and obedience.

German nineteenth-century nationalism defined nationality and citizenship as indistinguishable. Although individual Jews as economic citizens could prosper, the prevailing political system did not allow for improvement in the collective condition of Jewish communities.[126] Underpinning the debate on German Jewish emancipation was the debased image of the Jew as corrupt and dishonest. In response, the debates over emancipation revolved around a perceived need for Jewish regeneration, and the responsibility and conditions for this to take place.[127]

Historically, Jews of central and eastern Europe were not considered citizens of the state and as a result lived in autonomous communities. As Magnus summarises in his description of Cologne:

> Jewish toleration ... was extended only if perceived as beneficial to the granting authority. If Jews became unprofitable to their protectors because they became impoverished or because the burden of protecting Jews from popular passions or outside meddling became too great, the basis for toleration was undermined. Obviously, if Jews seemed a threat to the ruler's interests, no grounds for toleration existed.[128]

These autonomous communities required members to have mutual responsibility for the regulation of religious and civil functions while being obligated to manage state-imposed regulations and restrictions. They scrutinised the observance of religious law, public worship and the study of Torah, provided the synagogues, cemetery and *mikvot*, supervised the distribution of seasonal festival produce such as the wheat for *matzah*, enforced *kashrut*, supervised poor relief, and enforced sumptuary restrictions.[129] The self-governing authority incorporated the judicial systems and communal institutions required for a functioning society, including responsibility for a range of civic services from water supply to the removal of garbage.[130]

Jewish lives were controlled economically and socially, subject to restrictions on residential locations, population size, occupations and taxation.

Residential restrictions resulted in overcrowding in the limited space allocated, placing enormous pressures on housing and necessitating communal authorities to regulate living space, ensuring that all available space was used, controlling rents to ensure stability and affordability.[131] Residency permits were only available to household heads able to pay a fee and prove possession of property of a stated value. Without a residency permit, Jews were unable to start a family or engage in independent business.[132]

In Germany it was occupational restrictions that most defined the community. Excluded from ownership of land, guilds and thus trade occupations, Jews were largely constrained to small-scale commerce, money lending and pawnbroking.[133] In some areas Jews were forbidden to operate retail shops and consequently became pedlars, dealers in second-hand goods and casual traders. This trade evolved into the sale of agricultural products, grain and livestock, with Jews particularly involved in dealing in horses and cattle, activities not controlled by the urban guilds.[134] Jews also travelled to fairs and markets as far afield as Poland and Russia, procuring and selling merchandise, exchanges that presented opportunities for interaction with the wider society.[135]

Jewish education had been defined by the Torah and *halachic* law and held no requirements for a non-Jewish scholarship.[136] The German *Haskalah* argued for a separation of culture and religion, facilitating opportunities for Jews to live in the Jewish and in the secular worlds. Throughout the nineteenth-century, as emancipation evolved, Jews acquired German cultural habits and, in so doing, developed a new middle-class Jewish sensibility.[137] As with British Jews, German Jews saw education as a way of improving social status, participation and acculturation in wider society. And, as occurred elsewhere, improvements in secular education saw a diminishing of religious education and a corresponding fall in religious knowledge. In Prussia a secular education was reinforced by the state, which required students to attend state supervised schools.

By 1840, when only 10 per cent of Jewish students in Poland received a state-supervised education, 95 per cent of Jewish children in Prussia were studying in the educational system. By the late nineteenth century there 'were proportionally five times as many Jews in Prussian secondary schools (*Gymnasien*) as Jews in the population at large'.[138] This German secular education can be seen in the letters of families such as that of Emanuel Steinfeld, writing from Silesia in a high nineteenth-century formal German, while the Sheffield-based family of his wife, who had left Posen a generation previously, corresponded in English with the occasional Yiddish message or phrase.[139]

The experience of German Jewry from the eighteenth century has been defined as a cultural migration, with an 'abruptness and intensity' as new cultural contacts were experienced, not as an acculturation to the Christian majority, but specifically to the educated middle class through bourgeoisification.[140]

Bildung combined an educational framework with the importance of culture and the potential of humanity to express 'a cultured, well-bred personality, an autonomous, harmonious person of refined manners, aesthetic appreciation, politeness and gentility'.[141]

The Jewish community took to such concepts with enthusiasm. Jewish intellectuals in the emancipatory period expressed a 'passionate acquisition of European culture and proclaimed themselves eager to integrate into society'.[142] They became consumers and producers of culture in disproportionately high numbers, providing new spaces for the circulation of ideas and for wider social interactions.[143] Katz's oft-quoted statement that 'Jews have not assimilated into the German people, but into a certain layer of it, the newly emerging middle-class', defines the dichotomy of the emancipated German Jew.[144] But acculturation was restricted by persistent discrimination and many believed that social advancement could only be achieved through conversion to Christianity, consequently leading to significant numbers of proselytes and higher levels of intermarriage than occurred in Britain.

The differing legal status of Jews in the various German states was based on historical precedents. Prussia, the most powerful German state, was home to the majority of German Jews. In 1795, with the partition of Poland by Russia, Austria and Prussia, Prussia absorbed Greater Poland and redefined the provinces as Silesia, Pomerania and Posen, and in an attempt to 'Germanise' this population, exchanged Polish for German as the official language.[145]

In the early nineteenth century, Prussia was home to more than 50 per cent of German Jews, rising to 70 per cent fifty years later.[146] Following the Congress of Vienna (1815) the western part of the Duchy of Warsaw became the new Prussian Grand Duchy of Posen, a rural and agricultural region. By 1825, 68,100 Jews lived in this province, being 6.5 per cent of the total population, equating to two-thirds of the Jewish population of Prussia.[147] Unsurprisingly, the Posen area, where 95 per cent of the Jewish population resided in cities, was the place of birth of the highest proportion of non-English settlers to Melbourne.[148]

Many of the German Jews who arrived in Melbourne had previously lived in England. Jacob Abraham and his family arrived in Victoria on the *Ultonia* in May 1855, after residing for at least five years in England. The 1851 census lists him as a general dealer, living in Newcastle upon Tyne, sharing a house with his wife, two children, his brother and sister-in-law, nephew and three lodgers. His children had been born in Plymouth and Newcastle, indicating significant attempts at resettlement prior to his journey to Victoria.

At the other end of the social scale, Louis Beaver (previously Bibergeil), born in Bromberg, arrived in Manchester in 1840, escaping political repression.

Son of a doctor and nephew of the German scientist Aaron Bernstein, he began his career as a pedlar of jewellery, steel pens and other small items. Within four years he owned a number of successful Manchester jewellery shops and by 1861 had a home that required three live-in maids. Although he was an active participant in the Manchester Jewish community, this did not stop three of his children leaving for Melbourne, with sixteen-year-old Albert arriving in 1866, four years before his sisters Evelyn and Laura.[149] Albert married Australian-born Evelyn Bloomington, daughter of another Prussian merchant, Israel Bloomington. Both his sisters married German-born husbands.

Jamaica

The Sephardi community in Melbourne consisted of individuals and families from London and from many scattered Sephardi communities including Jamaica, Barbados, Gibraltar, Morocco, Egypt and Italy. For Melbourne, the largest non-English Sephardi community originated in Jamaica, and this community brought with it an alternative and singular model of Jewish inter-action and of Jewish urban familiarity. From the expulsion from Spain, the New World had provided economic and residential opportunities for Jews and although these at times proved inconsistent and sometimes impermanent, they forged new Jewish settlements, including the initial establishment of the large and significant communities of the Americas.

The unique economic networks of the Caribbean provided a transna-tional perspective for this community, one forged through its mercantile, familial and educational associations, connecting the Old and New Worlds with new linkages, providing an alternate world view. This was to be displayed in the Montefiore family, whose trading connections between the Caribbean and London included a family base in Barbados and international connections that took them to South Australia, Victoria, New South Wales, Madras and London.

The Jewish settlement of and emigration from Jamaica and other parts of the Caribbean is an example of how Jewish sub-diasporas utilised their connections jointly to build a community and an economic base, intersecting on a number of levels with British economic history and Anglo-Jewish history. The dispersion of the Sephardi community provided family connections across national boundaries, connections which were not necessarily severed by expulsion and migration, but which could be harnessed to allow financial collaboration and an international fluidity of capital.[150]

These were communities unconfined by national boundaries, transna-tional in outlook and connected by networks that stretched from Holland to England, France, Germany, North America and other parts of the Caribbean and through the *Converso* community back to the Iberian Peninsula.[151] They facilitated an import and export trade for the British and the Dutch and exploited their ambiguous or dual nationality to circumvent and disrupt trading embargos with the Spanish. This transnational strength could also be a liability; ambivalent national allegiance was a disadvantage in an era when economic demarcation was judged on a 'subject's true allegiance'.[152]

During the seventeenth and eighteenth centuries the centre of Jewish life in the British colonies of the Atlantic was not North America but rather the West Indies, and by 1769 Kingston was the second-largest Jewish community in the English-speaking world, with more Jews resident here than in all of the thirteen American colonies and Canada.[153] In 1720 Jews comprised 10 per cent of the white Jamaican population and in the early nineteenth century one-third of that of Curaçao, holding half the wealth and three-quarters of its commercial management.[154] This proportion was reflected in those coming to Melbourne more than a century later, with slightly more arriving from the Caribbean than from mainland America.

Jews, *Conversos* and Crypto-Jews had fled the Iberian Peninsula, with many establishing themselves in Holland. After the declaration of Dutch independence in 1579, their numbers dramatically increased, and in the new-found freedom were able to revert openly to practising Judaism.[155] Many of this community later migrated to the Caribbean, bringing with them not only the experience of acculturation in the multiethnic realm of medieval Spain, but also values and a collective memory that have been described as a 'blending of Iberian values and rabbinic Judaism [that] constituted a reinvention of ethnicity unequalled in the Jewish world'.[156]

Although Jamaica was controlled by Spain until conquered by the English in 1655, as personal property of Columbus's descendants, it was outside the direct authority of the Inquisition. While Jews could not practise openly, the first Jewish settlement in Jamaica is recorded in 1530, although it is unclear how many Jews were resident.[157] When the English expelled all Spaniards from the island, they allowed the 'Portuguese' (as the Jews were known), to remain, thus forming the nucleus of the Jewish community. Under English control, Jews were allowed openly to practise their religion, and a strong communal life developed, with the first synagogue established in 1704, followed by another four congregations by mid century. In the late eighteenth century Ashkenazi settlers began arriving and the first Ashkenazi synagogue was erected in Spanish Town in 1796.[158] The two groups remained culturally separate and were referred to as 'Spanish' and 'English' communities, although Ashkenazi Jewry were always a minority.

The Jewish community were viewed with suspicion, not considered equal citizens, were disenfranchised and subject to a variety of heavy and disproportionate taxes.[159] The granting of a franchise and full political rights did not occur until 1832, in parallel with the abolition of slavery, and only as 'they would be unable to uphold the image of the superiority of the white man if the franchise was to be extended to the free Negroes but denied the Jews'.[160] Jamaica was a community of 'betweenness', middlemen in a plantation society; people tolerated but not given full citizenship, caught between competing empires. Their ties to London, provided them with a competitive advantage, while maintaining Portuguese as the language for their business and communal correspondence.[161]

As with migration to the Victorian goldfields two centuries later, the typical seventeenth-century immigrant to Jamaica was 'single, male and from an urban trading background'.[162] Jews were primarily engaged in mercantile trade, particularly to Europe and British North America, as well as operating as shopkeepers, middlemen and smaller scale merchants.[163] Port Royal operated as a base for 2000 privateer vessels and Jews acted as agents for and purchasers of loot from privateers, as well as occasionally operating directly as privateers themselves.[164] Due to the high capital costs of establishing plantations and to the religious constraints of slave ownership, few Jews engaged in this field of activity.

Those migrating to Melbourne from the Caribbean were experienced in this slave economy, and almost all were individuals or children of parents who had been compensated for the loss of the slaves after 1834.[165] More specifically, the Lindo and Montefiore families had connections to slave trading, and the Lindos to privateering, and two branches of this family settled in the Australian colonies: Elizabeth Lindo and her husband, Benjamin Goldsmid Levien, in Melbourne and subsequently Geelong, while her nephew and Benjamin's cousin Alexander Lindo settled in Sydney. Elizabeth's father, Alexander, was born in Bordeaux of a Sephardi family and had settled in Jamaica by 1765.

Like most of the Jewish population, Lindo initially established himself as a merchant, but expanded his scope to include the purchase of privateer cargos before investing in substantial property holdings in Kingston and becoming one of the few Jewish plantation owners, as well as a slave factor. His company operated at an international level through financial arrangements with a London branch of the family.[166] Lindo's financial affairs became somewhat strained, initially through complications with his Jamaican partners and fatefully in 1802 through his decision to lend the French £60,000 to fund a proposed invasion of the British Caribbean from St Domingue.

It has been speculated that Alexander Lindo's rationale in funding such a venture against his adopted home may have been founded on the perception of Napoleon as the liberator of the Jews, particularly at a time when the Jewish community of Jamaica was disenfranchised and disproportionally taxed.[167] Unfortunately this decision cost him dearly when the French reneged on the loan. Lindo continued business from a base in London, where he died in 1812.

Among Lindo's assets at the time of his death were two plantations with a joint slave population of 639.

Kingston, March 29, 1786.

FOR SALE,

ON BOARD THE

SHIP ELLIOT,

Captain *John Clemenson*,

From WHYDAW,

On *Monday*, the 17th *April*,

898 Choice Gold Coast, Whydaw, Logos and Benin

SLAVES,

By ALEXANDRE LINDO.

Notice for a slave sale by Alexander Lindo, March 1786, Courtesy of the
National Library of Jamaica

The nineteenth century saw the development of a Jamaican Jewish professional class, beginning with the medical profession.[168] Solomon Iffla was a Jamaican-born and Glasgow-trained physician, who settled in Adelaide before moving to Melbourne. Iffla rose to prominence in Melbourne, where he was conspicuous as a magistrate, a council member for the Philosophical Society of Victoria and the vice president (1859), council member (1859–61) and subsequently life member (1860–72) of the Royal Society of Victoria. He represented the society on the 1858 Burke and Wills expedition committee. He also served the Jewish community, where for many years he volunteered his services as physician to the Jewish Philanthropic Society.

Dr Solomon Iffla c.1875, Port Phillip City Collection

From the late eighteenth century the Jamaican economy suffered a series of downturns. Liverpool increased in significance in the West Indies trade, reducing the importance of London, which was the principal connection for Jewish traders. From the late eighteenth century planters were able to import from and export to England directly, reducing the role of the middleman.[169] The equalisation of sugar duties in 1846 dramatically contracted the economic fortunes of the island.[170] Emigration and intermarriage reduced the once thriving Jewish community of Jamaica and many moved to take up the new opportunities Melbourne offered.

Notes

1   *Argus*, 27 November 1867, 5–7.
2   ibid., 6.
3   Doreen Massey and Pat Jess, *A Place in the World? Places, Cultures and Globalization* (The Open University, Oxford, 1995), 46 and 183.
4   Nancy L. Green, 'The Comparative Method and Poststructural Structuralism— New Perspective for Migration Studies', *Journal of American Ethnic History* 13, no. 4 (1994), 1.
5   Charlotte Elisheva Fonrobert and Vered Shemtov, 'Introduction, Jewish Conceptions and Practices of Space', *Jewish Social Studies* 11, no. 3 (2005), 3.
6   Eli Barnavi, *A Historical Atlas of the Jewish People, from the Time of the Patriarchs to the Present*, trans. Miriam Eliav-Feldon (Hachette Litteratures, Paris, 2002), vi.
7   Amnon Raz-Krakotzkin, 'Jewish Memory between Exile and History', in *Jewish Quarterly Review* 97, no 4 (2007), 532.
8   Julia Brauch, Anna Lipphardt and Alexandra Nocke, *Jewish Topographies, Visions of Space, Traditions of Place, Heritage, Culture, and Identity* (Ashgate Publishing, Aldershot, 2008), 6.
9   Robert Anchel, 'The Early History of the Jewish Quarters in Paris', *Jewish Social Studies* 2, no. 1 (1940), 45.
10 Barnavi, *Historical Atlas*, viii–ix; Barbara Mann, *Space and Place in Jewish Studies* (Rutgers University Press, New Brunswick, 2012), 100.
11 Mann, *Space and Place in Jewish Studies*, 25; Maurice Halbwachs, *The Collective Memory* (Harper & Row, New York, 1980), 12.
12 Oliver Valins, 'Institutionalised Religion, Sacred Texts and Jewish Spatial Practice', *Geoforum* 31, no. 4. (2000), 578.
13 Halbwachs, *The Collective Memory*, 13.
14 Nora, Pierre 'Between Memory and History: Les Lieux de Memoire', *Representations* 26, no. Spring (1989), 7–24.
15 See Amos Funkenstein, 'Collective Memory and Historical Consciousness', *History and Memory* 1 (1989); and Yosef Hayim Yerushalmi, Zakhor, *Jewish History and Jewish Memory, The Samuel and Althea Stroum Lectures in Jewish Studies* (University of Washington Press, Seattle, 1982).
16 Eszter Brigitta Gantner and Matyas Kovacs, 'Altering Alternatives, Mapping Jewish Subcultures in Budapest', in Julia Lipphardt, Anna Brauch and Alexander Nocke (eds), *Jewish Topographies, Visions of Space, Traditions of Place* (Ashgate Publishing, Aldershot, 2008), 145.
17 Joachim Schlor, 'Jews and the Big City, Explorations on an Urban State of Mind', in Julia Lipphardt, Anna Brauch and Alexander Nocke (eds), *Jewish Topographies, Visions of Space, Traditions of Place* (Ashgate Publishing, Aldershot, 2008), 229.
18 Peter Kvidera, 'Rewriting the Ghetto, Cultural Production in the Labor Narratives of Rose Schneiderman and Theresa Malkiel', *American Quarterly*, 57, no 4 (2005), 1132–3.
19 Fonrobert and Shemtov, 'Introduction, Jewish Conceptions and Practices of Space', 3.
20 Schlor, 'Jews and the Big City', 224.
21 Barnavi, *Historical Atlas of the Jewish People*, viii–ix.
22 Haya Bar-Itzhak, 'A Materialized Settlement and a Metaphysical Landscape in Legends of Origin of Polish Jews', in Julia Lipphardt, Anna Brauch and Alexander Nocke (eds), *Jewish Topographies, Visions of Space, Traditions of Place* (Ashgate Publishing, Aldershot, 2008), 165–6, 176.
23 Ralph Kingston, 'Mind over Matter? History and the Spatial Turn', *Cultural and Social History*, 7, no 1 (2010), 114.

24   Louis Wirth, 'The Ghetto', *American Journal of Sociology* 33, no. 1 (1927), 71.

25   Stephen Sharot, 'Jewish Acculturation in Premodern Societies', in Shlomo Deshen and Walter P. Zenner (eds), *Jews among Muslims, Communities in the Precolonial Middle East* (Macmillan, Great Britain, 1996), 46.

26   Richard Rürup, 'The Tortuous and Thorny Path to Legal Equality, "Jew Laws" and Emancipatory Legislation in Germany from the Late Eighteenth Century', *Leo Baeck Institute Year Book* 14 (1986), 67; Christhard Hoffman, 'From Heinrich Heine to Isidor Kracauer: The Frankfurt Ghetto in German-Jewish Historical Culture and Geography', *Jewish Culture and History* 10, nos 2–3 (2008), 59.

27   David Newman, 'Integration and Ethnic Spatial Concentration, the Changing Distribution of the Anglo-Jewish Community', *Transactions of the Institute of British Geographers* 10, no. 3 (1985), 380.

28   Benjamin Ravid, 'All Ghettos Were Jewish Quarters but not All Jewish Quarters Were Ghettos', *Jewish Culture and History* 10, nos. 2–3, (2008), 5.

29   Louis Wirth and Albert Reiss (ed.), *Louis Wirth on Cities and Social Life; Selected Papers* (University of Chicago Press, Chicago, 1964), 88.

30   Mann, *Space and Place in Jewish Studies*, 121.

31   Jacob Katz, *Out of the Ghetto; the Social Background of Jewish Emancipation, 1770–1870* (Harvard University Press, Cambridge, Mass., 1973), 19.

32   Wirth, 'The Ghetto', 62.

33   Wirth, *Louis Wirth on Cities and Social Life; Selected Papers*, 88.

34   Michael Goldfarb, *Emancipation, How Liberating Europe's Jews from the Ghetto Led to Revolution and Renaissance* (Simon & Schuster, New York, 2009), 119; Katz, *Out of the Ghetto*, 22.

35   Amitai Etzioni, 'The Ghetto—a Re-evaluation', *Social Forces* 37, no. 3 (1959), 256.

36   Jonathan I. Israel, *European Jewry in the Age of Mercantilism, 1550–1750* (Clarendon Press, Oxford, 1985), 33.

37   Ruth Gay, 'Inventing the Shtetl', *American Scholar* 53, no. 3 (1984), 335.

38   Alla Sokolova, 'House-Building Tradition of the Shtetl in Memorials and Memories (Based on Materials of Field Studies in Podolia', *East European Jewish Affairs* 41, no. 3 (2011), 120.

39   Lawrence A. Coben, 'A Note on Shtetl Definitions and the Dating of the First Shtetl', *East European Jewish Affairs* 41, no. 3 (2011), 203.

40   Gay, 'Inventing the Shtetl', 335.

41   ibid., 336.

42   David G. Mandelbaum, 'Change and Continuity in Jewish Life', in Marshall Sklare (ed.), *The Jews: Social Patterns of an American Group* (Free Press, Glencoe, 1960), 511–12.

43   Todd M. Endelman, *Comparing Jewish Societies* (University of Michigan Press, Ann Arbor, 1997), 51.

44   Parks, 'The Jewish Quarters of Interwar Paris and Tunis: Destruction, Creation, and French Urban Design', *Jewish Social Studies* 17, no. 1 (2010).

45   Daniel J. Schroeter and Joseph Chetrit, 'Emancipation and Its Discontents. Jews at the Formative Period of Colonial Rule in Morocco', *Jewish Social Studies* 13, no. 1 (2006), 171.

46   Laurence D. Loeb, 'Dhimmi Status and Jewish Roles', in Shlomo Deshen and Walter P. Zenner (eds), *Jews among Muslims: Communities in the Precolonial Middle East* (Palgrave Macmillan, London, 1996), 248; Walter P. Zenner, 'Syrian Jews and Their Non-Jewish Neighbors', in Shlomo Deshen and Walter P. Zenner (eds), *Jews among Muslims: Communities in the Precolonial Middle East* (Palgrave Macmillan, London, 1996), 168.

47   Daniel J. Schroeter, 'The Shifting Boundaries of Moroccan Jewish Identities', *Jewish*

Social Studies: History, Cultural, Society, 15, no. 1 (2008), 146.

48 Emily Gottreich, 'On the Origins of the Mellah of Marrakesh', *International Journal of Middle East Studies* 35 (2003), 288.

49 Emily Gottreich, 'Rethinking the "Islamic City" from the Perspective of Jewish Space', *Jewish Social Studies* 11, no. 1 (2004), 121.

50 Susan Gilson Miller, 'The Mellah of Fez, Reflections on the Spatial Turn in Moroccan Jewish History', in Anna Brauch, Julia Lipphardt and Alexander Nocke (eds), *Jewish Topographies, Visions of Space, Traditions of Place* (Ashgate Publishing, Aldershot, 2008), 102.

51 Haim Zafrani, 'Mallāh', in *Encyclopedia of Islam*, 2nd edn (Brill Online).

52 Susan Gibson Miller, Attilio Petruccioli and Mauro Bertagnin, 'Inscribing Minority Space in the Islamic City: The Jewish Quarter of Fez (1438–1912)', *Journal of the Society of Architectural Historians* 60, no. 3, (2001), 311.

53 Daniel J. Schroeter, 'The Jewish Quarter and the Moroccan City', in Yedida K. Stillman and George K. Zucker (eds), *New Horizons in Sephardic Studies* (State University of New York Press, New York, 1993), 70.

54 Schroeter, 'The Shifting Boundaries of Moroccan Jewish Identities', 151; Gottreich, 'On the Origins of the Mellah of Marrakesh', 297.

55 Schroeter, 'The Jewish Quarter and the Moroccan City', 70–1.

56 Mark Levene, 'Port Jewry of Salonika, between Neo-Colonialism and Nation-State', in David Cesarani (ed.), *Port Jews, Jewish Communities in Cosmopolitan Maritime Trading Centers 1550–1950* (Frank Cass, London, 2002), 125.

57 Jonathan D. Sarna, 'Port Jews in the Atlantic, Further Thoughts', *Jewish History* 20, no. 2, (2006), 213.

58 Lois Dubin, *The Port Jews of Habsburg Trieste, Absolutist Politics and Enlightenment Culture* (Stanford University Press, Stanford, 1999), 3.

59 David Cesarani (ed.), *Port Jews, Jewish Communities in Cosmopolitan Maritime Trading Centres, 1550–1950* (Frank Cass, London, 2002), 2.

60 Lois Dubin, 'Introduction, Port Jews in the Atlantic World', *Jewish History* 20, no. 2, (2006), 120.

61 Wim Klooster, 'Communities of Port Jews and Their Contacts in the Dutch Atlantic World', *Jewish History* 20, no. 2, (2006), 137.

62 David Sorkin, 'The Port Jew, Notes towards a Social Type', *Journal of Jewish Studies* 1, no. 1, (1999), 89–97.

63 Todd M. Endelman, 'The Legitimization of the Diaspora Experience in Recent Jewish Historiography', *Modern Judaism* 11, no. 2 (1991), 196.

64 Shmuel Feiner, 'The Pseudo-Enlightenment and the Question of Jewish Modernization', *Jewish Social Studies* 3, no. 1 (1996), 77; and Steven Singer, 'The Anglo-Jewish Ministry in Early Victorian London', *Modern Judaism* 5, no. 3 (1985), 279.

65 Judith Endelman as quoted by Sarna, 'Port Jews in the Atlantic, Further Thoughts', 216.

66 Green, 'The Comparative Method and Poststructural Structuralism', 285.

67 Hoffman, 'From Heinrich Heine to Isidor Kracauer', 46.

68 Steven J. Zipperstein, 'Jewish Historiography and the Modern City, Recent Writing on European Jewry', *Jewish History* 2, no. 1, (1987), 80; Bill Williams, *Jewish Manchester, An Illustrated History* (Breedon Books, Derby, 2008), 43.

69 Bettina Hitzer and Joachim Schlor, 'Introduction to God in the City, Religious Topographies in the Age of Urbanization', *Journal of Urban History*, 37, no. 6, (2011), 819–20.

70 Steven M. Cohen, quoted in ibid., 824.

71   Andrew Lees, *Cities Perceived, Urban Society in European and American Thought, 1820–1940* (Manchester University Press, Manchester, 1985), 29; and Hugh McLeod, *European Religion in the Age of Great Cities, 1830–1930* (Routledge, London, 1995), 184.

72   Israel Finestein, 'Jewish Emancipation in Victorian England, Self Imposed Limits on Assimilation', in Jonathan Frankel and Steven J. Zipperstein (eds), *Assimilation and Community: The Jews in Nineteenth Century Europe* (Cambridge University Press, Cambridge, 1992), 43.

73   Bill Williams, '"East and West", Class and Community in Manchester Jewry 1850–1914', in David Cesarani (ed.), *The Making of Modern Anglo-Jewry* (Basil Blackwell, Oxford, 1990), 20.

74   Bernard D. Weinryb, 'Jewish Immigration and Accomodation to America', in Marshall Sklare (ed.), *The Jews, Social Patterns of an American Group* (Free Press, Glencoe, 1960), 16.

75   Todd M. Endelman, *The Jews of Britain, 1656 to 2000* (University of California Press, Berkeley, 2002), 23.

76   Abraham Gilman, *The Emancipation of the Jews in England 1830–1860* (Garland Publishing, New York, 1982), 8.

77   Cecil Roth, *A History of the Jews in England* (Clarendon Press, Oxford, 1964), 252.

78   Holly Snyder, 'Rules, Rights and Redemption, The Negotiation of Jewish Status in British Atlantic Port Towns, 1740–1831', *Jewish History*, 20, no. 2, (2006), 149.

79   David Feldman, *Englishmen and Jews, Social Relations and Political Culture 1840–1914* (Yale University Press, New Haven, 1994), 30.

80   Michael Clark, *Albion and Jerusalem, The Anglo-Jewish Community in the Post-Emancipation Era* (Oxford University Press, Oxford, 2009), 236.

81   David B. Ruderman, *Jewish Enlightenment in an English Key: Anglo-Jewry's Construction of Modern Jewish Thought* (Princeton University Press, Princeton, 2000), 7.

82   Talya Fishman, 'Forging Jewish Memory, Besamin Rosh and the Invention of Pre Emancipation Culture', in Elisheva Carlebach, John M. Efron and David N. Myers (eds), *Jewish History and Jewish Memory* (Brandeis University Press, Hanover, 1998), 71.

83   Endelman, *The Jews of Britain*, 111.

84   Steven Singer, 'Jewish Religious Thought in Early Victorian London', *Association for Jewish Studies Review* 10, no. 2 (1985), 184.

85   Bill Williams, 'The anti-Semitism of Tolerance: Middleclass Manchester and the Jews 1870–1900', quoted in Bryan Cheyette, 'Jewish Stereotyping and English Literature, 1875–1920', in Anthony Kushner and Kenneth Lunn (eds), *Traditions of Intolerance, Historical Perspectives on Fascism and Race Discourse in Britain* (Manchester University Press, Manchester, 1989), 13.

86   Todd M. Endelman, 'English Jewish History', *Modern Judaism*, 11, no. 1, (1991), 91.

87   Steven Singer, 'The Anglo-Jewish Ministry in Early Victorian London', *Modern Judaism* 5 (1985), 279; and Vivian D. Lipman, *Social History of the Jews in England 1850–1950* (Watts & Co, London, 1950), 40.

88   Eugene Charlton Black, *The Social Politics of Anglo-Jewry* (Basil Blackwell, Oxford, 1988), 2.

89   Steven Singer, 'Jewish Education in the Mid-Nineteenth Century, A Study of the Early Victorian Community', *Jewish Quarterly Review*, LXXVII (1986–1987), 174–5.

90   Gilman, *The Emancipation of the Jews in England*, 57; and Michael Clark, 'Jewish Identity in British Politics, the Case of the First Jewish MPs, 1858–87', *Jewish Social Studies*, 13, no. 2, (2007), 102, 106.

91   Israel Finestein, "Jewish Emancipation in Victorian England: Self Imposed Limits on

Assimilation," in Jonathan Frankel and Steven J. Zipperstein (eds), *Assimilation and Community: The Jews in Nineteenth-Century Europe*, (Cambridge University Press, Cambridge, 1992), 39.

92 Todd M. Endelman, *Radical Assimilation in English Jewish History, 1656–1945* (Indiana University Press, Bloomington, 1990), 11.

93 Roth, *A History of the Jews in England*, 192.

94 Holly Snyder, 'English Markets, Jewish Merchants and Atlantic Endeavors: Jews and the Making of British Transatlantic Commercial Culture 1650–1800', in Richard L. Kagan and Philip D. Morgan (eds), *Atlantic Diasporas, Jews, Conversos and Crypto-Jews in the Age of Mercantilism, 1500–1800* (Johns Hopkins University Press, Baltimore, 2009), 51–5.

95 Endelman, *The Jews of Britain, 1656 to 2000*, 41.

96 Henry Mayhew, *London Labour and the London Poor*, 4 vols (Dover Publications, New York, 1968), 119; Endelman, *Radical Assimilation*, 115.

97 Endelman, *Radical Assimilation*, 114–18.

98 Roth, *A History of the Jews in England*, 201.

99 Endelman, *Radical Assimilation*, 10.

100 W. D. Rubinstein, *A History of the Jews in the English-Speaking World: Great Britain* (Macmillan, Basingstoke, 1996), 66, 68.

101 Vivian D. Lipman, 'Trends in Anglo-Jewish Occupations', *Journal of Jewish Sociology* 2, no. 2, (1960), 205.

102 Steven Singer, 'Jewish Education in the Mid-Nineteenth Century: A Study of the Early Victorian London Community', *The Jewish Quarterly Review*, 77, no. 2/3, (1986), 168.

103 ibid., 164, 168.

104 Ruderman, *Jewish Enlightenment in an English Key*, 6.

105 C. Russell and H.S. Lewis, *The Jew in London: A Study of Racial Character and Present-Day Conditions* (T.Y. Crowell & Co., New York, 1901), 217.

106 Vivian D. Lipman, 'Jewish Settlement in the East End 1840–1940', in Aubrey Newman, *East End 1840–1940. Proceedings of the Conference Held on 22 October 1980 Jointly by the Jewish Historical Society of England and the Jewish East End Project of the Association of Jewish Youth* (Jewish Historical Society of England, London, 1981), 26; Geoffrey Alderman, *Modern British Jewry* (Oxford University Press, Oxford, 1992), 6–7.

107 English Census, 1841, 1851, 1861.

108 Clark, *Albion and Jerusalem*, 237.

109 Mayhew, *London Labour and the London Poor*, 118.

110 ibid., 119; and Roth, *A History of the Jews in England*, 210.

111 Vivian D. Lipman, 'The Anglo-Jewish Community in Victorian Society', in Dov Noy and Issachar Ben-Ami, *Studies in the Cultural Life of the Jews in England* (Jerusalem Magnes Press, Hebrew University Press, 1975), 159.

112 Werner E. Mosse, *Jews in the German Economy, the German-Jewish Economic Elite 1820–1935* (Clarendon Press, Oxford, 1997), 17.

113 English Census 1851.

114 Cecil Roth, The Rise of Provincial Jewry, (JCR-UK Jewish Communities and Records, the Susser Archive, 1950), accessed 13 March 2013, <http,//www.jewishgen.org/jcr-uk/susser/provincialjewry/index.htm>; and Endelman, *The Jews of Britain, 1656 to 2000*, 51.

115 David Feldman, *Englishmen and Jews, Social Relations and Political Culture, 1840–1914* (Yale University Press, New Haven, 1994), 21.

116 Geoffery Green, 'Anglo-Jewish Trading Connections with Officers and Seamen of

the Royal Navy 1740–1820', *Jewish Historical Studies* 29 (1982–1986), 97.

117 Bernard Susser, 'Social Acclimatisation of Jews in 18th and 19th Century Devon', in *Exeter Papers in Economic History*, 3, (1970); Bernard Susser, *The Jews of South-West England: the Rise and Decline of Their Medieval and Modern Communities* (Exeter University Press, Exeter, 1993), 207.

118 Green, *The Royal Navy and Anglo-Jewry, 1740–1820, Traders and Those who Served*. Appendix 1 Register of Jewish Navel Agents; and Susser, *The Jews of South-West England*, 103.

119 Susser, *The Jews of South-West England*, 105.

120 Green, 'Anglo-Jewish Trading, 97, 113.

121 Susser, *The Jews of South-West England*, 258 see also *Voice of Jacob*, 13 March 1846.

122 Susser, 'Social Acclimatisation of Jews in 18th and 19th Century Devon', 207.

123 Susser, *The Jews of South-West England*, 60.

124 Gael R. Hammer, *Phillip Blashki, a Victorian Patriarch* (P. Blashki and Sons, Melbourne,1986), 2–3, 6, 10.

125 Sorkin, *The Transformation of German Jewry, 1780–1840*, 13.

126 Pulzer, *Jews and the German State. The Political History of a Minority, 1848–1933*, 79.

127 Sorkin, *The Transformation of German Jewry, 1780–1840*, 23.

128 Shulamit S. Magnus, *Jewish Emancipation in a German City* (Stanford University Press, Stanford, 1997), 16. For details on the economic activity of German Jewry see also Kaplan, *Jewish Daily Life in Germany, 1618–1945*.

129 Daniel Nussbaum, 'Social Justice and Social Policy in the Jewish Tradition. The Satisfaction of Basic Human Needs in Pozan in the 17th and 18th Centuries' (PhD thesis, Brandeis University, 1977), 148, 177.

130 Michael A. Meyer, Michael Brenner, Mordechai Breuer, and Michael Graetz, *German-Jewish History in Modern Times* (Columbia University Press, New York, 1996), 17.

131 Steven M. Lowenstein, 'The Beginning of Integration 1780–1870', in Marion A. Kaplan (ed.), *Jewish Daily Life in Germany 1618–1945* (Oxford University Press, Oxford, 2005), 98.

132 ibid., 99, 107.

133 Meyer et al., *German-Jewish History in Modern Times*, 30.

134 ibid., 129–30.

135 Nimrod Zinger, 'Away from Home, Travelling and Leisure Activities among German Jews in the Seventeenth and Eighteen Centuries', *Leo Baeck Institute Year Book* 56 (2011), 54; and Manfred Jehle, "Relocations" in South Prussia and New East Prussia. Prussia's Demographic Policy towards the Jews in Occupied Poland 1772–1806', *Leo Baeck Institute Year Book* 52 (2007), 26.

136 Keith H. Pickus, *Constructing Modern Identities, Jewish University Students in Germany, 1815–1914* (Wayne State University Press, Detroit, 1999), 26.

137 Meyer et al., *German-Jewish History in Modern Times*, 199.

138 Magnus, *Jewish Emancipation in a German City*, 61.

139 Private collections.

140 Christhard Hoffmann, 'Constructing Jewish Modernity. Mendelssohn Jubilee Celebrations within German Jewry 1829–1929', in Rainer Liedtke and David Rechter (eds), *Towards Normality? Acculturation and Modern German Jewry* (Mohr Siebeck, Tübingen, 2003), 30–1. For a discussion of German perceptions on Jewish cultural production see Jacob Katz, 'German Culture and the Jews', in Jehuda Reinharz and Walter Schatzberg (eds), *The Jewish Response to German Culture. From the Enlightenment to the Second World War* (published for Clark University by University Press of New England, Hanover, 1985).

141 Marion A. Kaplan, *The Making of the Jewish Middle Class. Women, Family, and Identity in Imperial Germany* (Oxford University Press, Oxford, 1991), 8.

142 Paula E. Hyman, *The Emancipation of the Jews of Alsace: Acculturation and Tradition in the Nineteenth Century* (Yale University Press, New Haven, 1984), 4.

143 Michael A. Meyer, 'Normality and Assimilation', in Rainer Liedtke and David Rechter, *Towards Normality? Acculturation and Modern German Jewry* (Mohr Siebeck, Tübingen, 2003), 22–3; Natalie Naimark-Goldberg, 'Health, Leisure and Sociability at the Turn of the Nineteenth Century. Jewish Women and German Spas', *Leo Baeck Institute Year Book* 55 (2010), 64.

144 Katz, 'German Culture and the Jews', 85.

145 Edward David Luft, *The Naturalized Jews of the Grand Duchy of Posen in 1834 and 1835* (Scholars Press, Atlanta, 1987), xi; Alan Levenson, 'The Posen Factor', *Shofar, An Interdisciplinary Journal of Jewish Studies* 17, no. 1 (1998), 73.

146 Ernest Hamburger, 'One Hundred Years of Emancipation', *Leo Baeck Institute Year Book* XIV (1969), 6. Although initially a Polish population, there was a continual influx of Germans during the first half of the nineteenth century, resulting in a greater number of Germans than Poles. Eliezer Sariel, '"In the East Lie My Roots; My Branches in the West". The Distinctiveness of the Jews of Posen in the First Half of the Nineteenth Century', *Leo Baeck Institute Year Book* 58 (2013), 176.

147 Artur Eisenbach, *The Emancipation of the Jews in Poland, 1780–1870* (Basil Blackwell in association with the Institute for Polish-Jewish Studies, Oxford, 1991), 287; Richard Rürup, 'Jewish Emancipation and Bourgeois Society', *Leo Baeck Institute Year Book*, XIV, (1969), 78.

148 Sariel, 'In the East Lie My Roots', 178.

149 Williams, *The Making of Manchester Jewry, 1740–1875*, 127, 350; Public Record Office Victoria, Index to Unassisted Inward Passenger Lists to Victoria 1852–1923; English Census 1861.

150 Thomas G. August, 'Family Structure and Jewish Continuity in Jamaica since 1655', *American Jewish Archives* XLI, no. 1 (1989), 34.

151 Arthur Kiron, 'An Atlantic Jewish Republic of Letters?', *Jewish History* 20, no. 2 (2006), 171; Adam Sutcliffe, 'Jewish History in the Age of Atlanticism', in Richard L. Kagan and Philip D. Morgan (eds), *Atlantic Diasporas, Jews, Conversos and Crypto-Jews in the Age of Mercantilism, 1500–1800* (Johns Hopkins University Press, Baltimore, 2009), 28.

152 Snyder, 'English Markets, Jewish Merchants', 51; Thomas G. August, 'An Historical Profile of the Jewish Community of Jamaica', *Jewish Social Studies* 49, nos 3–4 (1987), 312.

153 Eli Faber, *Jews, Slaves, and the Slave Trade: Setting the Record Straight* (New York University Press, New York, 1998), 58.

154 Thomas G. August, 'Jewish Assimilation and the Plural Society in Jamaica', *Social and Economic Studies* 36, no. 2 (1987), 111; and O. Alexander Miller, 'Colonial Capital, Advances in Understanding Caribbean Migration Experiences', *Social and Economic Studies* 57, nos 3–4 (2008), 157.

155 Gordon Merrill, 'The Role of Sephardic Jews in the British Caribbean Area during the Seventeenth Century', *Caribbean Studies* 4, no. 3 (1964), 35.

156 Marilyn Delevante and Anthony Alberga, *The Island of One People: An Account of the History of the Jews of Jamaica* (Ian Randle, Kingston, 2006), 13; C. S. Monaco, 'Port Jews or a People of the Diaspora? A Critique of the Port Jew Concept', *Jewish Social Studies* 15, no. 2 (2009), 152.

157 August, 'Family Structure and Jewish Continuity in Jamaica since 1655', 27; Delevante and Alberga, *The Island of One People*, 9.

158 August, 'An Historical Profile of the Jewish Community of Jamaica', 303 and 308.
159 Jacob A.P.M. Andrade and Basil Oscar Parks, *A Record of the Jews in Jamaica from the English Conquest to the Present Times* (Jamaica Times, Kingston, 1941), 9; Delevante and Alberga, *The Island of One People*, chapter 6.
160 Andrade and Parks, *A Record of the Jews in Jamaica*, 27.
161 Faber, *Jews, Slaves, and the Slave Trade*, 69.
162 Trevor Burnard, 'European Migration to Jamaica, 1655–1780', *William and Mary Quarterly* 53, no. 4 (1996), 790.
163 Robert Cohen, 'Early Caribbean Jewry, A Demographic Perspective', *Jewish Social Studies*, 45, no. 2, (1983) 126.
164 Andrade and Parks, *A Record of the Jews in Jamaica*, 106–7, 126–9.
165 August, 'An Historical Profile of the Jewish Community of Jamaica', 305. Although Jewish Law stipulates the legal position of slaves, records indicate that Jews certainly held slaves, University College London, Department of History, *Legacies of British Slave-Ownership* (University College London, 2019).
166 Jackie Ranston, *The Lindo Legacy* (Toucan Books, London, 2000), 50.
167 ibid., 54.
168 August, 'An Historical Profile of the Jewish Community of Jamaica', 307.
169 Merrill, 'The Role of Sephardic Jews', 48.
170 Miles Taylor, 'The 1848 Revolution and the British Empire', *Past & Present* 166, February (2000), 152, 158.

Chapter 2

Jewish Identity in a New Land

Yes gentle lady you sneer as you pass the Jew, but ask your Christian butcher how he kills his veal ... the explanation given will be sufficient to show that the custom alluded to, far from deserving reprobation, is rather entitled to our respect, both as a religious institution and as a safeguard to morality.
—*Argus*, 9 May 1851, 4

Jewish historiography charts the changing nature of collective Jewish identity, concentrating on the unique characteristics of specific time and place.[1] As we have seen in the previous chapter, communities responded to the challenges of modernity in individual ways, exhibiting varying levels of acculturation, although this did not necessarily lead to the communal loss of attachment to Judaism.[2] In new settler societies such as Melbourne, communal identity was structured from the values imported with settlers from their previous place of residence. In Melbourne these initial colonists were audacious individuals pursuing new opportunities, but also seeking to maintain the familiar in unfamiliar conditions, negotiating relationships and forming structural elements in a society that included convicts, emancipists and free settlers.

For Jews in New World cities, that newness offered an alternative and unique opportunity to become integrated participants in the development of these societies. In Melbourne, as in other new settlements, those establishing communities did so from scratch, which provided an opportunity to create and define a Jewish identity as an expression of the personal values of the members, integrated into the wider society and creating a community in their own image. They produced a unique response for the maintenance of the structural elements of Judaism. Every aspect required formulation and implementation, from the community's attempts to preserve Judaism through ritual and practice, to practical aspects such as the provision of kosher food and personal cultural identity.

These communal pragmatic responses are a reflection of the psychology of the early settlers to Melbourne, a self-selecting group of intrepid individuals immigrating to a fledgling community, which for the most religiously conservative would have been a massive step of profound implications, taking them outside the framework of a secure religious structure.[3] As Jews moved to the urban centres of Europe in the late nineteenth century, communal structures and the organisations that supported these were altered to suit the new conditions. This happened in Melbourne too, but unlike in Europe, those arriving came to a place devoid of all community.

By the mid nineteenth century, Melbourne had a Jewish population numerically equal to a midsized European city such as Lissa, but unlike these towns where the Jewish population comprised 40 to 50 per cent of the total, in Victoria this was around 0.5 per cent. Unlike many of their neighbours, they were already experienced urban dwellers, bringing with them Judaism practised in a modern urban setting. Melbourne also hosted a relatively homogenous Jewish population. The majority were of British birth or from the English-speaking world—Jamaica, the United States, New Zealand and South Africa—supplemented by a number of European Jews, many of whom had also lived in England. Others included a small number from Turkey, Egypt and North Africa.

A European Perspective

For the residents of the urban centres of Europe, modernity brought with it requirements to validate their contemporary faiths in light of new philosophical and scientific scholarship, while the rational philosophy of Descartes and the biblical critique of Spinoza further confronted Jewish and non-Jewish fundamental beliefs.[4] For Anglo-Jewry the demands of this new intellectual discourse was immediate and unmediated. English Jews had access to these new concepts and to the philosophical works of Voltaire, Locke, Newton, Stillingfleet, Cudworth and Bolinsbroke.[5] Previous values were also confronted through adaptations to older class systems, as new wealth generated by industrialisation and with urbanisation further loosened hierarchies. In response, governments acted to mediate these changes and to ensure maintenance of control.

For the Jewish community, secularisation held special challenges. Judaism is expressed through a range of commandments and prohibitions affecting the behaviours and the religious practices to which Jews are required to adhere in all spheres of their lives. Here there is no distinction between leisure and religious activity, so a response to modernity was often perceived as a laxity of religious observance.[6] As emancipatory processes defined new national and secular identities, there was a parallel reassessment of values, as Jewish communities questioned religious norms and the discipline of the rabbinic elite, developing a 'scepticism and religious permissiveness'.[7]

Adaptations included modifications to the internal and external manifestations of Judaism and cultural identity, shaping the intellectual and social life of the community. These were expressed through the adoption of many of the outward manifestations of their compatriots. Increased prosperity encouraged a consumer culture, and urban dwellers enjoyed the entertainments offered in a city, from the theatre to galleries and coffee houses, and in many cities Jews became prominent participants in cultural activity.[8] As Hyman considers in her analysis of the Jews of Alsace, 'Many Jews now discovered their individuality and embarked on a journey of self-definition freed from the constraints of a collective identity.'[9]

Linguistic assimilation also provided opportunities for cultural change, creating a Judaism that was 'religiously unified but culturally diverse', whereby 'each group displayed the markedly particular characteristics of its milieu'.[10] This was not an abandonment of Jewish identity; rather urbanisation encouraged new manifestations of Judaism, which was broadened to consider secular and religious issues. For English Jews this process had begun earlier than on much of the continent, and derived from a response and adaptation to the contemporary social values of English society. These external signs of acculturation are also evident in Melbourne, where the Jewish community also emulated many of the values and norms of their urban contemporaries.

Nineteenth-century Anglo-Jewry was not as orthodox as their eastern European brethren, but they were more orthodox in their practices than were contemporary wealthy urban Jews in America or in other parts of Europe. In general they observed the major Jewish holidays, kept the Sabbath and adhered to the laws of *kashrut*.[11] Whereas anti-Semitism in Germany led many to consider that social advancement could only be achieved by conversion to Christianity, this was a far rarer occurrence in England or in Australia. In the eighteenth century some English Jews responded to the rather more relaxed attitude towards religion by simply abandoning it, but they rarely chose the alternative—Christianity.[12] Following full political emancipation in the mid nineteenth century, abandoning Judaism, particularly for the wealthier Jews, was reversed. Instead, they sustained a nominal connection to Judaism, ignoring elements they considered obstacles to modernity, becoming 'nonobservant Orthodox Jews' and persevering in at least some association with Judaism and the Jewish community.[13]

The nineteenth century saw a sharp increase in the Jewish population of Europe, from 2 million at the beginning of the century to 7 million eighty years later. The period also witnessed enormous internal and external migration to urban centres. Of the many cities we now consider quintessentially 'Jewish', Odessa, Berlin, Vienna, Paris, London and New York became major Jewish centres only at this time. In all these cities debates arose surrounding the place of religion and the cultural frameworks of Judaism in a modern city.[14] A consequence of this new wave of urbanism was an identification by Jews with their new place of residence. Jews began to equate themselves culturally with these cities, to the extent that it has been said that 'Viennese Jews considered themselves politically Austrian, ethnically Jewish and more than ever, culturally Viennese.[15]

Communal Structure

In understanding Melbourne Jewry's adaptations in a new city, a number of areas of communal, personal and public expressions of Judaism require examination. The history of the Melbourne synagogues has been detailed in general histories and in the specific congregational histories, so their details do not require elaboration here, but reading the extant records does reveal attempts to maintain communal cohesion and perhaps financial pragmatism in their development.

In Victoria, in England and across the New World, Judaism was a matter of personal choice, requiring members to develop a collective consensus for its maintenance. Religious life provided a focus for networking, offering not only spiritual support and comfort, but also social and cultural interaction. In Melbourne this is clearly seen in the rapid establishment of communal social infrastructure. There is some conjecture over the exact date for the first services held in Melbourne. Isaac Hart, interviewed in 1895, stated that the first services were held in October 1840, presumably for the High Holidays of that year, at the home of David Benjamin.[16] Goldman places the services at the home of David Benjamin's brother, Solomon Benjamin, with the service conducted by Edward Hart and assisted by Michael Cashmore, Samuel Henry Harris and Isaac Lazarus Lincoln.[17] Hart was 'a welcome arrival and he was able to act as cantor and chant the prayers with grace and accuracy'.[18]

In 1841 formal congregational life in Melbourne was launched with the establishment of the 'Jewish Congregational Society', electing Michael Cashmore as its president, Solomon Benjamin vice president and a committee formed of Moses Lazarus, Isaac Lazarus Lincoln, Isaac Fonsaker and Henry Davis. That year, at the Port Phillip Hotel, the society held High Holidays services, attended by twenty-five coreligionists.[19] Establishing a management committee, they drew up organisational rules, which included a fine for non-attendance at committee meetings. In a society with voluntary communal allegiance, membership appears to have been problematic, as the committee initiated a weekly membership fee of six pence, while also decreeing a two-guinea fine for any Jews resident in the district who had not become a member within six months of arrival.

Even with these rules, maintenance of a *minyan* was challenging, as after the High Holidays of 1846 Asher Hymen Hart resigned as honorary reader. He was firm in stating his reason: 'I will not any longer (to be plain) submit to the insult of attending the Synagogue on Shabbats and Holydays without the means of celebrating public worship.' In response seven members of the congregation promised to attend every Shabbat service on penalty of a five-shilling fine, ensuring the *minyan* necessary for worship was guaranteed.[20] In 1843 they renamed the congregation ק'ק שארית ישראל, 'The Holy Congregation of the Remnant of Israel', a title popular with many New World synagogues and one that reveals the messianic hope of a dispersed population.[21] The central symbol of Jewish religious life is the Torah and the committee passed a resolution stating that 'the increasing population of the Jewish community in Port Phillip and their apparent anxiety for the establishment of our Holy Religion on a sure and firm basis renders it incumbent on the Committee of the Congregation to provide, amongst other necessities, a "Sepher Torah"', and authorised its procurement through Solomon Benjamin's agents in London.[22]

A cemetery was the first structural element created by the community. For settler societies cemeteries are not only a necessity for the burial of the dead, but also form an attachment and connection to a specific place for those who stay and for those who move on. For Jews, a cemetery is an imperative communal obligation and a number of religious teachings guide their location. Cemeteries must be situated beyond the outmost residences of a town and their size is defined by the minimum distances stipulated between graves.[23] In new communities, the reality of the settlement experience obliged provisioning of a cemetery in precedence over the construction of a synagogue.[24]

The death of Henry Davis's daughter in 1840 prompted the community to establish a place for her burial. They took an independent response, initially identifying land at Pentridge, which was purchased by Abraham Abrahams, but this proved unsuitable due to the rocky nature of the ground. By 1843 the tiny community estimated to number eighty to ninety had petitioned and gathered support from the colonial secretary, who surveyed and approved a site by May the same year.[25] The burial of Davis's daughter in a Jewish burial ground is interesting, as her mother Hannah Howell was not Jewish and had married Davis in church. Hannah was the sister to Judah Solomon's de facto wife

Elizabeth Howell (see chapter 4). As a founder of the Melbourne community, Davis obviously maintained a close connection to and identification with Judaism. Although two of his daughters converted to Judaism in Hobart Town in 1848, it would appear that the dead child had not, although this does not seem to have hindered her burial under Jewish rights.[26]

The issue of non-Jewish mothers continued throughout the development of the community. The construction of the synagogue in Bourke Street required identification of Melbourne's Jews and thus those eligible for membership. At a meeting in February 1848, the committee defined two tiers of membership, creating the category of privileged members for all those who had paid their subscriptions and 'were not married out or living openly in a state of concubinage'.[27] This stipulation gives an indication of the difficulty in maintaining Jewish families in a colony with few Jewish women. Privileged membership entitled voting rights and the prerogative to nominate as office holders. Those not eligible to become privileged members could obtain a seat on payment of six months membership in advance and seats were allocated in a preferential order based on membership status.

Melbourne had a sizable British and Caribbean Sephardi community. For twenty years from the mid 1850s, this community operated its own services according to their *minhag*, in the school room of the Melbourne Hebrew Congregation.[28] This was a lay-led service, conducted in the 1870s by London-born Moses Mendoza and Moroccan-born Lazarus Sicree.[29] The Sephardi community represented many of Melbourne's earliest settlers and some of its very high profile members were actively involved in communal and wider social and political circles. Interest in Sephardi liturgy was not confined to Melbourne. With the establishment of a synagogue in Ballarat, Charles Dyte unsuccessfully attempted to introduce 'Sephardi verses' into the services in this regional congregation.[30]

Even with the small pre–gold rush population, agitation was expressed by those settlers in Geelong for their own synagogue. In September 1849, following a request from Geelong for assistance with the burial of a child, the synagogue committee passed a motion that 'under present circumstances the committee were unanimous in their opinion of not sanctioning anything in connection with a separate congregation at Geelong'. This response is interesting. The distance from Geelong to Melbourne was not insignificant, and attendance at services would have required either a breaking of the Sabbath or holidays through travel or an overnight stay in Melbourne. The same resolution imposed a hefty financial burden on Mr Levy, the father of the late child, as a penalty for not being a financial member of the Melbourne congregation. They charged him £10 for the burial, with the expectation that other Geelong residents would act as guarantor.[31]

In 1857 following a number of disputes with the synagogue committee, its first minister, the Reverend Moses Rintel, resigned and established Melbourne's second synagogue, the East Melbourne Hebrew Congregation. Described in his obituary as 'the great leveller' and 'the pioneer of Judaism in this colony', the obituary continued, 'not a movement in the history of Victorian Judaism from its foundation to the present day, but breathes of the wise and careful forethought of Reverend Moses Rintel in its triumphant achievement'.[32] Rintel was Melbourne's longest-serving nineteenth-century rabbi, member of the Beth Din, and deeply involved in a number of Jewish and wider charitable organisations.

Rintel's concern for the maintenance of Judaism led to the establishment of a Jewish school in Melbourne that offered secular and Jewish subjects. He was engaged with Jewish welfare and politics both at home and internationally, as a long-standing committee member of the Jewish Philanthropic Society, and as one of the prime movers for the establishment of the Jewish Almshouse. His social welfare concerns were wider than his immediate community and he was also involved in a number of Jewish and secular friendly societies, including as president of the United Friends' Jewish Benefit Society, founder of the Order of Oddfellows, a Freemason and a member of the committee of management for the Benevolent Asylum.[33]

Judaism held interest for the general community, and articles appeared regularly explaining issues of belief and ritual. The confidence of the community's position in Melbourne society is exhibited in their use of the press for promotion of communal activities. More significantly, members of the community were not averse to conducting internal political and religious battles in public. Following the establishment of the East Melbourne Hebrew Congregation, Edward Cohen, president of the Melbourne Congregation, published a letter in the *Argus* notifying Melburnians that 'only a small proportion' of the community had joined the second synagogue and that 'the principal members of the Jewish community—nearly the whole of the British Jews in Victoria—held their meetings in the synagogue in Bourke-Street'.[34] Similarly, in 1869 papers around the country reported the ire of the East Melbourne Hebrew Congregation when the Melbourne Hebrew Congregation claimed at a meeting with the colonial secretary that they were the recognised body for Jews in Melbourne. They reported similar indignation over a long-running dispute about whether Reverend Rintel could claim to be the senior rabbi of Melbourne, a debate that reached such a level it was referred to the chief rabbi for arbitration.[35]

Acculturated Anglo-Jewry assumed that the wider society would accept the Jews as a religious community, allowing for a 'pride in being English and a pride in Jewishness'.[36] Similar values were expressed in Germany, where emancipation had created urban and integrated communities engaged in business with the broader community.[37] Moritz Michaelis spent some years in England before immigrating to Victoria and his attitudes and experience of Judaism were moulded by the many encounters in his life. Michaelis, born in Lügde near Bad Pyrmont, came from an Orthodox family, his father described as 'a learned and enthusiastic Talmudic Scholar' 'most respected in the neighbourhood by Jews and Gentiles alike'.[38] Educated in his hometown, he received training in Hebrew and Talmudic studies before being sent at the age of fifteen to begin study at a Gymnasium. He completed nearly two years there, but financial difficulties following his father's prolonged illness caused him to be removed from school and apprenticed to a wholesale and retail trading company. This position required Michaelis to travel, and he described the difficulties of keeping to the laws of *kashrut* in such circumstances:

> During my two visits to Leipsig, I had taken my meals at a Jewish restaurant where everything was exceedingly nice and clean. I there met an old gentleman from Bonn … On my asking him the reason for his absence from our restaurant he cried in great excitement, 'Have you been in there? That scoundrel! That scoundrel! I saw him buy the dressed geese and other poultry at the market.'
>
> … The Snow had been falling for some time and it continued during our journey to Halle, When we arrived there all the passengers felt the cold and rushed into the dining room. I went in also but did not sit down at table. Some of them, co-religionists, whose acquaintance I had made, chaffed me for not doing so. Being only nineteen years of age and very sensitive to ridicule, I thereupon seated myself and ordered a plate of soup. Scarcely had I swallowed a spoonful when I felt very sick and had to go out into the fresh air. This was the first time in my life I had to my knowledge eaten other that [*sic*] Jewish cooking, but according to the gentleman's statement I had already broken the law concerning food though unwittingly.
>
> From Halle to Cassel was a good two days' journey by coach … My religious scruples were such that rather than take another essay to eat non-Jewish cookery I lived on bread and butter and eggs, arriving at Cassel bitterly cold and literally famished.[39]

Michaelis relocated to Manchester to work with his brother for Samson and Leppoc, a firm of German commission agents. Arriving on the Day of Atonement, 23 September 1843, he endeavoured to attend synagogue, but as a non-member was refused admission, an action which so incensed him that he did not enter a synagogue for the ten years he spent in England. By the mid nineteenth century, the Unitarian chapel was proving a drawcard to the German Jewish community. Unlike in London, where the establishment were members of the Church of England, the industrial centres were the province of the industrial-mercantile elite of nonconformists.

Unitarianism 'was theologically relaxed, spiritually undemanding and politely rationalistic. Its ministers were frequently men of wide secular learning, intellectually sophisticated and tolerant of diverse opinions.' Its denial of the trinity removed for Jews the most baffling aspect of Christianity.[40] Men like Michaelis were drawn to experiment with the ideas of Unitarianism, to which he was introduced through a colleague. Never becoming a Unitarian himself, he was impressed by the preaching and rationality of the religion. Finding Unitarianism 'less acceptable to reason', he temporarily lost religious faith altogether, but maintained a study of Judaic works, including the Torah, Mendelsohn, Maimonides and Rashi in Hebrew, English and German:

> thus I became a Jew by conviction as well as birth though I still continued to visit the Unitarian Chapel at Strangeway, the minister being a very clever preacher. Do not misunderstand me, I did not again become strictly orthodox, and though I was then and have even continued, a true believer in God and our teacher Moses, I have not observed many of the ceremonial laws considering them non essential, whilst I yet feel convinced that with few exceptions they are beneficial alike to mind and body. Under these circumstances I could without hesitation answer your grandfather in the affirmative when he asked me before my marriage if I were a true Jew.[41]

Although claiming that he was never again 'strictly orthodox', Michaelis subsequently became actively involved in Melbourne's three synagogues, being respectively the treasurer for the Melbourne and the East Melbourne Hebrew congregations, a founder and president of the St Kilda Hebrew Congregation and committee member for the Melbourne Hebrew School, as well as a member of the Sabbath Observance and Jewish Aid Society committees and a founder of the newspaper the *Australian Israelite*.[42]

Jewish practice made an impression on the Victorian newspapers, with articles printing and reprinting explanations of ritual and observance. The mercantile nature of Jewish occupations meant that this was particularly apparent. It was summed up in 1864 by the *Star*:

The appearance of the streets of Melbourne ... was somewhat
singular during Monday, and in the absence, it may be said almost
total of the members of the Jewish community, a dull and vacant
look was given to the business portion of the city. Monday was
their day of atonement, and most religiously were the requirements of the occasion carried out. Without an exception every
Jewish shop and place of business has been closed, and few, if any,
of the Hebrew persuasion have visited the marts or resorts of
commercial men. Forming, as they do, so large a proportion of the
business population of Melbourne, the absence of Jewish merchants and dealers, even for a day, cannot fail to attract notice.[43]

In Castlemaine the newspaper showed respect and tolerance for the inconven-
ience this might cause the town:

Saturday next being the anniversary of the Jewish New Year, will
be observed as a strict holiday in Castlemaine by all members of
the 'persuasion.' We mention this fact lest ill-natured people
should place a wrong construction upon the closing of some business premises on the day in question.[44]

The gold rush and the mercantile occupations of the Victorian Jewish commu-
nity led to small and dispersed Jewish communities and families across Victoria.
The mining centres such as Bendigo, Ballarat and Castlemaine maintained a
Jewish life, with synagogues eventually being established in Bendigo (1856),
Geelong (1861) and Ballarat (1861), while there was a satellite community in
the seaside suburb of St Kilda prior to the foundation of the synagogue there.
In order to hold services on the most significant festivals, Torah scrolls and other
ritual items were lent from the metropolitan communities, with the expectation
that any donations received would be returned to them in recompense.

On occasion the rabbinical officers also travelled to remote locations.
Such was the case in January 1868 when Dutch-born Betsy Vanderberg
married local storekeeper Prussian-born Morris Brasch at a service conducted
by Moses Rintel at the bride's father's hotel in Beechworth. Connections to
Judaism and communal life were maintained by some rural dwellers through
memberships to metropolitan synagogues far from their place of residence.
The Moss brothers of Hay became members of the East Melbourne Hebrew
Congregation in 1867, two years later presenting it with silver plate for the
decoration of the Torah scrolls.[45]

But the community itself felt some disquiet at synagogue attendance,
religious engagement and reforming tendencies, and the correspondents'

reports to the Jewish press chart the communities concern. With the establishment of the St Kilda Hebrew Congregation in 1869, the members immediately established that they wanted to ensure decorum and make alterations to the services. Initially established as a 'Hebrew and German School and Synagogue combined', their minutes chart the debates to and fro over changes board members wished to make. In 1871 they attempted to experiment with alterations, eventually defining their own *minhag*. They advised that they would post a circular regarding the altered form of prayer a week prior to doing so, so that the congregation could form an opinion of the changes.[46] Throughout all congregations unease arose as to the decorum of the *mishibirach*, and in St Kilda they stipulated that the 'ordinary offering of money (*mishibirach*) be excluded from the service'.[47]

On the first day of Passover 1872, the lay reader Nelson Marks read a portion of the prayers in English from the seventh day service, much to the consternation of the *Australian Israelite*, 'considering that one main feature of this synagogue is to set an example to the younger generation, it seems to us a circumstance calling for extreme regret that any individual ... should assume the responsibility of turning topsy turvy the prescribed order of the service for the different days.'[48] In order to ensure that the congregation was familiar with the service and the expectations of decorum, they affixed the 'general regulations' to the desks, including a stipulation that 'communication with the female sex, such as bringing books, is prohibited'.[49]

Later that year the congregation again codified their *minhag* to ensure that 'the reading of the prayers which by their intrinsic values should occupy a more prominent position in the liturgy.'[50] A final transformation of the 1870s was the inclusion of women in the synagogue choir, and in the 1880s the organisation of a mixed choir.[51] The role of the clergy also changed, with expectations that they would and could provide meaningful sermons delivered in English. These too were advertised and reported in the press. Both city synagogues also introduced minor changes to create 'their own peculiar mode of worship'.[52]

Throughout the 1880s a number of letters were written to the Australian Jewish press expressing unease over issues of decorum and non-attendance in synagogue. These associated current liturgical practices with outmoded rituals requiring modernisation if they were to be of relevance to the community.[53] Although Reform Judaism had been established in various forms in England, Germany and America, the majority of the Melbourne community remained staunchly loyal to the chief rabbi and Anglo-Orthodoxy.

In appointing a reader and teacher, the community authorised a former board member, Isaac Hallenstein, then in England, to look for a suitable candidate, with a stipulation that the person would be able to preach in English.

With the appointment of Elias Blaubaum in 1873, there was a continual toing and froing over suitable changes to the program.

Connecting them firmly to the British Empire was the inclusion of an English 'Prayer for the Royal Family', a prayer that found a place in the liturgy of most of the synagogues within the British Empire, and in many instances emblazoned in carved tablets in pride of place beside the Ark.

The first attempts to introduce Reform Judaism to Melbourne were initiated in the 1880s, led by Abraham Michael Samuell and Rabbi Dattner Jacobson. Samuell had been inspired by Reform Judaism after experiencing this confessional practice while in America. In 1882 he attempted to establish a synagogue with a 'philosophy of modern Judaism'. As he was a believer in observance of the Torah, his modifications were aimed not at dismissing the core elements of religion, but at re-evaluating blind adherence to the letter of the law.

His proposal included holding services on Sunday, which initially appealed to a number of Melbourne's Jewish shopkeepers and tradesmen who found it necessary to work on the Sabbath. Recognising a lack of Hebrew proficiency in the community, he proposed services predominantly in English, and in an attempt to appear modern, providing for mixed seating and a mixed choir, as well as affording full membership to men with non-Jewish wives. The holding of Sunday services was unthinkable to most in the community, and after the preliminary meeting the idea did not progress.[54]

Samuell attempted again three years later, this time with the support of Dattner Jacobson, previously the rabbi at the Melbourne Hebrew Congregation, but who had proved too controversial for the committee and had been removed from his post. Together they briefly formed the Temple of Israel and conducted a service at a Collins Street church, at which Jacobson gave a sermon and a non-Jewish woman played the organ, but this again did not succeed and no further services were held.[55]

A board member of the St Kilda Synagogue created the next push for radical change. The architect Nahum Barnet, a prolific correspondent to the Australian papers, was a constant commentator on religious issues. While adamant in his belief in the importance of the connection with the chief rabbi, he was also critical of communal apathy and expressed a desire to adapt services to add meaning for his contemporaries, writing:

> The younger members of our faith, the intellectual and the educated, are fast drifting into religious nihilism, and the institutions which generally bind and strengthen a community are drooping into decay ... whose duty is it to revive the all but moribund religious zeal of the people? ... I look, then, to our clergy. It is their

duty, nay—it is an obligation they owe the Divine Master whom they serve to rescue us from this mortal death.[56]

Continuing the theme twenty years later, commenting on the Anglican Church's attempts to adapt the *Book of Common Prayer*, he wrote that 'The pruning knife is sadly needed in the ritual of the Synagogue.'[57]

Perhaps the most persistent agitator for change was Prussian-born but English-educated Isaac Jacobs. Jacobs, a founder of the St Kilda Synagogue, was spurred on by what he considered religious apathy engendered through outmoded forms of worship. Jacobs published two pamphlets on the issue. In *Conservative Reform in Jewish Observance* he noted:

> We may reasonably assume that no revision of the liturgy, or modernisation in the mode of rendering Divine Service, is likely to be effected here until some reformer of outstanding ability comes along, and arouses the majority of our people to bring about by communal action such changes in our synagogue services as would be calculated to attract more of our men and women, especially those of the better educated class, and get them to listen to, and take part in a service better calculated to bear good fruit than the present time in some of the orthodox Synagogues; and something that will reflect more of the spirit of the present enlightened age, and less of that of the hoary past.[58]

This pamphlet is noteworthy for the depth of research Jacobs undertook, quoting and then critiquing a number of contemporary sources from Britain, America and Germany. In this battle he was pitched against a conservative opponent, another stalwart of the St Kilda congregation, Phillip Blashki, who would not countenance any changes to liturgical practices.[59] The vision of Jacobs and Samuells was not fulfilled until 1930. Following a trip to England by Castlemaine-born Ada Phillips (nee Crawcour), formal connections were established with one of the influential founders of British Liberal Judaism, Lily Montague, and a viable Reform Congregation was established.

Although commentators decried apathy, maintenance of Judaism was an important sign of merit for many in the community and individual observance was worthy of comment in obituaries. Henriette Leishershonn, incidentally mother of Isaac Jacobs, is described in the *Hebrew Standard* as a woman who 'strictly adhered to the orthodox practices of her faith and was a regular attendant at the services of the St Kilda Hebrew Congregation. As a mark of respect the synagogue doors were opened whilst the funeral cortege passed.'[60] Although Moritz Michaelis claimed not to be an 'observant Jew', his wife Rachel Gotthelp was described in her obituary as 'a devout Jewess withal ... carefully supervising the religious and moral education of her children'.[61]

Henriette Leishershonn, Private Collection

Communal identity requires the interlinked activities of personal and public participation. Without individuals exhibiting cultural connections to the decisions they make, no communal activity can take place. The remote setting of the Australian colonies and the realities of a new settler society created challenges for the practicalities of observance and religious maintenance.

Without existing communal structures or the formal establishment of Jewish education and training, the community was required to take responsibility for important elements of ritual and practice. The first sanctioned *mohel* in Melbourne, Isaac Lazarus Lincoln, undertook the role for the fledgling community, acquiring training from a non-Jewish doctor. Lincoln, born Isaac Lazarus, son of Polish-born Jonas Lazarus and his wife, Rosa Nathan, took the name Lincoln from the city of his birth in Lincolnshire. First settling in New South Wales in 1834, Lincoln was an early investor in Victoria, purchasing land in Seymour in 1845.[62] Economic prosperity seems to have eluded him, due either to the economic conditions of Victoria in the 1840s or to his lack of business acumen. Initially establishing himself as a draper in Collins Street, he then tried his hand as an auctioneer and commission agent, prior to relocating to Seymour, where in 1846 he established the Lincolnshire Stores. Lincoln's fortunes declined further, and in 1849 he was declared insolvent, accused of poor bookkeeping and of gambling. The family sailed for California, only to be drowned on the return voyage a year later.[63]

Lincoln was intimately involved with the establishment of the Melbourne Hebrew Congregation. Described as 'zealous and pious', he could not be formally accredited as *mohel*, as any authorisation would have required a personal examination by the chief rabbi. In lieu of this, the Melbourne Hebrew Congregation issued a certificate stating that 'he had acted as *mohel* for seven years to the entire satisfaction of the community'.[64] Interestingly, Lincoln appears to have been pragmatic in his willingness on occasion to circumcise the children of non-Jewish mothers in variance with *halachic* law. In other areas he proved to be a traditionalist. Where Chief Rabbi Solomon Herschel condoned modern medical practices, sanctioning the use of chloroform to anaesthetise an infant prior to circumcision, Lincoln would not.[65]

Lincoln was prepared to circumcise two sons of Nathaniel Nathan, although their mother was not Jewish. Nathan, convicted in 1830 for stealing clothing, was granted a ticket of leave in New South Wales in 1838, although this was revoked after he was found to have committed 'highly disorderly and immoral conduct' with Harriet Smith (who became pregnant), an assigned servant to Abraham Elias.[66] After being released from jail, he was sent to Melbourne where he married Louisa Darcy although, as discussed below, this was likely to have been a bigamous marriage.

Lincoln circumcised Nathan's first son, Samuel, on 3 August 1843, as the child was considered a 'special case'. In 1848, Nathan wrote to the Melbourne Hebrew Congregation requesting a conversion for his family. The same letter also contained an application for the circumcision of a second son. The committee took a somewhat noncommittal approach, replying that 'as the officers of the congregation had no control over Mr Lincoln the *mohel* they could not interfere in the matter', but this view was revised by the time of the birth of Nathan's third son, Chaim, and on this occasion permission was refused.[67]

In 1850, the committee was still debating whether the children of non-Jewish mothers could be circumcised, and requesting clarification from their newly appointed rabbi, Moses Rintel. His response was that 'a child of a Jewish mother and Christian father can be circumcised, but there was nothing that would stop a Christian mother's child being circumcised. Nothing in the laws to stop this', stressing that there was no religious objection, but that he would only undertake the procedure if it was sanctioned by the committee.[68] But two months later the committee had again hardened its stance, passing a resolution preventing Rintel from circumcising or burying anyone without the committee's express permission.[69]

Conversion

In modern societies, maintaining Jewish identity and communal behavioural norms are a challenge. For Jews, cultural survival and communal solidarity are grounded in the family unit and supported through communal organisations. Endogamy is important and reinforced by the orthodox Jewish law that children follow the religion of their mother. Maintaining this tradition and the hereditary line of Judaism was a major preoccupation not only of the community of colonial Victoria, but also a pattern repeated in the early settler society of America and in the urbanising centres of central and western Europe.

In Victoria, the makeup of society was a major contributing factor. The demographics of nineteenth-century Victoria meant that there was a far greater number of men than women, inevitably resulting in significant rates of out-marriage by Jewish men, and thus the potential loss of their children from Judaism. Prior to the discovery of gold, the population of Victoria was very small and the Jewish population was minute, estimated at 117 in 1846 and rising to 364 by 1851.[70]

Although the gold rush greatly increased the number of Jews in Victoria, it did not solve the gender imbalance, so that by 1857 the total Jewish population had risen to 2181, of whom only 665 were women. Four years later, the proportion had improved, and the total Jewish population had risen to 2903 the majority of this increase being female, bringing the number of Jewish women in the colony to 1046. But this increase did not alleviate the problem for Jewish men unable to find Jewish brides, continuing the inevitable response of men finding non-Jewish partners.[71]

The Jewish community of England considered that under the agreement allowing their readmission, a prohibition existed on conversion. Amsterdam, with its more tolerant tradition and high numbers of *Conversos*, had been a convenient and pragmatic destination for British conversions. The differing settlement patterns and diverging congregational structures in the Australian colonies resulted in a lack of uniformity in the attitudes and management of conversion. The New South Wales Court Act of 1787 ensured that 'British law landed with the First Fleet', and this was reiterated in 1828 with Imperial Act 9 Geo IV c83, ensuring that all statutes and laws in force in England would apply to New South Wales and Van Diemen's Land. These included the 1698 Blasphemy Act, which prohibited the conversion to Judaism of English Christians.[72]

The practicalities of establishing a Jewish community in an environment with a gender imbalance required some expediency. In Hobart the community took a pragmatic approach, creating a Beth Din of lay members and converting women when required. With the appointment of religious functionaries, the system was regularised. Melbourne had a more conservative approach and in 1844 in the absence of a formally appointed Beth Din, the Laws of the Melbourne Hebrew Congregation stated that 'no application of conversion to the Jewish faith be received by this congregation or entertained in any shape'.[73] In July 1845 Asher Hyman Hart put forward a proposition to the congregation that:

> All persons of the Jewish Faith wishing to have their wives and females that they may be cohabiting with up to this day 27 July 1845 be made 'Geurists', shall make application to the Honorary Secretary in writing within one month from this date and that the President shall write in the name of the Congregation to the 'High Priest' [*sic*] of London.[74]

Hart also raised the issue in a letter dated 27 June 1848 to the chief rabbi, which included a substantial list of procedural and *halachah* enquiries, the final of which was:

> the desire to know whether, under favourable circumstances, you would authorise the making of female proselytes, there being one or two cases that have very frequently been brought under our notice, but which we have invariably refused to entertain, not thinking it a matter for laymen (most of whom are young and inexperienced in such affairs) to legislate upon?[75]

This led to a situation where Jewish men chose not to marry, rather living unmarried with the mothers of their children, a situation that did nothing to resolve the religious identity of these offspring. In November 1851, the then president of the Melbourne Hebrew Congregation, Michael Cashmore, wrote again to the chief rabbi on this topic:

> I must crave your particular indulgence for a little while, as the subject assumes a new feature by your reply than it ever has and is a matter itself most important to our community, because there are several members of our faith who have unfortunately been in the Colony for some years past; they arrived at a time when no Jewish females were to be found, and in consequence have

become united with Christian women; they, however, do not wish to sever from the faith of their fathers, but on the contrary, are ready to support the same and are more desirous of initiating their children in the true faith of Israel.[76]

The marriage records across all three synagogues show that at least twenty-nine marriages were formalised in synagogue of relationships previously contracted under civil law, and at least three by couples who had already produced families out of wedlock. Some appear to be the result of delayed conversions. Such was the example of the hawker Samuel Marks, who in 1874 remarried Louisa Jane Cheetham, seventeen years after their first wedding.

Other couples appear to have been married in a synagogue sometime after civil ceremonies. Couples living in mining towns or other areas without access to a synagogue would also sometimes marry civilly prior to the formalisation of their relationship in a metropolitan synagogue, although that would not explain why Melbourne residents Katie Raphael and Leopold Lobascher married in Carlton six weeks prior to their wedding at the Melbourne Hebrew Congregation in 1887.

The difficulty of conversion in Victoria also led some who could afford it to seek assistance directly from London. Four cases have been identified in the London records. At least two of these cases were of Melbourne families, and indicate the importance of the correct and recognised conversion procedures. Nathaniel Nathan, mentioned above, who was a married man with a daughter at the time of his transportation, did not obtain a *get* from his first wife Edal, but left her for twenty-three years as an *agunah*.

Nathan was a founding member of the Melbourne Hebrew Congregation, although living with a non-Jewish common law wife. In 1845 he was one of the five members of the Melbourne Hebrew Congregation who requested an ultimately unsuccessful meeting 'to consider the priority of making converts'. Although two of his sons were circumcised by Lazarus Lincoln as 'special cases', his request for conversion was refused, contained in the same resolution which passed the ambiguous ruling on the circumcision of his second son.[77] To remedy this position, Nathaniel and his family sailed to London and, although technically an adulterer, he was accepted by the Beth Din, where on 18 April 1853 he divorced his first wife. On 30 January 1854, Louisa Darcy and the five children were converted; she and Nathaniel were married a week later, with Nathaniel signing the marriage register as a 'widow'.[78]

In the 1860s, Melbourne's two synagogues put themselves under the auspices and jurisdiction of the chief rabbi of the United Kingdom, Nathan Adler. In 1861, to ensure proper protocols were established, Rabbi Adler attempted to instigate a multi-staged procedure. To ensure that the community was satisfied with the applicants' credentials, a joint committee of the synagogues would receive applications and make recommendations, before requests were sent to London for his approval. When the joint committee of the two congregations broke down, the chief rabbi required the wardens of both congregations to support the application before he would entertain support.

The final process was undertaken through a Beth Din established in 1864, expressly for this purpose. The Beth Din initially comprised Moses Rintel, Isaac Pulver and Samuel Herman (the rabbi of the Ballarat Hebrew Congregation).[79] The Beth Din was established only for conversions and to supervise issues and procedures pertaining to *kashrut* and it was initially not authorised to hear cases of divorce, although this was later added to its responsibilities.[80]

Although in letter after letter the chief rabbi reiterated that he did not approve of conversions, he appears to have taken a pragmatic approach to the issue:

> Since I am in office, I have always set my face against proselytisation because a long experience has convinced me that by facilitating the same—consequences as serious and disastrous to the religious, moral and social state must arise in our Communities.
>
> I have only given my way to your request and to those of other congregations to allow the Rev Messrs Herman, Rintel and Pulver to make גיור. However I have such permission only in urgent and <u>exceptional</u> cases, when there was no religious objection whatsoever and by special request of the Warden.[81]

Conversions would only be considered where initial marriages had been contracted under civil law, rather than in a Christian ceremony.[82] Complications arose not only for the wives of Jewish men but also for children born prior to the mother's conversion. Although a number of the sons of such unions were circumcised, the chief rabbi also required them to undergo a conversion, which included immersion in a *mikvah*.

The two congregations did not see eye to eye on the matter. Initially the East Melbourne Hebrew Congregation appears more readily to have agreed to conversions, while the Melbourne Hebrew Congregation stalled, even after candidates had been approved by the chief rabbi. The East Melbourne Hebrew Congregation seems to have been operating at a somewhat independent pace, and in 1872 during a spat with Reverend Ornstein over the seniority of Melbourne's rabbis they reported the case to the chief rabbi of a circumcised son born to a non-Jewish housekeeper. Apparently paying the housekeeper off, the father had subsequently married a Jewish woman and produced a large family. The elder son was reaching bar mitzvah age and had no knowledge of his maternity. In order to solve the problem, Reverend Rintel convened his own 'Beth Din', with Woolf Davis and Isaac Friedman, converting the child and enabling the bar mitzvah to take place.[83]

The Beth Din was constituted for the Melbourne metropolitan area only. In 1862 a Rabbi Sappir arrived in the colony, and converted a woman in Bendigo. This came to the attention of Rabbi Adler, who wrote to the Melbourne Hebrew Congregation expressing his disapproval: 'I cannot acknowledge those whom he has made proselytes.'[84]

In a society with so few Jewish women, families tried their best to maintain their religious and cultural connections, and the letter of the law was maintained with some strength. In November 1864 a member of the Melbourne Hebrew Congregation wrote to Rabbi Adler, requesting his wife be converted urgently. She was the daughter of a Jewish father, and had maintained a Jewish household, 'keeping all the Feasts and Festivals' and his sons had been circumcised, and he claimed that his children had attended the Jewish school. One of his daughters had recently died, and the community would not bury her as a Jew, although he has 'sat Shiva and had prayers led during the week ... it would cause us everlasting sorrow and bring dif crase [sic] on my children.'[85]

Those seeking conversion for their wives and families included those who were actively engaged in synagogue life. In 1869 a member of the Melbourne Hebrew Congregation, Jacob Hart, married and went on to produce a number of children. He subsequently applied to the Melbourne Hebrew Congregation for his family's conversion, before remarrying in synagogue in 1878. The letter of support from the congregation described him as a 'contributing member ... and a constant attendant at synagogue on Sabbaths and Festivals during the past twenty years'.[86]

Hart's obituary in the *Jewish Herald* describes him as an 'invaluable member' of the Jewish community, who had been actively involved in assisting in religious burial practices for the community, and a board member to the Melbourne Hebrew Congregation. Having been unwell for some time, he died at the age of fifty-eight after a mishap stepping off the train. On his death he left five orphan children unprovided for and who were taken in by a cousin, Isaac Davis, and his wife Rosetta Nathan at the Orrong Hotel. The Melbourne Hebrew Congregation held a meeting to raise subscriptions on behalf of the family, at which Sir Benjamin Benjamin noted that 'the loss of Mr Jacob S. Hart was one the community could ill afford, and the place of the late gentleman would not easily be filled'.

Ephraim Laman Zox continued: 'there was no one more respected in the community ... he had no hesitation in saying that the services rendered ... were of such a valuable and disinterested nature that he would not easily be replaced. No difference was made whether the family requiring his assistance was rich or poor, at the bedside of the sick and the dying, or administering the last solemn rites to the dead, he was always to be found, rendering assistance at a time when the relatives of the dead were steeped in grief, and carrying out the rites in a manner that had reflected the greatest credit in the eyes of their non-Jewish neighbours, who had repeatedly expressed their appreciation of them.'[87]

With the establishment of a third metropolitan synagogue in St Kilda, the issue of conversions remained as complex as before. In 1879 that congregation wrote to the chief rabbi requesting clarification on British practices for the burial of people who had not been married by Jewish rites. Again Adler's reply shows his understanding of the pragmatism needed in the Australian situation, 'although their ought to be a distinction made in the burial of persons who were married כדת משה וישראל [according to the law of Moses and Israel] and this is not in order to inflict punishment on the dead but to deter the living from acting wrongly'. He went on to clarify that those who had been married in a church could not be buried in a Jewish section of a cemetery, and that the funeral could not be conducted by a minister of the congregation.[88]

These rules were obviously not entirely enforced. On 14 June 1869, the 39-year-old Jamaican-born publisher Alexander Lindo Henriques died. Fourteen years earlier Alexander Henriques had married his Jamaican-born bride, Janette Gibson, at St Peter's Eastern Hill under the rites of the Church of England. On his death he was buried in the Jewish section of the Melbourne General Cemetery, but within weeks his wife was agitating to have him disinterred and reburied in the Christian portion of the cemetery.[89] This compelled both the Melbourne and East Melbourne boards to seek expensive legal advice on how to proceed; eventually his wife reinterred him in the Church of England section of the cemetery.

In a fluid community such as that in Victoria, obtaining proof of someone's identity could be difficult. In 1870 Mr Greenbaum reported to the board of the East Melbourne Hebrew Congregation that he had inadvertently circumcised the son of a Mr Solomon, subsequently learning that the child was the son of a non-Jewish mother. In the discussion that ensued, the president of the board, Louis Gerschel, admitted 'inducing' Greenbaum to undertake the circumcision. Greenbaum was exonerated for his mistake, and a letter was sent to the chief rabbi, explaining the situation, who replied in March the following year cautioning him 'never again to circumcise a child born of a Christian mother and a Jewish father'.[90]

Furore over conversion led to a sensational court case and the removal of the Reverend Dr Dattner Jacobson as minister to the Melbourne Hebrew

Congregation. In 1878 he gave a lecture advocating conversion in some circumstances. This led to a week of very public outcry and debate, with daily letters to the *Argus* supporting or decrying his ideas. 'I would like to ask those who are so anxious for the conversion of Christians to Judaism whether there is a single instance on record in which Judaism has been embraced from an honest conviction in the teaching of that faith.' In the same issue Edward Asher wrote that, 'With all due respects to the Christian community at large, I should say that if a Christian becomes converted to the Jewish religion, and that having been educated in the Christian religion will not, and cannot ever have Jewish feelings with regard to the Jewish religion.'

The Reverend Blaubaum of the St Kilda Hebrew Congregation also entered into this debate, arguing 'Can a Gentile women who married a Jew, even if she be converted, be expected to acquire in a short time all that religious knowledge which it takes a child seven or eight years to master?' In defence of Jacobson's position, 'A Jew' replied: 'now it is another matter, and we young Jews are not treated as Jew, but as citizens. Our birth is ignored or remembered as a thing of credit … To marry thus is not to ignore Jewish life, but to extend its sphere, not to destroy our national traits, but to enrich them.'[91]

Three years later, Jacobson, who had been in difficulties with his board, became embroiled in a legal dispute over his conversion of the son-in-law of a friend of Julius Mathews. It was revealed that Jacobson had converted the man for a fee, in order for him to marry a Jewish bride, without the approval of the Beth Din. Mathews circulated a letter of condemnation of Jacobson, who countered that the letter defamed him for 'fraud and deceit' and 'that he had been guilty of conduct unfitting him to be the minister of the congregation'.[92] Jacobson then sued for libel in the Supreme Court, again igniting a very public argument, the salacious details reported daily, and in the process he lost the support of the principal members of the congregation. He was awarded £300 of the £5000 he had claimed, finally resigned and left the colony.

By the 1870s, following the introduction of civil divorce, the Beth Din was empowered to make decisions in this area of *halachah*, and the records of the Melbourne Hebrew Congregation contain a copy of a get from a London divorce, believed to be a 'template' for the Melbourne congregations to follow.

Wills

Ensuring offspring remained Jewish was a preoccupation of many families, even under the difficult demographics of the era. The examination of wills shows that many parents were willing to disinherit their children if they married outside their faith. London-born Elias Ellis arrived in Melbourne from Sydney in November 1846, following a fire that destroyed his premises, causing an estimated £2000 damage and leaving him insolvent.[93] Melbourne proved a more lucrative location, and at his death on 21 February 1866 his estate included seven properties in Carlton, contiguously situated on the corner of Cardigan and Queensberry streets.

Appointing Moses Rintel and his son Angel Ellis as executors, Ellis bequeathed property in trust for his wife's lifetime. Following her death, all but one of his surviving children were to receive a portion of this property.[94] The exception was his son Maurice, who had married a Catholic and was raising his children in that faith. Ellis's will stipulated that if his unmarried sons 'marry persons not being Jewesses and professing the Hebrew faith' then they were to forfeit their inheritance. He, like the majority of Jewish parents, left his property in equal shares to his sons and daughters. In this instance, as with many other Melbourne Jewish wills, Elias Ellis also protected the interest of his daughters, specifying individually for each daughter that their share of this property was to be 'free from the debts and liabilities and control of any persons who may become her husband'.

Twenty years later the will of Szymanski Leon, dated 11 December 1882, is even more prescriptive, defining his children's obligations concerning their inheritance and the maintenance of their Jewish faith. In his will he leaves annuities to his sister, half siblings, niece and nephews, as well as property to his children. Bequeathing equal shares in property to his two daughters and son, he stipulates:

> as long as they respectively shall profess and faithfully observe all the ordinances of the religion of the Jews and shall not intermarry with any person not of Jewish birth and religion … I declare that my mind and will to be that any child of mine renouncing the Jewish faith and ceasing to profess and observe the ordinances of the Jewish religion or marrying anyone not of the Jewish people and persuasion and professing the Jewish religion and observing the ordinances shall cease to be entitled to any interest in my estate and shall take no share thereof under this my Will … and the share of any child of mine so becoming disinherited shall be disposed of in like manner as if such a child had died leaving no issue.[95]

Personal Names

As Jews in the Western world achieved levels of acceptance and emancipation, they self-consciously transformed some of the outward symbols of Judaism, including adapting the names of their children and creating names for their religious and cultural institutions that reflected their new political circumstances.[96] Jews have been relatively fluid with their surnames, which often reveal the political, social and economic history of their acquisition. Traditionally Jews used a patriarchal form, linking individuals to their fathers through the term Ben (son of) or Bat/Bas (daughter of), a practice that placed the emphasis on the individual within the family.

The development of larger urban centres required more specific forms of individual identity and by the tenth and eleventh centuries it was common for Jews living in larger urban environments to have acquired family names, but the practice waxed and waned with fluctuating economic circumstances.[97] Following the imposition of the Napoleonic Code, European Jewry acquired surnames. As they were required or enforced, names were selected based on a variety of placenames, occupations or through acronyms. In order to protect individuals from legal restrictions such as limitations on marriage, or in an attempt to avoid compulsory army conscription, Jewish families sometimes consciously gave children different family names or their mother's surname.[98]

The family of Alfred and Ernest Kornblum, born in Tost, Silesia, described the origins of their family name from the Napoleonic edict of 1806, when their grandfather Abraham was walking in a field near his home in Gleiwitz, Silesia, with several of his brothers discussing the name they would take. As no agreement could be reached each took a different name. One, indicating a tree, decided to call himself after that and became Baum, while a second brother called Solomon, determined this as a surname, while Abraham, who was admiring the blue flowers in the field, resolved on Kornblum.[99]

Although many studies have considered the acculturation of immigrant communities through the transformation of names, Jews arriving in England appear generally to have taken a limited range of surnames, most of which clearly define them as Jewish.[100] Many of those arriving in England before the mid nineteenth century may not have had surnames or changed them on arrival to more obviously Anglo-Jewish names, favouring English versions of biblical names, both for their personal and family names. Thus the Rypinskis arriving in Manchester in the 1840s immediately became Jacobs, while at the same time in Sheffield, Michael son of Levi became Levinson.

This biblio-centric focus led to names such as Abraham, Aaron, Isaac, Jacob and Solomon as favoured alternatives for both family and male personal names. Other Jewish names reflect the tribal ancestry of the bearer such as Cohen (Khan, Cohn, Katz) or Levi (Levien, Levitt, Levy). German Jews devised Germanic versions of these names such as that of the Melbourne merchant Joseph Katzenstein.[101] First names can be diminutives of biblical names, so that Eliezer could be Lesser, Leser or Lesyser; Isaac, Itig; Jacob, Kopel, Kofman, Kopleman and Solomon, Salaman, Salmon or Zalman.[102] Jews had sometimes taken names from their place of origin. As they moved around

Europe these names were either retained, indicating a place of origin, or changed to reflect the new location. A number of families in Melbourne retain placenames including Horowitz, Englander and Hollander.

The Sephardi community historically had family names adopted from their Arab or Christian neighbours, and these were generally retained, a sign of the importance of Sephardi identity. The origins of these names can reveal their history of hidden Judaism, reflecting names that were common Spanish first names or surnames. Names such as Mendez and Henriques were borrowed from their Christian neighbours, while Lopez originates as a common Spanish first name.[103] Among those migrating to Melbourne were many Londoners with distinctly Sephardi surnames, such as Fonseca, Mendoza, Mendes, Mocatta and Montefiore. These were joined by a number of Jamaican Sephardi families such as the Belinfante, de Leon, de Pinto, Henriques, Lopez, Lindo and Mosquita families. Identifying other Sephardi residents of Melbourne without obviously Spanish derived names requires additional information, such are the Sephardi origins of Edward Cohen and Jamaican-born Hyman Joseph.

Some names appear to have been corrupted entirely through the process of immigration. Saicob Silberberg's is a miss-transliteration from Yaakov (Jacob), while his marriage record of 1832 in Cora Kalwaria, Poland, lists him as Jankel Calle, a Yiddish diminutive. 'Saicob' is spelt differently on a number of his documents, while his shipping record lists him as Jacques, a name with at least some phonetic linkage to Yaakov. Jews used religious and secular names, sometimes using one for their community affairs and the other for their civic and business activities. Thus Henrietta Salomons was the daughter of Yehiel Prager, known in business as Israel Levien Salomons.

The first names chosen for children reflect the class and ethnic identification of a parent.[104] As the acculturation process changes over time, some names become more fashionable, so that by the 1870s we witness the appearance of contemporary secular names such as Joan, May or Gladys for women, while men acquired names such as Clarence, Harold or Frank, although biblical names retain a parallel vogue. A few families showed great patriotism to their new land, providing first and second names with significant Australian connections; consequently, we have the first Jewish child born in Victoria and grandson of Henrietta Salomons (Prager), Jonas Felix Australia Levien or Eureka Isabel Sicree, daughter of Moroccan-born Lazarus Sicree.

Some Jews had unexpected names: Noel Syron Lopez de Leon, son of Jamaican-born Rebecca Lopez and David de Leon, similarly Dutch-born Christina Van Eyl, while there remains a popularity in the Jewish community for Isobel/Isabella, a name associated with the expulsion of Jews from Spain. The fluidity of names is also reflected by individuals who adapt their names for class reasons such as the interchangeability of Lewis and Louis. Until the outbreak of the First World War and the hostility to Germanic names, few Jews anglicised their names further, although during the course of the nine-teenth century the Ottolangai family became Langley. The anti-German feeling during the war years led the Littens to transform their name to the less Germanic Raphael, while the British army insisted that the son of Alfred Kornblum discard his German surname and anglicise it to Kaye.

Ashkenazi Jews traditionally name children after deceased relatives, while the Sephardi allow for the naming of a child after a relative who is still alive; thus naming patterns can reflect cultural backgrounds. In examining families in Melbourne, there are instances of fathers and sons sharing first names. This could be an indication of Sephardi origin, or a sign of acculturation forming fashionable family linkages.

Such was the case for London-born Abraham Benjamin Isaacs, named after his father, Benjamin, whose origins are unknown, while his mother was Rachel Rodrigues. London-born photographer Alexander Fox named a son born in Fitzroy in 1865 Alexander after himself. It can only be assumed that Fox is an Ashkenazi name.[105] Other families carry names through generations: draper Michael Cashmore, son of Joseph Cashmore and Alice Nathan, produced nine children born in New South Wales and Victoria. Of these, Joseph Michael shares his father's and grandfather's names, while his eldest daughter, Alice, is named after her still-living grandmother.

Public Manifestation

In the nineteenth century, associational activities were a vital component in the delineation of the middle class.[106] The way Jewish community members chose to position themselves in the wider community illustrated not only their attempts at communal maintenance but also their status as equal members in mainstream society.

Without suitable structures, the initial tiny Melbourne Jewish commu-nity was unable to maintain the strict rules of *kashrut*. It was not until the appointment of Moses Rintel as reader, *shochet* and *mohel* in January 1849 that kosher meat could be slaughtered.[107] As with other aspects of Jewish ritual and practice, kosher food appears to have fascinated the wider Melbourne commu-nity, with many articles on the subject appearing in the metropolitan and regional press. In 1851 the *Argus* published a long opinion piece on the morality of the kosher killing of animals, favourably comparing their treat-ment to non-Jewish butchering.[108]

The importance the community gave to ensuring a supply of kosher meat is reflected in the inordinate amount of time the various synagogue boards put into its organisation and monitoring. The issue of kosher meat in

Melbourne reached the attention of the chief rabbi in London, who wrote to the wardens of the Hebrew Congregation in 1853:

> I hereby beg to inform you that several complaints have been made to me relative to the insufficient supply of lawful meat at Melbourne. I deeply regret that a Congregation which had given repeated proof of religious zeal by the costly enlargement of their synagogue and by other similar accomplishments should neglect a matter which is of such vital importance to the preservation of our faith. The difficulty of obtaining Kosher meat temps many young men to eat forbidden foods; having once commenced it is very difficult for them to cease, and a habit is thus formed which not only endures throughout life but even descends to further generations. Such a growing evil must be crushed at the root, and energetic measures should at once be taken to provide an ample supply of kosher Meat.'[109]

The number of advertisements promoting kosher food and the commentary surrounding *kashrut*, place the issue in the public eye. Local shops ran competitive advertisements in the Melbourne and Ballarat papers, particularly prominent in the lead up to Passover, where advertisements marketed a range of kosher cakes, *matzah* and wines.

From 1850 Isaac Pulver had somewhat of a monopoly on the supply of kosher food, as member of the Beth Din overseeing Jewish religious laws, *shochet* and manufacturer of kosher products. Pulver's multi-continent career had commenced as minister to the Jewish community of Cheltenham, England, prior to sailing for Cape Town in 1849, where he was appointed the community's first minister and *shochet* and in these roles participated in the consecration of the new synagogue.[110] Apparently finding the 'ideas of the congregants difficult to comprehend', he resigned from the post and arrived in Melbourne hoping to seek wider commercial opportunities.[111] Pulver was appointed to the Beth Din, where he exercised considerable intellectual authority. His three-year contact as *shochet* brought with it an annual salary of £250, which was supplemented by an additional £100 from the purveying butchers Easton and Bennet of Stephen Street.[112]

Until the 1850s there was no *matzos* manufacturing in Victoria and all had to be imported from Sydney at great cost. By 1856 several members of the community vied for the honour of becoming Melbourne's first *matzos* baker, with the privilege falling to the partnership of Isaac Pulver and S. Mendel. A large advertisement appeared in the *Argus* in February 1856, authorising Messrs Pulver and Mendal as manufacturers of *matzos* and Passover cakes under the auspices of Reverend Rintel and an especially appointed subcommittee of the Melbourne Synagogue.[113] Interestingly this sizeable advertisement starts with large Hebrew characters spelling out the word *Matzot* (מצרת), requiring the publishers of the *Argus* to have acquired Hebrew type, perhaps in expectation of more advertisements of this sort.

Pulver's Passover advertisement for 1861 describes his *matzos* and cakes as 'clean, pure and kosher'. His monopoly was, however, challenged directly by the Polish born 'French' pastry chef Saicob Silberberg, whose advertisement in the *Argus* explicitly states: 'No Monopoly ... authorised by the officers of the Mickva Yisrael Melbourne Synagogue, will SUPPLY the finest KOSHER PASSOVER CAKES ... 120 Bourke St.'[114] The rift between the congregations seems to have been healed somewhat by 1874, where Leon Josephson, who had purchased Pulver's business, advertised *matzos* under the authority of both Melbourne congregations.[115]

In the 1850s and 1860s several firms were advertising other Passover produce. These included Pirani of 9 Queen Street, who were offering kosher wines and cordials; the hotelier Barnett Isaacs, who advertised Passover accommodation complete with kosher rum at the Duke of Kent Hotel and later ran similar advertisements for Passover kosher rum on his relocation to the London Tavern.[116] In larger regional areas, shops such as those of Louis Vince in Ballarat were placing sizable advertisements in their local paper advertising kosher groceries.[117]

מצות THE Hebrews of Victoria are hereby informed that the Passover Cakes manufactured by Messrs. Pulver and Mendel are under the immediate supervision of the Rev. M. Rintel and a sub-committee of the Synagogue appointed for that purpose.

Persons desirous of securing Kosher Motzes for Pesach are therefore respectfully informed that they may rely upon those obtained from the above.

By order of the Warden,
A. BARNARD, Secretary.
Synagogue Chambers, January 5616.

NOTICE.

In reference to the above, Messrs. Pulver and Mendel beg to inform the Jewish members that they are now ready to supply orders and to deliver the same at 1s. 2d. per lb. in any part of Melbourne free of expense.

Messrs. P. and M. beg to assure those who may favor them with their orders, that their Motzes are of the very best quality, and equal in every respect to English-made Motzes; also that they have bestowed the utmost attention to have the meal ground as fine as possibly can be.

Kosher Sweet Cakes of various descriptions.
N.B.—Early orders will greatly oblige.
Address Mr. Pulver, 118 Queen-street. 17

Advertisements for Passover cakes, Argus,
9 February, 1856

Sabbath Maintenance

For minority groups such as the Jews of Melbourne, maintaining religious practices in a diverse city required a negotiated interface with the wider community, raising questions irrelevant in small self-contained communities with a Jewish majority.[118] Melbourne's economy created issues requiring innovative responses in order to maintain traditional religious practices. Just as the maintenance of Jewish institutions required a new conceptualisation of space and identity, so too did engagement with civil society. In 1841 the opening hours of shops confronted Jewish values of social justice and challenged Jewish ritual practices for the proprietors and shop assistants alike.

Twenty-five of the forty-seven drapery stores in Melbourne were operated by Jews, particularly clustered around the north side of Collins and Elizabeth streets, and these shops operated until well into the night. In February 1841 the drapers attempted to restrict trading hours, by agreeing to close at 8 pm, thereby improving the conditions of their employees and maintaining the Sabbath.

Of the fourteen who signed the advertisement in the *Port Phillip Gazette* proclaiming these new hours at least half were Jewish, including the businesses of Michael Cashmore, Isaac Lazarus Lincoln, E. & I. Hart, D. & S. Benjamin, M. Lazarus, I. Simeon and Harris and Marks.[119] Their initiative was supported the following week, when a group of fifteen grocers also announced that they would close their premises at 8 pm.[120] Three years later, Moses Benjamin would advertise that he 'did not conduct business between 6 pm on Friday and 6 pm on Saturday'.[121]

These schemes did not go entirely smoothly. The issue that hosted the grocers' advertisement contained a letter signed 'Studeo', expressing concern that young men, usually employed in shops, but now with greater leisure time would not have adequate diversions for their new hours of relaxation and could be led into ill pursuits. The letter also suggested this provided an opportunity for education and self-improvement.[122] Obviously not all who had committed to these trading hours fulfilled their promise, perhaps seeing a competitive advantage, as within a fortnight the following letter was published in the paper:

> Sir,—I presume to draw your attention to the circumstances of a certain Draper in this town Mr _, who having signed the declaration against keeping business open after 8 o'clock, is still in the habit of admitting customers after that hour clandestinely—such a breach of honor and common honesty towards fellow tradesmen should not be allowed to pass with impunity, and such conduct

should be held up to the public reprehension by the exposure of the party to that odium which he justly merits.

I am your's obediently
LANARIUS[123]

The problems of religious observance and commerce continued. In 1864 the *Jewish Chronicle* reported that the Jewish shopkeepers in Melbourne were closing their premises for the High Holidays, while the issue of Sunday trading by Jewish traders was championed in the Jewish and wider papers. In 1874 a Mr Bukh in Ballarat was convicted for operating his business on a Sunday, which involved the employment of his apprentices. The *Australian Israelite* criticised him for violating the laws of the land, pointing to the injunction 'The law of the country in which we are must under all circumstances be obeyed', but also arguing that the issue required resolution in a manner 'befitting a liberal, tolerant and enlightened community. No one can shut his eyes to the fact that it is very hard upon a Jew that he should be prevented from pursuing his ordinary business on a day which is to him the same as any other.'[124] The *Argus* took a stronger view, arguing that:

> We are fond of boasting of our religious liberty, and point to the removal of disabilities, the imposition of which can only be defended on political grounds, as an evidence of our trust in the validity of Christian principles and the ultimate triumph of Protestant truth ... During fifty-four days of every year ... we forbid our Jewish fellow subjects to carry on their lawful callings—in other words, we handicap industry with over seven weeks and a half of enforced idleness ... We are not discussing the question now as to whether a nation, the great majority of which is Christian, is justified or not in insisting on the general observance of its weekly holy day by all the people that are within its gates; but we simply point out the fact, in order to show that the edifice of religious freedom is still awaiting completion.[125]

The 1880s saw a rise in a Sabbatarian movement in the Protestant Churches of Victoria, set to counter what they perceived as a secularisation of society. This was particularly focused around attempts to open museums and galleries and increase the provision of public transport for Victorians on Sundays. Slightly earlier, the Jewish community had attempted to impose a parallel tightening of religious observance. In 1872 an influential group of Jewish men met to form a Sabbath Observance Society. Many of those at the initial meeting admitted that they were culpable in opening their places of business on the Sabbath and discussed the possible economic cost to their closing.

Henry Raphael noted the impact of emancipation on the Jewish community when he 'contemplated the outcry that would be raised if Jews were compelled to work on the Sabbath, but now happily being free agents, they absolutely elected of their own account, to violate this great principle of our faith.'[126] Several of those at the meeting noted that employment in the public service required Saturday attendance, and Edward Cohen offered to take up the issues with government. Two years later he headed a deputation to the chief secretary, arguing that Jews were disadvantaged by the Christian concept of the Sabbath, arguing that the Sabbath was on a Saturday, as initiated at Mount Sinai.

The deputation presented eight points, including the disturbance to the Jewish Sabbath by traffic and other activities on the streets, that Jews were economically disadvantaged by not being able to undertake their business on a Sunday, but closing on a Saturday, therefore losing a day's trade in comparison with their competitors. Arguing that 'Christians should be likewise enforced to respect and keep holy the seventh day of the week which is the true and divinely appointed day of rest ... And we therefore pray that the Government will be pleased to take such steps as to prevent a recurrence of similar proceedings.'[127]

At the inaugural meeting of the Sabbath Observance Society, Moritz Michaelis explained that 'he had experienced many religions ... [although] ... in none other was there to be found the feeling of geniality and contentment so conspicuous as in the Sabbath observing Jew.'[128] The initial meeting and subsequent committee included the rabbinical leaders and many of the board members of the metropolitan synagogues, and also included two men whose family arrangements would seem to put them outside mainstream orthodoxy, but whose attendance at the meeting implies a maintenance of the connection to the religion of their birth. Sidney Montefiore had married his Irish-born bride at St Andrews Brighton in 1857; and the politician Jonas Felix Levien was married to his first cousin, daughter of a non-Jewish mother, and whose children became Anglicans.

By the following week the committee had sent a letter to the three metropolitan congregations, asking that members be made ineligible for office if they did not keep the Sabbath, although this was rejected by the St Kilda Hebrew Congregation as not being practicable while the East Melbourne Congregation postponed discussion on the issue.[129]

In a similar vein, in 1874 the Melbourne Hebrew Congregation sent a letter requesting support in asking the University of Melbourne to exempt students from classes on the Sabbath, a move supported by an editorial in the *Australian Israelite*. Here again, the community felt empowered to assert itself against the structures of wider society and established institutions, although there appears to have been a pragmatic pushback to the suggestion.[130]

Philanthropy

The accumulation of wealth and education served personal and communal interests; Jews were able to speak publicly as Jews, to represent the community, and to refashion Jewish society through philanthropic actions. This emancipatory outlook has been described thus: 'The Jewish public sphere was a discursive network mediating between the twin realms of Jewish economic life-capitalist production and philanthropic distribution.'[131] This maintenance of Jewish identity provided practical support, facilitated personal networks and provided intellectual outlets through participation in benevolent associations, and Jewish social and cultural organisations such as debating and literary societies.

Tsedakah is a powerful feature of Jewish communal life and formal provision for charity was made almost as soon as a Jewish presence was established in Melbourne. In 1841 the Jewish community formed a Poor Society, although not all in the community considered it necessary. Asher Hyman Hart argued that the community was so small that each knew the circumstances of the others and that 'the natural tie of Jew and Jew was strong enough without requiring any formal pledge to assist another'.[132] The 1840s was a time of financial instability in Victoria as elsewhere and the communal records paint a somewhat harsh reality. In 1849 Lewis Davis requested assistance in waving the £4 charged for burial of his child, to which the Melbourne Hebrew Congregation replied that 'they did not want to make a precedent'.[133] This unsympathetic attitude was soon replaced by a communal responsibility in the form of the Melbourne Jewish Philanthropic Society (Melbourne's first 'philanthropic' organisation), whose first meeting at the Rainbow Tavern on 19 November 1849 defined its objectives:[134]

> to assist the poor and distressed in cases of sickness and medical aid and a weekly stipend to maintain themselves while unable to˙ attend to their usual avocations, and secondly to afford temporary aid to deserving objects who may require it in such a form and at such times as shall be found expedient by the committee.[135]

The Philanthropic Society was followed in 1857 by the Hebrew Ladies Benevolent Society, initially to assist women in their confinement. Later the remit was extended to provide financial assistance to distressed women of the

Jewish faith during their confinement, a responsibility extended two years later to 'sick women and children of the Jewish faith, providing financial assistance and also providing funds to ensure a brit'.[136] Both organisations were supported by individuals in the community and from the donations made at *brit milah*. The Philanthropic Society also received state support. Other *tsedakah* boxes collected for charity funerals and the poor of Jerusalem.

The two Melbourne congregations also regularly held joint services to raise money for the Melbourne Hospital. Although many members of the community had settled as a part of an extended family migration, others in this new society had no extended family network to call upon in times of need and both societies provided financial and medical assistance. On 5 September 1858 the Philanthropic Society received a request for assistance for six-year-old Rachel Nathan, the orphaned daughter of Michael Nathan, who had been taken in by Mr Simmons of Stephen Street. Simmons applied for assistance for her support and the committee resolved to investigate and establish whether Rachel had any other family who may be responsible for her welfare.[137]

Both organisations received applications from individuals and families for support to relocate to another colony or to return to Britain. Two of the children of the pugilist Daniel Mendoza had been separately transported to Tasmania for theft. At a meeting on 12 August 1854, a request was received from Isaac Mendoza for help to travel to Launceston, where he said that his sister Sophia was willing to take care of him. He was provided with £3. In a few instances, the application was to leave Victoria for either another Australian colony or another part of the English-speaking world.

At the same meeting an appeal was received from a Mr Beck for a passage to Sydney or the United States. The committee possibly took an economic view and provided him with £4 for a fare to Sydney.[138] The most distressing case appears to be that of Dr Dattner Jacobson. The Philanthropic Society and Hebrew Ladies Benevolent Society raised funds to assist him and his family to leave for America. Initially they were provided with £5, but the president of the Benevolent Society noted during a visit the 'starving condition of the family' and she left a discretionary sum of £2 for the purpose of providing food.[139]

Eventually Jacobson sailed to America to take up a post in Chicago and later in New Orleans, while his wife stayed in Melbourne, where she again sought financial assistance from the Melbourne Hebrew Congregation, eventually receiving a *get* (although no civil divorce appears to have been sought). Their daughter opened a kindergarten in the Oddfellows Hall, catering for both Jewish and non-Jewish children, before attempting to establish the first Jewish boarding school in Australia, one 'intended to meet a long felt want'. It does not appear that this was achieved and she too eventually emigrated to America.[140]

Those immigrating could also arrive without resources. At a meeting of the Philanthropic Society on 14 September 1857, relief was granted to two immigrants who had just arrived on the *White Star*, £6 to fourteen-year-old Solomon Cohen (listed on the shipping manifest as Samuel aged 11) and £3 to Isaac Greenfield, a passenger on the same ship.[141]

Assistance was also called upon for the management of Jewish practice, with effort expended by the Philanthropic Society for the provision of *matzos* at Passover. With a growing Jewish population, in 1862 the Philanthropic Society applied for a grant of land on which to build an almshouse. Reporting the laying of the foundation stone in 1870, the *Illustrated Australian News for Home Readers* commented:

> The Jews are everywhere remarkable for their kind consideration and treatment of the poor brethren amongst them, and the pro-posed erection by the Jewish community in Melbourne of almshouses for their aged and decayed people is in accordance with the charity which is characteristic of the race.[142]

Designed by George Johnson, each almshouse contained a parlour, kitchen and bedroom, and included a veranda to assist with ventilation. Their location on St Kilda Road placed this institution among a number of other charitable organisations that catered for Melbourne's needy residents, although this too was contentious, with many in the community questioning both appropriate-ness and the location of the institution. In 1885 the almshouses were extended and renamed in commemoration and honour of the century of the birth of the philanthropist Sir Moses Montefiore.[143] The minutes, fundraising and high-profile events such as subscription balls were widely advertised and reported in the Melbourne papers as integral elements of Melbourne's social and charitable life.

The maintenance of Jewish practices for the poor, infirm, imprisoned and otherwise needy attracted the attention of many in the community. This need was also recognised in wider circles, with the Society for Promoting Morality obtaining advice from the Jewish community on the assistance provided to prisoners. Reverend Ornstein explaining that the rabbis made regular visits to Pentridge Prison to conduct services, coordinating with the Philanthropic Society on the release of the prisoner, ensuring that they had money, clothes and assisting with finding employment or transport to their location of preference.[144] Funds were raised from charitable endeavours across

the world, the poor were given charity burials, and the communal and spiritual needs of those in the various asylums were considered.

Proposed design for Jewish Almshouses, Illustrated Australian News for Home Readers,
24 January 1870

Jews also sat on the boards of various charitable institutions, although the
Melbourne Blind Asylum appears have excluded Jews and Catholics from its
management, and was accused of proselytisation by the Jewish community,
with a letter to the Jewish press suggesting that the community refrain from
supporting the institution.[145] This came to a head in the case of resident Fanny
Krakower. As her parents were in West Australia where her father was seriously
ill, a guardian had been appointed for her in Melbourne. In 1875 it was
reported that she kept Sabbath and knew her prayers, and was occasionally
visited by women of the community, and that the community had been
ensuring that she participated in the major festivals.

But two years later, when her guardian asked permission for her to celebrate Passover, the matron of the institution refused. After interventions by
many members, of the community including Reverend Rintel and Reverend
Blabaum and members the asylum's board of management, the matron argued
that as it was a Protestant institution, she would not comply. In reporting the
incident the *Herald* concluded, 'This certainly does appear to be a most reason-
able request, and if the committee desire to restore public confidence in the
management of the institution, they cannot refuse it.'[146] In a more benign case,

the community supported a Miss Woolff, described as having 'an affliction since birth which demanded unceasing care' and who was an inmate of the Benevolent Asylum. In 1872 the Hebrew Ladies Benevolent Society arranged for her to be released to celebrate the Passover holidays.[147]

For the wider community two Jewish mutual aid societies were formed in the 1850s, the first the Jewish Benefit Society, with Solomon Iffla acting as the medical officer and in 1863 a Jewish Mutual Aid Society was formed allowing members to pay a small weekly fee that would entitle them to medical advice and an allowance in the event of incapacitation.

Philanthropic interests were not confined to Jewish causes; Jews were actively involved in hospitals and benevolent charities throughout the colony, transferring their focus as they moved from the goldfields to Melbourne. Particularly as the twentieth century dawned, a number of locally born Jewish women became associated with wider charitable roles. Jane Benjamin was president of the House Committee of the Jewish Almshouses; Annie Cohen was a committee member for both the Foundling Hospital for the Unmarried Mother and Her Child, Berry Street, the Melbourne District Nursing Service and a number of Jewish charities.[148]

An advocate for free kindergarten education, Ray Ellis used her professional capacity as an author to campaign for her chosen cause, publishing articles across the Victorian press.[149] Interested in the wider medical interests of her female cousins, she was secretary to the Queen Victoria Hospital, while her society connections led her to become a founding and long-standing member of the management committee of the Lyceum Club.[150] These individuals were recognised for their charitable activities, energy and social connections rather than for their religious affiliations, although the two could be bound together. Perhaps the most overt example is a memorial to Edward Cohen in the Royal Melbourne Hospital, complete with iconography presenting the priestly blessing bestowed by Cohenim through the raising of the hands.

'The narrow confines of nationality opened themselves to give way to the judging and crowning of the world.' So argued Dr Bernard Lilienfeld, in a speech aimed at raising funds for the erection of a statue in Melbourne in honour of Shakespeare by the German community.[151] Jews formed part of a complex multicultural society of Germans, Italians, African Americans, Swiss and Chinese willing to chance the unpredictability of the Victorian goldfields. Many German Jews retained a dual identity as Germans and Jews, expressed in their participation in the German Association, founded in 1850. The association's initial aim was to support German immigrants, particularly those seeking employment but hindered by their lack of English. It later lobbied on a range of political issues including proposed changes to the Naturalisation Act and arguing for equal representation for equal taxation.

At the outbreak of the Franco-Prussian War the association became a political and consciousness-raising organisation, arguing the German cause.[152] The 1867 visit by the Duke of Edinburgh (son of a German father) provided an opportunity for the community to show its loyalty to the British crown by staging a major procession, which included a German band assisted by the band of the 14th Regiment and that of the Collingwood Rifles.[153]

The German Association's committee included a number of high-profile Victorian Germans including the artist Eugene von Guérard and the botanist Ferdinand von Mueller. A number of its committee members were German Jews, including Bernard Lilienfeld, honorary physician to the Melbourne Hospital, the Victorian Eye and Ear Hospital, honorary secretary to the Medical Society and medical officer for the Hebrew Ladies Benevolent Society.[154] Other active Jewish participants included Louis Monash, the father of Sir John Monash, secretary to the association in the 1850s.[155]

Isaac Katzenstein was also active as a public face of the organisation during the few years he resided in Melbourne. Katzenstein appears to have been a highly cultured individual acknowledged 'in literary and artistic circles' and amassing a significant art collection, which was sold at public auction on his emigration to Egypt in 1868. This collection was described possibly with some hyperbole as 'the largest and most valuable private art collection in the Australias' and included furniture, watercolours, drawings, engravings, sculpture and a large collection of framed and bound photographs. Reflecting Katzenstein's world view, the collection was international in scope and utilised the new technology of photography, with 120 images of artwork from international collections held in museums in Germany, London and Rome.[156] His brother Joseph shared his interest in art, and although Joseph's collection was far more modest, it revealed his complex identity in an English colony, as among a number of English landscapes were four busts of members of the German royal family.[157]

Judaism had been challenged by the scientific and philosophical concepts of the European Enlightenment, while the growth and attraction of cities brought new challenges. Urban life has been conceived as a duality of influence: places to which small communities could seek guidance, while simultaneously places of assimilation and loss of Jewish identity, pressing communities to respond to the freedoms that social and political emancipation offered them.[158]

Bringing the experiences gained in London, Germany, eastern Europe and the Sephardi world to a developing urban context, the Melbourne Jewish community—children of these intellectual and social challenges—did not lose their identification with or their practice of Judaism. In an isolated environment such as Melbourne, they sought to structure their lives around Jewish ritual and practice, proclaiming their identity and recognising this as a part of a dispersed diasporic experience. In Melbourne and in other centres, issues of Jewish interest, explanations of Jewish practices and reprinting of articles from the Jewish press appeared in Australian newspapers, exhibiting a high level of acceptance and integration into the wider community.

Notes

1   Charlotte Elisheva Fonrobert and Vered Shemtov, 'Introduction: Jewish Conceptions and Practices of Space', *Jewish Social Studies* 11, no. 3, (2005), 3.

2   Steven J. Zipperstein, 'Jewish Historiography and the Modern City: Recent Writing on European Jewry', *Jewish History* 2, no. 1, (1987), 86. Traditional forms of observance were maintained longest in small town settings, while the political imperatives of the state influenced practice in France and Germany: Hugh McLeod, *Secularisation in Western Europe, 1848–1914* (St Martin's Press, New York, 2000), 3.

3   In a similar vein Heilman describes how the religiously conservative chose not to migrate to America, considering it *treyfe medine*, a contaminated state, outside the one thousand years of 'traditional' European Judaism: Samuel C. Heilman, 'Orthodox Jews, the City and the Suburbs', in Ezra Mendelsohn (ed.), *People of the City: Jews and the Urban Challenge* (Oxford University Press, Oxford, 1999), 20.

4   David B. Ruderman, *Connecting the Covenants, Judaism and the Search for Christian Identity in Eighteenth Century England* (University of Pennsylvania Press, Philadelphia, 2007), 5; Shmuel Feiner, *The Origins of Jewish Secularization in Eighteenth-Century Europe*, trans. Chaya Naor (University of Pennsylvania Press, Philadelphia, 2010), 11.

5   David B. Ruderman, *Jewish Enlightenment in an English Key: Anglo-Jewry's Construction of Modern Jewish Thought* (Princeton University Press, Princeton, 2000), 9.

6   Feiner, *The Origins of Jewish Secularization in Eighteenth-Century Europe*, 10.

7   ibid., xi; Andrew Lees, *Cities Perceived: Urban Society in European and American Thought, 1820–1940* (Manchester University Press, Manchester, 1985), 5.

8   For a discussion on German Jewish participation in cultural activities see Jacob Katz, 'German Culture and Jews', in Jehuda Reinharz and Walter Schatzberg (eds), *The Jewish Response to German Culture, from the Enlightenment to the Second World War* (University Press of New England, Lebanon, NH, 1985).

9   Paula E. Hyman, *The Emancipation of the Jews of Alsace, Acculturation and Tradition in the Nineteenth Century* (Yale University Press, New Haven, 1984), 1.

10   Yosef Hayim Yerushalmi, 'Exile and Expulsion in Jewish History', in Benjamin R. Gampel (ed.), *Crisis and Creativity in the Sephardic World 1391–1648* (Columbia University Press, New York, 1997), 13.

11   Todd M. Endelman, 'Communal Solidarity among the Jewish Elite of Victorian London', *Victorian Studies* 28, no. 3 (1985), 497–8.

12   Todd M. Endelman, *The Jews of Georgian England, 1714–1830: Tradition and Change in a Liberal Society* (University of Michigan Press, Ann Arbor, 2002), 132; Michael Goldfarb, *Emancipation: How Liberating Europe's Jews from the Ghetto Led to Revolution and Renaissance* (Simon & Schuster, New York, 2009), 116.

13   Endelman, *The Jews of Georgian England*, 154; Endelman, 'Communal Solidarity among the Jewish Elite of Victorian London', 492, 514.

14 Bettina Hitzer and Joachim Schlor, 'Introduction to God in the City: Religious Topographies in the Age of Urbanization', *Journal of Urban History*, 37, no. 6, (2011), 820.

15 Lisa Silverman, 'Jewish Memory: Jewish Geography', in Arijit Sen and Lisa Silverman (eds), *Making Place: Space and Embodiment in the City* (Indiana University Press, Bloomington, 2014), 175.

16 *Leader*, 15 June 1895, 11.

17 Morris Goldman, *The Jews in Victoria in the Nineteenth Century* (Self-published, Melbourne, 1954), 33.

18 John S. Levi and G.F.J. Bergman, *Australian Genesis: Jewish Convicts and Settlers, 1788–1860* (Melbourne University Press, Carlton, 2002), 286.

19 Joseph Aron and Judy Arndt, *The Enduring Remnant: The First 150 Years of the Melbourne Hebrew Congregation 1841–1991* (Melbourne University Press, Carlton, 1992), 5.

20 Levi and Bergman, *Australian Genesis*, 289.

21 Jonathan D. Sarna, 'The Jews in British America', *Jewish History* 20, no. 2, (2006), 520. In 1861 the Ballarat Synagogue took the same title.

22 Goldman, *The Jews in Victoria in the Nineteenth Century*, 46.

23 David Newman, 'Integration and Ethnic Spatial Concentration: The Changing Distribution of the Anglo-Jewish Community', *Transactions of the Institute of British Geographers* 10, no. 3, (1985), 364.

24 Lee Shai Weissbach, *Jewish Life in Small-Town America: A History* (Yale University Press, New Haven, 2005), 40.

25 This was adjacent to the Melbourne Cemetery on land that now forms part of the Queen Victoria Market. Colonial Secretary's Correspondence, Public Record Office Victoria, VPRS 17.

26 John S. Levi, *These Are the Names: Jewish Lives in Australia, 1788–1850* (Miegunyah Press, Melbourne, 2006), 205–7.

27 Melbourne Hebrew Congregation (ed.), 'Minutes of the Melbourne Hebrew Congregation' (Melbourne Hebrew Congregation Archive, 1847–1851), 18 February 1848.

28 Aaron Aaron, *The Sephardim of Australia and New Zealand* (Aaron Aaron, 1979), 24–6.

29 *Australian Israelite*, 4 October 1872, 4.

30 Aaron, 'The Sephardi Presence in Australia', date accessed 4 July 2015, <http:// jewishhistoryaustralia.net/sephardim/Sephardi_Australia.pdf>.

31 Melbourne Hebrew Congregation, 'Minutes of the Melbourne Hebrew Congregation', 16 September 1849.

32 *Jewish Herald*, 21 May 1880, 6–7.

33 *Jewish Herald*, 21 May 1880, 6–7; Thad. W.H. Leavitt, *Australian Representative Men* (Wells & Leavitt, Melbourne, 1887), 176.

34 *Argus*, 30 December 1859, 6.

35 *Illustrated Australian News for Home Readers*, 29 November 1869, 226; *Argus,* 6 October 1869, 6; *Ballarat Star*, 8 October 1869, 3.

36 Israel Feinstein, 'Jewish Emancipation in Victorian England: Self Imposed Limits on Assimilation', in Jonathan Frankel and Steven J. Zipperstein (eds) *Assimilation and Community: the Jews in Nineteenth-Century Europe* (Cambridge University Press, Cambridge, 1992), 39.

37 Todd M. Endelman, 'German Jews in Victorian England: A Study in Drift and Defection', in Jonathan Frankel and Steven J. Zipperstein (eds) *Assimilation and Community: the Jews in Nineteenth-Century Europe* (Cambridge University Press, Cambridge, 1992), 58, 62.

38 *Australian Leather Journal*, 15 December 1902, 562; Moritz Michaelis, *Chapters from the Story of My Life* (Norman Brothers, Melbourne, 1899), 7.

39 ibid., 21–2.

40 Endelman, 'German Jews in Victorian England', 67–8.

41 Michaelis, *Chapters from the Story of My Life*, 64–5.

42 J. Ann Hone, 'Moritz Michaelis (1820–1902)', in *Australian Dictionary of Biography* (National Centre for Biography, Australian National University, Canberra, 1974), vol. 5.

43 *Star*, 11 October 1864, 2.

44 *Mount Alexander Mail*, 30 September 1864, 2.

45 East Melbourne Hebrew Congregration, 'Minutes; December 1860 – October 1875', (Australian Jewish Historical Society Collection, State Library of Victoria), 15 September 1867 and 25 July 1869.

46 St Kilda Hebrew Congregation, 'Minutes of the St Kilda Hebrew Congregation', in (Australian Jewish Historical Society Collection, State Library of Victoria), 28 October 1871.

47 ibid., 15 September 1872.

48 *Australian Israelite*, 26 April 1872, 5.

49 St Kilda Hebrew Congregation, 'Minutes of the St Kilda Hebrew Congregation', 24 May 1874.

50 ibid., 7 May 1877.

51 ibid., 3 October 1875, 17 May 1877.

52 *Australian Israelite*, 17 May 1872, 4.

53 *Jewish Herald*, 12 March 1880, 3; 11 February 1881, 4; 20 May 1881, 5.

54 Hilary L. Rubinstein, *The Jews in Australia: A Thematic History* (William Heinemann Australia, Port Melbourne, 1991), 312.

55 Werner Graff, Malcom J. Turnbull and Eliot J. Baskin, *A Time to Keep, the Story of Temple Beth Israel 1930–2005* (Hybrid Publishers, Melbourne, 2005), 7–8.

56 *Jewish Herald*, 1 February 1901, 6; *Jewish Herald*, 20 January 1888, 7.

57 *Jewish Herald*, 14 October 1910, 10.

58 Isaac Jacobs, *Conservative Reform in Jewish Observance* (Alex McKinley & Co, Melbourne, 1910), 7–8.

59 John S. Levi, *Rabbi Jacob Danglow: The Uncrowned Monarch of Australian Jews* (Melbourne University Press, Carlton, 1995), 34.

60 *Hebrew Standard of Australasia*, 17 November 1899, 5.

61 *Jewish Herald*, 15 February 1901, 6.

62 Levi, *These Are the Names*, 488; Goldman, *The Jews in Victoria in the Nineteenth Century*, 32.

63 *Argus*, 6 February 1846, 3; *Argus*, 2 August 1849, 2. Lincoln's son Jonas was the sole survivor.

64 Melbourne Hebrew Congregation, 'Minutes of the Melbourne Hebrew Congregation', 8 October 1848.

65 Anthony P. Joseph, 'Patterns of Migration 1850–1914', paper presented at the *International Academic Conference of the Jewish Historical Society of England and the Institute of Jewish Studies*, University College London, London, 1996, 337.

66 Levi, *These Are the Names*, 665.

67 Melbourne Hebrew Congregation, 'Minutes of the Melbourne Hebrew Congregation', 10 January 1848.

68 Melbourne Hebrew Congregation, 'Minutes of the Melbourne Hebrew Congregation', 15 December 5611 (1850).

69 ibid., 21 February 1851.

70   Census for Victoria for the Year 1851 (John Ferres for the Government Printing Office, Melbourne, 1851).

71   Victoria. Registrar-General's Office, Census of Victoria, 1861 (John Ferres, Government Printer, Melbourne, 1864).

72   Jeremy I. Pfeffer, *'From One End of the Earth to the Other': The London Bet Din, 1805–1855, and the Jewish Convicts Transported to Australia* (Sussex Academic Press, Brighton, 2008), 313.

73   ibid., 314.

74   Levi and Bergman, *Australian Genesis*, 291.

75   Quoted in Goldman, *The Jews in Victoria in the Nineteenth Century*, 59.

76   Quoted in ibid., 63.

77   Melbourne Hebrew Congregation, 'Minutes of the Melbourne Hebrew Congregation', 10 January 1848.

78   Pfeffer, *'From One End of the Earth to the Other'*, 318.

79   East Melbourne Hebrew Congregation, 'Minutes, December 1860 – October 1875'.

80   Rabbi Nathan Adler, Letter, 22 October 5624, *Australian Israelite,* 27 September 1872, 5

81   Rabbi Nathan Adler, Letter, 4 December 5624 (Melbourne Hebrew Congregation Archive).

82   Rabbi Nathan Adler, Letter, 19 August 5623 (Melbourne Hebrew Congregation Archive).

83   East Melbourne Hebrew Congregration, 'Minutes; December 1860 – October 1875', 21 May 1872.

84   Rabbi Nathan Adler, Letter, 5 April 5622 (Melbourne Hebrew Congregation Archive).

85   Letter to the Chief Rabbi, 15 November 1864.

86   Simon Cohen and Nathaniel Levi, Letter, 26 November (Melbourne Hebrew Congregation Archive).

87   *Jewish Herald*, 9 October 1889, 10.

88   St Kilda Hebrew Congregation, 'Minutes of the St Kilda Hebrew Congregation', 1 July 1879.

89   East Melbourne Hebrew Congregation, 'Minutes; December 1860 – October 1875', 1 August 1869.

90   ibid, 2 October 1870 and 7 March 1871.

91   *Argus*, 10 May 1878, 6; *Argus*, 8 May 1878, 7; *Argus*, 7 May 1878, 6.

92   *Argus*, 17 March 1878, 4.

93   Levi, *These Are the Names*, 229–30.

94   Will of Elias Ellis, Public Record Office Victoria, Index to Wills, Probate and Administration Records 1841–2009, VPRS 7591 P01 24.

95   Will of Szymanski Leon, Public Record Office Victoria, Index to Wills, Probate and Administration Records 1841–2009, VPRS 7591 P02 78.

96   Michael A. Meyer, *Jewish Identity in the Modern World* (University of Washington Press, Seattle, 1990), 37.

97   Benzion C. Kaganoff, *A Dictionary of Jewish Names and Their History* (Schocken Books, New York, 1977), 12, 16, 35.

98   Justin Kaplan and Anne Bernays, *The Language of Names* (Simon & Schuster, New York, 1997), 57.

99   Geoffrey Kaye, 'Alfred Kaye: A Study in Adaptation' (unpublished manuscript) 1932–35, revised 1969), 1.

100   Hyman considers changes to naming patterns as one of the initial steps of acculturation. Hyman, *The Emancipation of the Jews of Alsace*. For examples of

acculturation through naming in the New World see A.D. Lavander, 'United States Ethnic Groups in 1790: Given Names as Suggestions of Ethnic Identity', *Journal of American Ethnic History* 19, no. 1 (1989); Susan Cotts Watkins and Andrew S. London, 'Personal Names and Cultural Change: A Study of the Naming Patterns of Italians and Jews in the United States in 1910', *Social Science History* 18, no. 2 (1994); Stanley Lieberson and Eleanor O. Bell, 'Children's Names: An Empirical Study of Social Taste', *American Journal of Sociology* 98, no. 3 (1992); Rudolf Glanz, 'Jewish Names in America', *Jewish Social Studies* 23, no. 3 (1961).

101 Kaganoff, *A Dictionary of Jewish Names and Their History*, 24.

102 ibid., 50.

103 Aaron Demsky, *Pleasant Are Their Names: Jewish Names in the Sephardi Diaspora* (University Press of Maryland, Bethesda, 2010), 45.

104 Lieberson and Bell, 'Children's Names', 515.

105 Kaganoff, *A Dictionary of Jewish Names and Their History*, 153.

106 Rainer Liedtke, *Jewish Welfare in Hamburg and Manchester, c. 1850–1914* (Oxford University Press, Oxford, 1998), 10.

107 Goldman, *The Jews in Victoria in the Nineteenth Century*, 52, 62.

108 *Argus*, 9 May 1851, 4.

109 Letter dated 21 November 5614 (1853) as quoted in Goldman, *The Jews in Victoria in the Nineteenth Century*, 112.

110 Solly Berger, 'The Pre-History of the Great Synagogue: The Cape Town Hebrew Congregation, 1841–1905', <http://www.gardensshul.org/attachments/article/20/Early%20History%20by%20Solly%20Berger.pdf>, 3.

111 Goldman, *The Jews in Victoria in the Nineteenth Century*, 91.

112 ibid., 115.

113 *Argus*, 9 February 1856, 7.

114 *Argus*, 11 March 1861, 7; Letter from Joan Flight, undated, private collection; *Argus*, 24 February 1858, 3.

115 Goldman, *The Jews in Victoria in the Nineteenth Century*, 185; *Argus*, 24 February 1874, 7.

116 *Argus*, 11 March 1861, 7; *Argus*, 27 March 1858, 7; *Argus*, 25 March 1869, 7; *Argus*, 31 March 1869, 8.

117 *Ballarat Star*, 5 April 1865, 3.

118 McLeod, *Secularisation in Western Europe, 1848–1914*, 141.

119 *Port Phillip Gazette,* 20 February 1841, 2.

120 *Port Phillip Gazette,* 27 February 1841, 2.

121 *Port Phillip Patriot and Melbourne Advertiser*, 29 January 1844, 3.

122 ibid., 3.

123 *Port Phillip Gazette*, 13 March 1841, 2.

124 *Australian Israelite*, 15 May 1874, 308.

125 *Argus*, 13 May 1874, 4–5; *Jewish Chronicle*, 24 July 1874, 271.

126 *Herald*, 20 August 1872, 3.

127 *Herald,* 30 March 1874, 3.

128 ibid.

129 East Melbourne Hebrew Congregation, 'Minutes; December 1860 – October 1875', 3 April 1872; St Kilda Hebrew Congregation, 'Minutes of the St Kilda Hebrew Congregation', 24 June 1872.

130 'Minutes of the St Kilda Hebrew Congregation', 1 June 1874; *Australian Israelite*, 19 June 1897, 348.

131 Derek Jonathan Penslar, *Shylock's Children: Economics and Jewish Identity in Modern Europe* (University of California Press, Berkeley, 2001), 5.

132 Quoted in Hilary L. Rubinstein, *The Jews in Victoria 1835–1985* (George Allen & Unwin, Sydney, 1986), 5.

133 Melbourne Hebrew Congregation, 'Minutes of the Melbourne Hebrew Congregation', 21 October 1848.

134 Rodney Benjamin, *A Serious Influx of Jews: A History of Jewish Welfare in Victoria* (Allen & Unwin, St Leonards, 1998), 6.

135 Melbourne Jewish Philanthropic Society, 'Minute Book of the Melbourne Jewish Philanthropic Society', 1849–1862 (Australian Jewish Historical Society Collection, State Library of Victoria), 19 November 1849.

136 Hebrew Ladies Benevolent Society, 'Minutes of the Hebrew Ladies Benevolent Society', in (Australian Jewish Historical Society Collection, State Library of Victoria), 17 May 1857 and 25 May 1859.

137 Melbourne Jewish Philanthropic Society Minute Books, State Library of Victoria, Box 4252/1 MS 15380, 5 September 1858.

138 ibid., 12 August 1854.

139 Hebrew Ladies Benevolent Society, 'Minutes, Hebrew Ladies Benevolent Society', in (Australian Jewish Historical Society Collection, State Library of Victoria), 21 December 1885.

140 *Argus*, 22 Dec 1887, 4; *Jewish Herald*, 6 July 1880, 4.

141 Public Record Office Victoria, *Australia, Assisted and Unassisted Passenger Lists, 1839–1923;* Melbourne Jewish Philanthropic Society Minute Books, State Library of Victoria, Box 4252/1 MS 15380, 14 September 1853.

142 *Illustrated Australian News for Home Readers*, 24 January 1870, 30.

143 *Jewish Herald*, 11 December 1885, 6.

144 *Australian Israelite*, 2 August 1872, 5.

145 *Australian Israelite*, 8 March 1872, 4; *Australian Israelite*, 12 April 1872, 2.

146 *Australian Israelite*, 15 January 1875, 225; *Herald*, 12 April 1877, 3.

147 *Herald*, 18 April 1872, 4.

148 *Argus*, 30 June 1909, 6.

149 For example, *Shepparton Advertiser*, 17 September 1925, 3.

150 A.S. Ellis, 'The Cousins, Descendants of Solomon and Caroline Phillips' (unpublished manuscript) 1990.

151 *Argus*, 21 May 1860, 5.

152 *Argus*, 9 September 1850, 2; *Age*, 13 March 1856, 3; *Argus*, 31 December 1856, 5; *Argus*, 27 September 1866, 5; *Geelong Advertiser*, 6 September 1870, 3.

153 *Ballarat Star*, 2 December 1867, 4.

154 *Argus*, 23 December 1871, 7; *Argus*, 15 February 1877, 6; *Argus*, 7 April 1873, 5; *Illustrated Australian News for the Home Readers*, 20 June 1868, 13. See also Thomas A. Darragh and Robert N. Wuchatsch, *From Hamburg to Hobson's Bay: German Emigration to Port Phillip (Australia Felix) 1848–1851* (Wendish Heritage Society of Australia, Melbourne, 1999). Unfortunately Darragh and Wuchatsch do not consider any Jews as being a part of the German community, ignoring even those who held consular representation for German territories.

155 Geoffrey Serle, *John Monash: A Biography* (Melbourne University Press in association with Monash University, Melbourne, 1982), 3.

156 *Argus*, 22 February 1868, 2; *Argus*, 25 February 1868, 6.

157 Will of Joseph Katzenstein, Public Record Office Victoria, Index to Wills, Probate and Administration Records 1841–2009, VPRS 28 P01 1045.

158 Steven M. Lowenstein, 'Was Urbanization Harmful to Jewish Tradition and Identity in Germany?' in Ezra Mendelsohn (ed.), *People of the City: Jews and the Urban Challenge* (Oxford University Press, Oxford, 1999), 81.

Chapter 3

Family Identity

In 1896, many Australian city and regional papers reported on the generosity and philanthropic activities of wealthy Jewish New Yorker Lazarus Morgenthau. He had 'found a new and romantic way of distributing some part of his wealth', through a fund set up to support the provision of dowries for poor but 'healthy' brides, of 'all religions'.[1] Marriage for Jews, as with others, was not always so generous or romantic: in 1865 the *Geelong Advertiser* carried an advertisement from Ludwig Hyman stating that he would 'not be responsible for Mrs Hyman's debts from this date'.[2]

In analysing the complexity of family relationships and family history, it is useful to adopt a six-pronged methodological and historiographical approach, taking into account demographic, legal, economic, social, psychological and behavioural issues. This approach will be applied to examine the distinctive nature of the family relationships of Victorian Jewry.[3] Utilising a range of demographic and familial information as the basis of a prosopographical study, a detailed understanding of the community's demographic structure can be perceived. Melbourne's expansion resulted from both intercolonial and international immigration and was facilitated by natural growth. Analysis of the place of birth of Melbourne's residents has revealed the cosmopolitan composition of the community.

While the traditions of Judaism are transferred generationally, they are reinterpreted by the legal and social frameworks of their time and place, subtly altering the values and actions disseminated to following generations. For new settlements the relationship between marriage and colonisation is inseparable as the new arrivals construct and define a new society, one based on multiple identities and divided families. For Jews, this heterogeneity is compounded by a duality of identity expressed through the legal judicial codes in which they operate (that of Jewish law represented by the Beth Din and that of civil authorities).

In contrast to central and eastern Europe, in Britain and Australia, Jews were included in a civil legal framework that recognised Jews as citizens. Civil law is based on the rituals and moralities of the dominant society and in England and Australia the precepts of Christianity at times conflicted with the traditions that framed Jewish law. On occasions the differences provided a pragmatic alternative for individuals, enabling them to resort to either secular or religious courts to find the most advantageous determinations for personal matters such as dowries, inheritance rights and divorce.[4]

In Victoria, as family law developed, an observable shift from religious practices to civil jurisdiction can be detected. Although the synagogues of Melbourne placed themselves under the authority of the chief rabbi of the British Empire, the difficulty of communications, the unrestricted nature of citizenship and the circumstances arising from a new and isolated society required pragmatic responses by the community. Even with the establishment of a Beth Din in 1864, many theological issues and their practical outcomes required communication with London, the only religious alternative being an unauthorised local response.

Whereas in England scholarship on family history stresses the importance of religion and the various forces of evangelicalism and non-conformism in shaping the values and preconceptions of families in the early modern and modern periods, for Jews, the models and influences differed. Religious and traditional adaptions were influenced by patterns of acculturation and alterations in the legal status and practice of Jewish communities, rather than by religious reforms. Family life holds a central position in Judaism, and detailed examinations have been made on exemplars of the Jewish experience: medieval Jewry; the golden age of Jewish Spain; Jews under Islam; nineteenth-century Germany, with further attention to eastern Europe in the early modern period and immigrants to America. But Jews are absent from more general historical studies of family structures.

This omission provides an opportunity to study Jewish family patterns through a 'deviant case' analysis, isolating the characteristics of Jewish family patterns that have enabled communities to maintain their distinctive traditions.[5] The Mishna clearly creates mechanisms for the formal organisation of family and societal relationships, including permitted and expected consanguineous relationships, the status of minors, *ketubah* (marriage agreements), betrothal, divorce, adultery and vows. Although this religious legal framework is central, the negotiation of these issues in the diaspora has varied. Social, cultural and class expectations of families shape the educational, economic and demographic experiences of individuals, and these are rarely static. This sculpting of the legal framework creates an 'inward acculturation', one that transforms and creates new customs adapted through the intersection of religious and secular laws.[6]

Jewish traditions are characterised by strong family ties, a consequence of the focus of Jewish life and observance in the home. These values were promoted by middle-class Jews seeking to acculturate into wider society, and perceived as a sign of Judaism's adherence to ideals of bourgeois domesticity.[7] In contrast to a women's peripheral role in the synagogue, her remit within the home was to actively diffuse Judaism within the family.[8] This responsibility in the domestic setting could be a double-edged sword, whereby women's failure to impart Judaism adequately was considered the cause of assimilation and the breakdown of 'traditional' strengths.[9]

Research can establish a number of extended kinship relationships in the Melbourne Jewish community at a business and personal level. A number of widows immigrated to be with children already settled in the colony; widows can be seen living with children, nieces and nephews; bequests were left to male and female family members; financial support was provided to children and in-laws; business partnerships were developed between extended family members; while long patterns of chain migration, sometimes over several decades, indicate transnational connections, communication and support.

One such case is witnessed in the inquest of the death of Esther Woolf and Julian Emanuel Jacobs. Esther and her husband, Nelson Samuel Marks, were living in a single-storey rented house, on the corner of Jackson and Acland streets, St Kilda, in late December 1877. While Nelson Marks was away in Gippsland on business, his wife was at home with their 'adopted' nephew Julian Emanuel Jacobs, his cousin Miss Levinson and another nephew, Henry Robert Woolf, an apprentice to Marks in business as a manufacturing chemist. The reason for this extended family group is unknown, although Henry Robert Woolf's father died in New Zealand when Henry was a baby. On the other hand, while the Levinson and Jacobs families each had twelve children, it is unclear why their relatively well-off parents were not caring for these two children, and why they were living with the childless Marks family. Julian's parents also lived nearby in St Kilda, while the Levinsons had recently moved from Ballarat to Victoria Parade. Tragically, in the early morning of 16 December, a large storm blew over Melbourne, and a five-metre high, heavily decorated chimney fell from the house, killing both Esther Woolf and Julian Jacobs who were asleep in a back bedroom.[10]

Marriage

Although linked to the divine *mitzvah* of procreation, for Jews marriage is not a sacrament; rather it is a legal transaction, defined as such by the *ketubah*, which outlines the contractual arrangements of both parties. These specify the husband's obligations to provide for his wife, her contribution by way of a dowry, and the potential financial obligations of the groom in the event of a divorce.

As states promulgated civil marriage legislation, the autonomy of Jewish legal frameworks was challenged. In Britain, where no legislation defined the legal status of Jewish institutions, marriage customs acquired a de facto legal status. This status was formalised as Britain attempted to regulate marriage through the passage and amendment of marriage acts. Recognition was given to the explicit requirements of the community, as in these acts Jews (and Quakers) were granted unambiguous exemptions, privileging their respective marriage traditions.[11] From the mid eighteenth century, in an attempt to prevent clandestine marriages, to regulate marriage and to bring it under the auspices of the Established Church, England instigated and subsequently amended legislation regulating and codifying matrimony.[12] The first of these, the 1753 Hardwick Act, formalised the process, requiring all marriages to be preceded by the publishing of banns announcing the couple's intention to marry, limiting the solemnisation of a marriage to a church or chapel between specified hours, and introducing official registration of these unions. The act specifically excluded marriages by Jews and Quakers:

> Provided likewise that nothing in the Act contained shall extend to … nor to any marriages amongst the people called Quakers, or amongst the persons professing the Jewish religion, where both the parties to any such marriage shall be of the people called Quakers or persons professing the Jewish religion respectively.[13]

This exemption and similar exclusions in further legislation were deemed to denote the validity of Jewish and Quaker marriages, although the lack of a specific and explicit legal framework caused some confusion for both individuals and the courts. This exception was still ambiguous ninety years later when a further amendment was introduced though 'An Act to remove doubts as to Quakers' and Jews' marriages solemnized before certain periods (10 and 11 Vict., c.58)'.

> Whereas doubts have been entertained as to the validity of marriages amongst the people called Quakers and amongst persons professing the Jewish religion, solemnized in England before the

first day of July one thousand eight hundreds and thirty-seven ...
according to the usages of those denominations respectively; and
whereas it is expedient to put an end to such doubts; be it therefore declared and enacted ... That all marriages so solemnized as
aforesaid were and are good in law provided that the parties to
such marriages were both Quakers or both persons professing the
Jewish religion respectively.[14]

With the British settlement of Australia, these exemptions were transferred to
the colonies. In New South Wales, as early as 1836 the 'Act to prevent
Clandestine Marriages and to provide for the issuing of Licences' again
exempted marriages by Jews and Quakers, reiterating the wording of the original British acts:

Provided always and be it further enacted That nothing in this Act
contained shall extend to any marriages amongst the people called
Quakers or among persons professing the Jewish religion when
both the parties to any such marriage shall be of the people called
Quakers or persons professing the Jewish religion respectively.[15]

These clauses were followed in Victoria in 1859 in an 'Act to amend and
consolidate the Laws affecting the Solemnization of Marriage', which, as with
the Hardwick Act a century before, endeavoured to regularise marriage within
Victoria by defining those authorised to officiate at a wedding, when and
where weddings could be performed and delineating the administrative procedures. Again specifically excluding Jews and Quakers from the provisions, the
Act stated:

shall nevertheless within three months next following be trans-
mitted to the registrar of the district within which it was
celebrated by the person celebrating or witnessing the marriage
or by one of the parties thereto stating the date and place of such
marriage and the name designation and usual residence of each of
these parties.[16]

Consanguinity

Judaism is transferred matriarchally and communities are maintained through
endogamous marriages, with reluctant provision for conversion. In the colonial context, endogamous marriages were characterised by the small numbers
of interrelated families and constrained by the disproportionate numbers of

Jewish men to women. Jewish patterns of consanguinity can be contrary to English and Christian practices and thus the legal standing of these unions was ambiguous. Marriages between cousins were common and, unlike in Britain, where they were illegal, marriages between an uncle and niece, and those of a man to his brother's widow, are not only acceptable but in the case of the levirate marriage, biblically sanctioned.[17]

These patterns of consanguinity were clearly exhibited in 1870s Prussia, where twenty-three out of 1000 Jewish marriages were between relatives (compared to ten for Catholics and fourteen for Protestants).[18] In the Melbourne community a number of discernible forms of endogamy appear, with a prevalence of families marrying among themselves; repeat marriage between particular families; 'occupation endogamy'; and only occasionally 'geographical endogamy' of spouses born in the same location.[19] Historically, family marriages were used to support the retention of property, identity, occupation or class and undertaken especially when the number of eligible partners was limited. Although widely practised by Anglo-Jewry, the legality of consanguineous marriages was unclear and in June 1837 a Bill was passed in the House of Commons 'For removing Doubts respecting the Validity of certain Marriages amongst Persons professing the Jewish Religion'. This legislation aimed to define the issue of consanguinity for Jews:

> THAT no Marriage already or hereafter to be celebrated between any two persons professing the Jewish Religion shall be impeached or rendered void or voidable by reason of consanguinity or affinity unless the same be within the degrees of consanguinity or affinity prohibited by Mosasic Law, according to its interpretation as received by persons of the said Religion.[20]

Although the Bill passed in the House of Commons, it appears not to have been passed by the House of Lords, and the Jewish community and the London Beth Din continued to maintain their historical cultural practices.[21]

Many families intermarried over several generations. The descendants of Livorno-born Israel Ottolangui and his London-born wife, Miriam Amelia HaLevy, settled in Australia over a fifty year period, following the 1830 transportation of their nineteen-year-old son known as David Langley, sentenced to life for stealing 12 shillings worth of cheese.[22] Among those who settled in Melbourne, two other sons, Moses and Aaron, married sisters Emma and Renya Bensabat, the daughters of Jacob Bensabat and Rachel Rodrigues.

Moses and Emma's son Ben Joshua Ottolangui subsequently married his double cousin Sarah, daughter of Aaron and Renya. A third Bensabat daughter, Sarah, married George Mendes. On Sarah's death, George married his wife's niece, Amelia Ottolangui, the daughter of Moses and Emma. Although cross-generational family marriages were outside British law, large families such as the Bensabat's produced lineages where age and generations merge. The Sephardi habit of naming family members after those who are living as well as those who are deceased leads to an even more complex interconnecting of this family, with names reappearing over generations and among family members.

Marrying one's uncle was a particular Sephardi tradition, but the pattern can also appear in Ashkenazi families. German-born Isadore Gross migrated to England where, in 1857 he married Polish-born but English-educated Jane Jacobs.[23] Their daughter Adeline married her father's brother William Gross before both families migrated to Melbourne. In 1908 in St Kilda, Adeline and William's daughter Truda married her mother's first cousin, the lawyer Bertram Levinson. This connection is made stronger by the families' previous geographical connections, with the Gross family's place of birth in Schwetz, Prussia, only 25 kilometres from that of Jane Jacobs' father Elias, in Graudenz.

Wedding of Truda Gross and Bertram Levinson, 1908, Private Collection

Dowries

Although lineage, family wealth, learning and commercial talents were the four factors customarily favoured in the selection of Jewish marriage partners, individual families prioritised these according to their specific aspirations. Jewish families considered identifying potential marriage partners and undertaking financial negotiations on behalf of the bridal couple as a *mitzvot*. Although a good name and religious observance were important, dowries could also be a defining element in the marriageability of women. While marriages provided opportunities for judicious political, professional, friendship and business alliances, the transfer of property through the mechanism of a dowry enabled the consolidation of wealth. According to Jewish custom, dowries are assets that a wife contributes to the marriage and entrusts to the charge of her husband. These can include 'cash, real estate, jewels, stocks or other transferrable wealth'.[24]

If the marriage was dissolved by either the husband's death or divorce, the dowry was returned to the wife.[25] Dowries were not unique to Jewish practice; rather, they were both a historic precedent in Ashkenazi society and a prevailing practice in the wider society. In a European context, dowries doubled as insurance for political and economic insecurity, often forming a critical fund for residential permits in urban centres, as well as leverage capital for the establishment and support of business for a mercantile community.[26] As a predominantly middle-class, urban and mercantile society, Melbourne Jewry could utilise the transfer and acquisition of wealth to create social and economic alliances. With tight endogamous marriages, Judaism and Jewish traditions were maintained.

Dowry provision is often visible in wills. In 1888 Isaac Levi died, leaving four daughters and a son. His will divided his estate into equal shares, stipulating that upon marriage the daughters were to receive £500 each as a 'marriage portion', this sum to be deducted from their total share. As with many others, Levi's will further specified that if any child were to marry outside the Jewish faith, their total allocation would be reduced to £200.[27] A wife's dowry could be leveraged for business ventures. The dowry of Rosetta Levinson was invested by her husband, Alfred Kornblum, in the establishment of a new business with his brother-in-law in Ballarat, a firm that subsequently became Kornblum and Co, with premises in Melbourne's Flinders Lane, and in London.[28]

Age at Marriage

'At eighteen a man marries' is a much quoted statement from the Mishna, and traditionally seen as representing the ideal upper age for marriage. In eastern European communities marriage marked a transition from childhood to adulthood, and for wealthy or scholarly families, unions of young teenage couples were contracted swiftly following a boy's bar mitzvah.[29] These adolescent couples did not set up independent households of their own; rather, they began married life in the confines of the bride's family, supported for a period known as *kest*.[30] At the other extreme, civil authorities in the German territories attempted to restrict the growth of Jewish communities through the control and constraint of Jewish fertility by the imposition of various repressive marriage regulations. This resulted in high instances of late marriage or non-marriage.

Following the second partition of Poland in 1793, southern Prussia (the Province of Posen) imposed a minimum age for marriage of twenty five, levied high fees for marriage certificates and enacted a property valuation of one thousand talers (greater than most families could afford), resulting in many couples forgoing a wedding and merely cohabiting.[31] The autonomous and semi-autonomous nature of many of these communities occasionally sanctioned approaches of non-compliance through the strategic use of poor record keeping and by communal provision of dowries for the poor. In other areas where these restrictive quotas were imposed, many couples failed to register their unions with the civil authorities. As Jews acculturated in the developing cities of western Europe without these restrictive constraints they adopted later marriage patterns, as is reflected in the marriage patterns of Melbourne Jewry.

In examining the extant marriage records of the three Melbourne congregations, it becomes evident that not all marriages were those of previously unmarried individuals. The records also include weddings of widows, divorcees, those who had previously been married by registration or licence and those who had children prior to marriage. The experience of migration also allowed for some 'remaking' of an individual's past, so the numbers of those who had previously been married or cohabiting may not always be clear.

Although the individual's age at marriage is not always reliable, what can be surmised is that for first marriages in the Melbourne congregations, women were marrying at approximately twenty-two years, while men were on average marrying at twenty-nine years, older than their British contemporaries.[32] Not only were the grooms older but the age disparity between husband and wife was also greater. The average deviation in Britain was five years whereas in Victoria it was seven.[33] This pattern compares more closely to American Jews of German descent, where men waited until they were financially established after immigration, marrying in their late twenties or early thirties.

In Melbourne a paucity of women resulted in some younger brides, who married in their late teens and early twenties.[34] There, the oldest cohort of Jewish grooms appears in the 1860s, coinciding with the end of the gold rush and the consolidation of the Victorian economy in its wake. Marriage requires the expense of establishing a household and consequently some occupational stability.[35] The postponement of marriage by this male cohort would appear to be attributed to the disruption that the social and economic conditions of the gold rush created.

Melbourne saw the marriage of around fifty brides who were minors, although no grooms so young. The youngest bride identified was fourteen-year-old Port Macquarie–born Annie (Agnes) Cohen, niece of politician and businessman Edward Cohen. Annie married London-born Simeon Frankel, the acting minister for the Launceston Jewish community.[36] The Frankel family's immigration and settlement followed a pattern reminiscent of many. Simeon's father, Jacob, born in Breslau, Prussia, had migrated to England, where he studied with the chief rabbi, Solomon Herschell, before taking up employment as a cantor in Kent.[37]

Migrating with his family to Hobart when Simeon was two, Jacob was a founder of the Hobart Synagogue and assisted with services. In 1849, following the death of his wife Sarah Moses, he moved to San Francisco, while his children went with their aunt and uncle to Sydney. Returning to Melbourne in 1857, the 44-year old Jacob married 24-year-old Mary Marks. Years later he relocated again, this time to New Zealand, where he stayed until his death at age eighty-eight.[38] Simeon's peripatetic life took him from London to Hobart, Sydney, Launceston and Melbourne before he finally returned to settle in Sydney, where for forty years he was secretary to the Great Synagogue.[39]

A number of older couples celebrated marriages up to twenty-five years after civil ceremonies had taken place, an indication of the brides' conversion to Judaism. The nearly 17 per cent of grooms marrying at thirty-five years or older signifies the immigration transition, lack of Jewish marriage partners or possibly a remaking of lives, without indicating previous marriages.

While the place of birth of a minority of the population is unclear, 87 per cent of brides had been born in Australia or another English-speaking country and were unlikely to have been independent immigrants; rather, they settled either as one of a family group or as a result of chain migration. This would indicate the potential for greater support networks and a less dislocated experience than for those who travelled independently.

Although the majority of brides gave no occupation, generally describing themselves as a 'lady', those who indicated a livelihood were almost all either in the clothing industry or teachers. Fanny Solomons states on her 1882 marriage certificate that she is a 'lady', but in her divorce testimony she says that she had been a paid employee in her father's shop and as a housekeeper to her brothers.[40] If the records are any indication of workforce participation, they imply that few women were engaged in paid employment prior to marriage; and marriage may have offered an opportunity for families to shift the financial burden of extra members.

Small but consistent variations in the age of brides occur in the three synagogues. The 1860s saw the marriages of the youngest cohort of brides, those of the East Melbourne Hebrew Congregation marrying at around twenty or twenty-one, a year and a half earlier than those of the Melbourne Hebrew Congregation. The East Melbourne Hebrew Congregation consistently had the youngest brides, and one-quarter of these were born outside the English-speaking world. Place of birth appears to have significantly affected age at marriage.

While those from Victoria, South Australia and New South Wales married at approximately twenty-two, an age comparable to those of Prussian birth or from Russian Poland, those from Tasmania married slightly later, in line with their German counterparts. With the exception of thirty-year-old Amelia Benjamin from Australind, Western Australia, the oldest group were from America, who married on average at 25.1 years. This pattern is largely reflected in their partners, with central and eastern European men and many from the colonies marrying prior to turning thirty, with late marriage characteristic of those born in Denmark, Germany, Holland and Britain.

A strategy often utilised by poorer European women unable to afford a dowry was to migrate to the New World or marry older widowers. Although the socioeconomic position of European wives is not visible in the data, this does not appear to be the case for Victoria. It could be assumed that the direct and indirect expense and difficulty of travel reduced the viability of this option. Melbourne had twice as many Jewish widowers as widows; what is perhaps unexpected is that equal proportions of these men and women were marrying younger spouses.

Women remarrying younger partners had an average age difference of less than ten years; widowed men who married tended to be considerably older than their partners. The marriage in March 1860 at the East Melbourne Hebrew Congregation of 38-year-old Bavarian widow Sophia Newman nee Hecht and 25-year-old Prussian-born George Victor, both storekeepers of Golden Point (Ballarat), may have been facilitated by a common German background or be a reflection of the paucity of women on the gold fields.

Combining a number of records from various sources indicates that poverty (and possibly the lack of a dowry) could well have been a facilitating factor in the marriage on 3 February 1883 of 23-year-old Melbourne-born Sarah Emden, listed as a servant living at the Jewish Almshouse, to Ludwig Hyman, a Geelong-based but Vilna-born tailor, twenty-seven years her senior and responsible for the advertisement repudiating responsibility for his first wife's debts in the *Geelong Advertiser* of 1865. The Emden family had settled in Victoria in 1855, where Sarah's father, Elias, a slipper maker by trade, had been employed as the beadle to the Melbourne Hebrew Congregation, a position that included onsite accommodation.[41]

The family was compelled to move when, in an attempt to reduce synagogue costs, Elias' position was amalgamated with two others.[42] Even though he was an employee of the synagogue, the family could not make ends meet. On at least three occasions in 1855 and 1856, Elias applied to the Melbourne Jewish Philanthropic Society for relief; his income was supplemented in the late 1850s by small gratuities earned as a messenger and meetings assistant for the society. In February 1860 he resigned, stating that 'he did not wish to have anything further to do with this Society in any capacity'.[43] Notices placed in the *Argus* announcing family marriages proudly list the Emden family as 'late of London', but their fortunes had slipped by the time of Sarah's marriage and the family were living in the Jewish Almshouse, where Elias was employed as caretaker.

Family alliances could also spread over generations and through shared life experiences. On 7 July 1877, 29-year-old Dinah Levy married her 62-year-old widowed uncle, George Gershon Harris, at the Melbourne Hebrew Congregation. Dinah Levy was the daughter of emancipist Lazarus Levy and his wife, Rebecca Harris, a former servant. This was a family inter-married with several others that had arrived in Australia due to criminal convictions. Lazarus's older brother, Phillip, also a convict, married Mary Moses, the daughter of 'Money Moses', convicted with Lewin and Ellis Casper of the 1839 Great Gold Dust Robbery. In 1846 in Hobart his younger brother, Samuel, married Ellis Casper's daughter Sarah.

Place of Birth

To investigate further the demography of the Melbourne Jewish community requires a more nuanced understanding of the place of birth. It has been considered that the three synagogues had differing constituencies, with the Melbourne Hebrew Congregation the most 'Anglo', East Melbourne for the 'foreign Jews' and St Kilda defined by its long-standing and high-profile Rabbi Danglow, who arrived in Melbourne to take up his post in 1905.[44]

Unsurprisingly, considering the population spread of European Jewry, those from the German territories and Russian Poland made up the majority of the non-English-speaking immigrants. While just over one-third of grooms and approximately 12 per cent of brides were born in non-English speaking countries, this number is somewhat misleading, as many of those born outside the English-speaking diaspora had migrated to Britain or the Australian colonies as children or spent considerable time in Britain working as young adults.

The experience and expectations of this subgroup may have differed from those of their immigrant peers. Leaving that aside, the German territories followed by the bordering areas of Russian Poland provided the highest number of non-English speaking marriage partners. It is difficult to determine the motivating factors for immigration, but concentrations of immigrants from this area would imply that the restrictions placed on these communities were decisive push factors. Throughout the nineteenth century, Germany, like Britain, witnessed enormous mass emigration. The cost of travel from Europe was significant, restricting emigration to those with at least some means. Research indicates that mid-century emigration was unlikely to occur from the highest levels of profession or skilled occupations or the lowest occupations. Australian immigration would be similar to that identified in America, where it has been noted that many European immigrants earned more than those who remained in Europe, perhaps because the brightest (or more courageous) were likely to emigrate.[45]

By far the majority of marriage partners in this study came from English-speaking countries (77.23 per cent)—87.4 per cent of brides and 63.5 per cent of grooms—with marriages conducted between individuals born in Britain, the Australian colonies, New Zealand, the United States, Jamaica, Gibraltar and South Africa. Concentrated in these figures are the large numbers from Britain, who constituted 42.4 per cent of brides and 43.3 per cent of grooms.[46]

Wider research on patterns of female immigration has noted that women tended to be the majority of short-distance migrants (partly explained by the fact that they often travelled to nearby centres to undertake domestic service).[47] Although the incidence of Jewish women undertaking domestic service appears low, women arrived in Melbourne from New Zealand at twice the rate as men, with Dunedin as the primary location of birth. While 41.3 per cent of brides were Australian-born, only 17.3 per cent of grooms were from the Australian colonies. This raises the question, what happened to the other Australian-born sons?

Although high concentrations of Jews in central Europe resided in historic Poland, the majority lived in the east, particularly in three areas: Ruthenia-Ukraine (south-east, 44 per cent), Lithuania-Belarus (north-east, 27 per cent) and Malopolska (central, 17 per cent). Those in Melbourne came from what had been Great Poland, home to only 12 per cent of the Jewish community and subsequently divided between Prussia and the Russian Empire.[48] Due to economic and political conditions, the Jewish population in this area was highly urbanised with only an estimated 2 to 5 per cent residing in villages.[49]

In Great Poland, the Prussian Province of Posen provided the largest concentration of Jews in the German territories and this was one of the four principal German territories from which international migration occurred in the nineteenth century.[50] In this province five towns had communities of more than two thousand (Posen, Lissa, Kempden, Krotoschin and Inowrazlaw). This distribution is not reflected in the Melbourne marriage records, with only Posen and Krotoschin providing any significant numbers (and then it is not clear if 'Posen' refers to the city or the province), with twelve from Krotoschin and fourteen individuals identifying Posen, six from Melbourne, seven from East Melbourne and one from the St Kilda records.[51]

Also in the Prussian-controlled area Chodziesen/Kolmar (now Chodzież, Poland), a city north of Posen, provided thirteen marriage partners (seven from the East Melbourne Hebrew Congregation, four from St Kilda and two from the Melbourne Hebrew Congregation). In the Russian-controlled territories of the former Great Poland, the Province of Plock provided significant numbers to Victoria, with at least eleven individuals from East Melbourne listing Plock as their place of birth, while Kutno (Kutney) in the same province was home to another nine, eight from East Melbourne and one from the Melbourne Hebrew Congregation. The Warsaw region also produced a significant population in Melbourne, with eleven marriage partners, eight married in the East Melbourne Hebrew Congregation, two in the Melbourne and only one in St Kilda.

The demographics of the various synagogues are represented in their marriage patterns. For the Melbourne Hebrew Congregation, 93.56 per cent of brides came from an English-speaking background compared to 75.75 per cent of grooms. Reflecting the later establishment of the St Kilda Hebrew Congregation with its dominance by Anglo-German Jewry, 91.11 per cent of brides came from an English-speaking background while Australia was the birthplace of only 59.58 per cent of their spouses; 33.93 per cent of grooms came from Germany, including 27.7 per cent from Prussia. The East Melbourne Hebrew Congregation had the least number of English-speaking partners, with 74.56 per cent of brides and 39.55 per cent of grooms.

The differences in liturgy and expectations sometimes caused disharmony. In 1871 the *Australian Israelite* printed a letter from a disgruntled member of the East Melbourne Hebrew Congregation who complained

> I know full well, Sir, that as an Englishman I am regarded by my fellow worshipers in that place with the utmost contempt. I know that they claim exclusive possession of the knowledge of the correct working of the Judaic system, and that while they regard me as 'a good Jehudee', they yet shrug their shoulders at what they consider my ignorance, saying, 'After all what does he know, he's only an Englishman.'

The following week, in response the president, American-born Henri Hart, expounded on the importance of the cosmopolitan nature of the community and its outlook, 'for the tendency of the age of liberality of sentiment in all matters affecting our people, who, by the will of the Almighty, are cosmopolitan in every sense of the word'.[52]

For those from a non-English-speaking place of birth, geographic endogamy does not appear to play a large part in determining marriage partners.[53] Occasionally marriages occurred between couples from the same town or village in Europe; whether these were a result of arranged marriages (of either relatives or acquaintances) or coincidence cannot be determined. Such was the 1854 marriage of Hamburg-born couple Herman Heynemann and Helen Cohen and the 1874 marriage of Hyman Cohen from Ozorków, Russia, and Eva Harris of the same town. Others such as that of Aaron Joseph from Constantinople, Turkey, and Fanny Morelle from Hoorn, Holland, show the diversity of the unions in the community.

As with the lack of geographic endogamy in the marriage partners, the eastern European Jews do not appear to have developed an identity separate from others in Jewish Melbourne. Although the East Melbourne Hebrew Congregation has been considered the home of eastern European Jews, this is somewhat simplistic.[54] This congregation certainly had a higher proportion of Prussian and Russian/Polish grooms (52.45 per cent), but only 19.74 per cent of their wives were from Prussia or Russia/Poland. In the absence of marriage in geographically endogamous patterns, historical ties to place of birth may have been harder to maintain.

While family connections were certainly sustained by letter, and through the circulation of communal publications, newsletters, minutes and newspapers, unlike America or in the aftermath of the Shoah, geographic or ethno-specific organisations were not established, while many were eager to be naturalised (see chapter 4). The identity of those Jews from Great Poland is also difficult to determine; academic debate has focused on whether the population considered themselves German Jews or Polish Jews (with a more traditional outlook).[55] Throughout the long nineteenth century, political allegiances shifted rapidly as territory was claimed by advancing armies and Great Poland shifted from Polish to Prussian, French, back to Prussian and subsequently German control, before being reabsorbed into Poland at the end of the First World War.

These geopolitical shifts, coupled with the restrictive laws imposed until full emancipation was achieved in 1871, fostered a Jewish identity ahead of a national consciousness. Prior to 1871, the pressure exerted by the Prussian state towards the Jewish community, opposing its traditional autonomy while withholding equal rights, was a probable facilitating factor in emigration to the Australian colonies. Furthermore, Posen was not a centre of religious conservatism, rather one that took up Reform Judaism at an early date. In

1847, 89 per cent of those participating in a vote in Krotoschin believed that rabbis should have an academic education, while in nearby Inowraclaw 100 members of the community were also members of the Progressive Party, supporters of Reform Judaism. In Posen a large Reform synagogue capable of seating 900 was built in the 1850s. Those settling in Australia may or may not have been directly involved in any of these modernising tendencies, but their choice to come to Australia, with its predominately Anglo Judaism, may reflect these enlightenment tendencies.

Occupational endogamy provided an opportunity to consolidate personal relationships and financial resources; on occasion this could be reinforced by a shared migration experience. Jewellery, watchmaking and pawnbroking were traditional Jewish occupations; all are skills easily portable in times of economic or political unrest. At a rudimentary level they can amount to little more than hawking, but with skill they become highly valued trades. The associated occupation of pawnbroking derives from the historic insistence on Jews to engage in money lending, releasing Christian merchants from the Church's injunctions against usury. Pawnbrokers in Victoria often developed into 'financiers' or gold buyers supporting a number of commercial and personal financial investments.

The Levinson family migrated from Posen to Sheffield in the 1840s and although the 1847 Jewish population of Sheffield was assessed at fifty-six, two generations of the family found Sheffield-born partners in Ballarat. These families had much in common: all three were families of jewellers and children of parents who had migrated from Prussia in the 1840s, while Hyman Levinson, Louis Lazarus Meanowski and Simon Cohen were simultaneously committee members of the Ballarat Synagogue, and were at various times business partners.

In Ballarat in 1876 the marriage took place of the thirty-year-old jeweller Mark Levinson and eighteen-year-old Amelia Meanowski, the daughter of the jeweller and pawnbroker Louis Lazarus Meanowski. The 1851 census for Sheffield lists Prussian jeweller Simon Cohen as one of three 'visitors' to the Levinson home in Pond Hill, Sheffield. As the Jewish community moved from the goldfields to Melbourne, these connections were maintained and the subsequent generation saw the marriage of 41-year-old Michael Maurice Levinson and 29-year-old Daisy Cohen, daughter of Simon Cohen, then both resident in St Kilda.

Divorce

As marriage is a contractual arrangement, the conditions of which can be severed under particular circumstances, although interpretations of these vary in Talmudic and other philosophical discussions.[56] Divorce is effected by the husband, who provides a writ of repudiation in the form of a *get*, which formally severs the union, and with this the *ketubah* and any dowry is returned to the wife.[57] Although men instigate divorce and formalise the process through the *get*, wives have the right to apply for a divorce on specific grounds.[58]

Although a framework for Jewish divorce was provided in biblical and Talmudic teachings, attitudes to divorce and its moral and legal elements were shaped by the social norms of the surrounding society. Its application was restricted by changes to the jurisdiction provided to Jewish courts and the capacity of Jews to seek legal action in civil courts. European Christian societies considered marriage a sanctified and indissoluble contract manifesting God's will and requiring wifely submission.[59] In Europe, the gradual shift from absolutism to a concept of a civil society 'transformed the standard of the moral good from a conflation of Christian principles with the public good ... to a secularized concept of the public good', and this became the primary driver for moral and political decision-making in the nineteenth century.[60]

These were not uniform changes in attitude; rather, they reflected the nascent changes in political and social attitudes occurring throughout Europe, particularly following Napoleon's introduction of the Civil Code. The nexus between Jewish legal frameworks and those of the state was particularly complex and underscored in the divergent concepts of divorce. The Russian Civil Code considered matrimonial matters the responsibility of individual confessional groups, thus allowing autonomous decision-making by Jewish communities; the Hapsburg Empire took a centralist approach, divesting authority for marriage to religious bodies while simultaneously subjecting them to civil conditions; in post-revolutionary nineteenth-century France, rabbis attempted to reform Jewish practice to conform with civic norms.[61]

The special status accorded Jewish matrimonial practices in Britain does not appear to have provided clarity on the thorny issue of divorce. Henriques argues that although there were statutory regulations providing for Jewish marriages, Jewish divorce remained outside religious jurisdiction, subject to civil law.[62] The evidence, as we will consider below, would seem to somewhat contradict this argument. It would appear that by formally distinguishing Jewish marriages as a separate category Jews were afforded the opportunity to maintain a parallel system of family law.

The issue of transportation to the colonies raised some unique challenges for Jewish convicts, their families and their communities. The English courts could grant a divorce after a 'desertion' of seven years, a procedure that could be employed by the wives of non-Jewish convicts to resolve the issue of their permanent separation, but this is not the case in Jewish law.[63] Desertion by a husband is in itself not a ground for divorce and a deserted woman is considered to be *agunah*, prohibited to remarry until her husband has provided a *get*. It would appear that the English Beth Din facilitated divorce for women who might be left in this predicament due to the transportation of their husbands. What is unclear is whether after seven years these women could also apply to the civil courts and obtain a civil divorce, thus removing any civil legal impediments to remarriage.

While in many instances wives and children followed their convict husbands, or families came en masse with a convicted loved one, divorce was an option taken in some circumstances. Several emancipists who settled in Victoria had divorced prior to embarkation. The most dramatic case was Samuel Lazarus Levy, sentenced for life in 1808, whose wife's predicament warranted the arrival in Sydney in 1830 of Rabbi Aaron Levy, the first rabbi to visit the Australian colonies, apparently to organise a *get* for Levy's long-suffering wife.

Perhaps the most illustrative example is that of the Solomon family, who as partners in the Port Phillip Association were the first Jews associated with Victoria, and represent clearly the complexity of experiences of conversion, divorce and out-marriage of the Anglo and Australian Jewish communities. Following the conviction in 1830 of the brothers Judah and Joseph Solomon for inciting the theft of goods from the pawnbrokers Abraham Abrahams and Wolf Myers in Sheerness, their death sentences were commuted and both were transported for life to Van Diemen's Land. Although the pair are believed to be brothers, Joseph Solomon's wedding certificate of 8 May 1806 lists his father as Isaac Stakenman, with the Hebrew name as 'Abraham our Father', implying he was a convert.[64] Prior to leaving England, Joseph divorced his first wife, Judith Lazarus, in a dramatic ceremony, reported in *The Times*:

> Their feelings were sensibly affected at leaving their native country, particularly Judah, who had long resided in Sheerness. On Thursday last, the ceremony of divorcement, according to the Jewish custom, took place at the Fountain-inn, Sheerness between Joseph Solomons [*sic*] and his wife. It was performed by the High-Priest and Chief Rabbi, who arrived for the purpose in a coach and four. The husband was permitted to come on shore, under an escort, and in irons; and after the ceremony, he returned on board, to suffer that expatriation his guilt had brought upon him.[65]

The openness of this divorce would imply either that the Jewish community's practices were outside and alien to those of civil society, or that they were accepted in Britain. The complications of this family did not end here. The story of the financial success of the Solomon brothers has been well documented, facilitated by the £60 investment they took with them, enabling the establishment a mercantile empire while still ostensibly under conviction.[66] But it is their family relationships that concern us here. Both Solomon brothers joined the Hobart Hebrew Congregation on its formation in 1842, although a year later, upon his marriage by special licence to Mrs Eliza Backhouse at St John's Church, Joseph left. Joseph's four children by his first wife subsequently joined him in Van Diemen's Land, all marrying non-Jews, and he and his children were all buried as Christians. In 1838 his daughter Frances married Anthony Cottrell, who with Judah's son Michael established extensive property holdings in Port Phillip.

At the time of his transportation, Judah had eight children and a pregnant wife, Esther Abrahams (nee Levy), believed to be the widowed daughter-in-law of the Abraham Abrahams who was either the victim of or a complicit partner in their theft.[67] In 1825 Judah had acquired sufficient wealth to build a £500 mansion complex in Hobart, which included a storehouse, residence and business premises that he named Temple House. Judah's choice of appellation for his house reflected its use as the premises for the first Jewish services in Tasmania and was a public display of Judah's identity. He was the financial benefactor and treasurer for the fledgling community, donating land for the site of the Hobart Synagogue, as well as donating £200 and lending the community a further £250 for the synagogue's construction.

Yet Judah offered this financial support while cohabiting with his non-Jewish housekeeper, Elizabeth Howell, by whom he had a son, Joseph. It was this son who eventually inherited his father's properties on the Saltwater River (Maribyrnong River) in Port Phillip.[68] Unfortunately for Judah, in December 1832 his wife, Esther, arrived with three of their daughters, to reclaim her marriage and half his fortune. Judah attempted to renounce Esther, declaring that under Jewish and English law his absence of more than twelve years entitled him to remarry. The couple battled and lobbied publicly for a number of years and it is believed that this impeded Judah's attempts to gain a pardon.[69] Three of Judah's daughters married Jewish husbands and settled in Melbourne, Rachel to Samuel Barnett, Louise to John Davis. His daughter Sarah married her cousin Joseph, son of another brother, Samuel, in a Christian ceremony, and settled in Port Phillip, where the couple purchased land in Melbourne's second land sale. Judah's son Michael not only followed him to invest in Port Phillip but also into crime and to divorce.

Michael Solomon had landed in Tasmania in 1829 with another uncle, Henry Solomon, and his wife, Elizabeth. In 1835 he settled in the Port Phillip District at Moode Yalla, Yarra Yarra, also holding licences for land in Keilor and Carrum, and working in partnership with his brother-in-law at Solomon's Ford on the Saltwater River.[70] In 1840 he married a cousin, also called Sarah

Solomon, in Tasmania's first Jewish wedding.[71] After being declared insolvent, Michael Solomon, like his father before him, attempted a brazen robbery against his mother-in-law's second husband, Simeon Benjamin.[72] The motivation for this audacious theft was apparently the reneging of a condition imposed by the Hobart congregation on Elizabeth Solomon in her attempt to marry Simeon Benjamin.

The congregation's stipulation was that prior to her marriage she settle £1000 from her late husband's estate on her children and donate £25 to the synagogue, which would have significantly eased her son-in-law Michael Solomon's financial position.[73] 'After a long trial ... by a highly respectable and intelligent jury', he was found guilty and sentenced to 'transportation beyond the seas for fifteen years'.[74] Although Michael Solomon received a ticket of leave in 1852, a *get* was issued on 29 January 1859 dissolving his marriage to Sarah under Jewish law, making this couple the first Jewish marriage and divorce in Tasmania. Later that year he married a second time, in a Presbyterian ceremony to Elizabeth Salmon.[75]

Divorce also reflects the changing attitudes to personal autonomy, particularly the willingness of women to accept unacceptable or unpleasant personal relations. In Victoria, the fluidity of society allowed husbands to desert wives by going 'upcountry' or leaving the colony altogether. Such was the case of Rosetta Phillips and Alexander Fox. Life as a photographer on the goldfields had been somewhat peripatetic, and the couple moved from Bendigo to Melbourne, where Fox struggled to make a living. In 1865 while resident at 41 King William Street, Alexander and Rosetta gave birth to their son, the artist Emanuel Phillips Fox. Apparently unable to support his family, Fox separated from and reunited with his wife, finally abandoning Rosetta in the position of an *agunah* and leaving her to care for six sons and a daughter.[76]

In Victoria, civil divorce was introduced three years prior to the establishment of a Beth Din, providing a process for applications to be assessed. It would appear that as civil society grappled with the concept of divorce, the Jewish community acquiesced to civil law. Articles appeared in the papers stating the Jewish law was no longer binding in England, while by 1895 the subject was of interest as far afield as the Riverina, where it was reported that the *Jewish Chronicle* had been calling for divorce reform to alleviate the plight of deserted wives, and praising the advanced arguments put forward:

> the most conservative people in existence are the Jews ...
> Therefore we regard it with triumph to our cause that the 'Jewish Chronicle' this month endorses marriage reform in a leading article ... All honour to the Rabbis! As the Irish would say more

power to them! The heads of the Jewish Church are in advance of our own.[77]

Other than for convicts sent to the colonies, religious divorce in Victoria appears to have been rare, and only one previous marriage of a new spouse born in an English-speaking country appears in the records (although a number of those immigrating from Europe indicate previous divorces on their marriage records). Julius Mathews was divorced for adultery in England, some-time before his immigration to Victoria in the early 1850s and his subsequent remarriage to Anna Horwitz in 1857. Mathews' legal adversary Dr Dattner Jacobson provided a *get* to his wife prior to leaving for the United States.

Prior to 1890, when more lenient divorce laws were enacted, only about thirteen cases per year were heard.[78] The records indicate that a few Jewish women took advantage of the new civil legal framework to end abusive relationships and formalise their status after desertion by their husbands. This would indicate that the community had moved away from an autonomous religious legal framework to engagement with civil law. The Divorce and Matrimonial Causes Act 1861 provided for judicial separation on the grounds of 'adultery or cruelty or of desertion without cause for a period of two years'. Divorce proceedings could be brought against wives on the grounds of adultery, while wives could only apply for a divorce if they could prove adultery and another matrimonial offence such as rape, incest, bigamy, sodomy or cruelty.[79]

These civil laws were relaxed in an 1883 amendment that provided custody to mothers, maintenance payments to wives who had fled abusive husbands, and allowed for remarriage after the finalisation of the proceedings.[80] Whereas seven categories for divorce were available in Russia—'domestic strife, primarily over monetary matters and in-laws; physical and psychological abuse; adultery; licentiousness; childlessness; insanity; and religious conversion'[81]—they appear to be far more limited in Victoria (both in number and in reason), responding directly to the legal framework as outlined in the Act.

Many couples with marital difficulties refrained from taking the far-reaching step of instigating a divorce, as we can see by Ludwig Hyman's 1865 advertisement quoted above, but some did. Not all couples could afford the associated costs. Only four Jewish divorces have been identified for the period 1861–95, each instigated by the wife on the grounds of desertion and cruelty, and all were from poor families with significant financial strains. The case of Krakow-born Eva Silberfeld and Dunedin-born Louis Levy in 1895 perhaps raised the most issues. The couple was married in 1889, when Louis referred to himself as a 'commission agent'. His wife claimed that he almost immediately began drinking, refused to work and left the family with no income. Louis had been employed by the jewellers P. Falk and Co, and to assist the couple, his mother Mathilda Seba and father-in-law Bernard Silberfeld provided money to purchase more stock, which he chose instead to gamble and drink away.

By August 1890, with one small son, Eva was forced to sell the household furniture to pay their debts. Her father, Bernard, brought the family to Coleraine, where he was living, and provided them with a home and furniture, again setting Louis up in business. In March 1891 Louis threatened to kill his pregnant wife and after the birth of her second child again threatened her life. The police were called and he was committed to the lunatic asylum. By February 1892 the couple were again cohabiting, this time in St Kilda. Eva's father had supplied £50 to establish Louis in business and credit had also been supplied by her uncle, John Silberfeld.

Again Louis took the money, his stock, her watch and jewellery and pawned it all for drink. By the time his father-in-law arrived, Louis was so drunk he could not stand. He again asked Bernard for money and when he refused, Louis asked him to take Eva and the children to Coleraine, as he was going to commit suicide. She fled to Coleraine and gave birth to a third son. Louis moved to his mother's home in Bendigo, where he was arrested for drunkenness, again sent to the lunatic asylum, released, rearrested and re-incarcerated, before apparently fleeing to Sydney. In her attempt to petition for divorce, Eva tried to contact her husband over several months.[82] The Act stated that a reversal of a divorce can be granted 'on the grounds that it was obtained in his or her absence'.

In two of the three divorce cases examined the wives had attempted to communicate with their deserting husbands. In both cases the husband's families refused to assist, either declining to provide an address or refusing to forward correspondence, as a result of which the cases dragged on for considerable periods of time. In the Lobascher case of 1894, the plaintiff Fanny Solomons was explicitly informed by her husband's sister that she would not provide Fanny with the address of the husband (he was believed to have fled to London) as the divorce was 'washing dirty linen before the public'.[83] The greater ease with which central and eastern European Jewish communities were able to manage divorce in the mid nineteenth century is reflected in the records, with two women and five men remarrying after religious divorces in Prussia and Russian Poland.

The Melbourne Jewish community was formed by settlers from the urban centres of England, the New World and Europe. They were predominantly Anglo-Jewish in background, while many more had also spent time in Britain prior to relocating to Victoria. This was not a community that maintained strong allegiances to their countries of birth; rather, they experienced the Jewish world in its diversity. They rarely married people from their home towns and did not form organisations that were culturally specific to their place of birth. Lured by the opportunities of a new settlement and free of religious restrictions, they married and began families utilising the dual legal frameworks under which they lived.

They brought the experience of negotiating Judaism and Jewish practices under a variety of civil and judicial processes, while maintaining Jewish traditions of consanguinity and divorce. Not shy of expressing their opinions of themselves and their place in Melbourne, they created space through their organisations and public debates. Lacking significant numbers of potential Jewish marriage partners, and although outwardly opposed to conversion, the records indicate that this occurred even though it could engender a hostile public communal reaction.

Notes

1   *Maitland Weekly Mercury*, 3 July 1897, 13.
2   *Geelong Advertiser*, 20 April 1865, 4.
3   Lawrence Stone, 'Family History in the 1980s, Past Achievement and Future Trends', *Journal of Interdisciplinary History* 12, no. 1 (1981), 55.
4   Lois Dubin, 'Jewish Women, Marriage Law and Emancipation: A Civil Divorce in Late-Eighteenth-Century Trieste', *Jewish Social Studies, New Series* 13, no. 2 (2007), 68.
5   Paula E. Hyman, 'Introduction: Perspectives on the Evolving Jewish Family', in Steven M. Cohen and Paula E. Hyman (eds), *The Jewish Family, Myths and Reality* (Holmes & Meier, New York, 1986), 5.
6   Ivan G. Marcus, *The Jewish Life Cycle: Rites of Passage from Biblical to Modern Times*, The Samuel & Althea Stroum Lectures in Jewish Studies (University of Washington Press, Seattle, 2004), 5.
7   Paula E. Hyman, 'The Modern Jewish Family: Image and Reality', in David Kraemer (ed.), *The Jewish Family: Metaphor and Memory* (Oxford University Press, Oxford, 1989), 177.
8   Marion A. Kaplan, *The Making of the Jewish Middle Class: Women, Family, and Identity in Imperial Germany* (Oxford University Press, New York, 1991), 70, 66; Tamara K. Hareven, 'The Home and Family in Historical Perspective', *Social Research* 58, no. 1 (1991), 67.
9   Gershon David Hundert, *Jews in Poland-Lithuania in the Eighteenth Century* (University of California Press, Berkeley, 2004), 3–4.
10   *Age*, 18 December 1877, 3; Public Record Office Victoria, Inquest Deposition Files, VPRS 24, P0000, Unit 369.
11   Feinstein argues that this reinforced the 'alien' character of the Jewish community, creating a contradictory dilemma for those striving for emancipation. While eager to preserve the legal recognition of Jewish marriage, they simultaneously wanted to 'divest the Jews of any further special category in matrimonial law'. Israel Feinstein, *Jewish Society in Victorian England: Collected Essays* (Vallentine Mitchell, London, 1993), 55. See also M.C.N. Salbstein, *The Emancipation of the Jews in Britain: The Question of the Admission of the Jews to Parliament, 1828–1860*, The Littman Library of Jewish Civilization (Fairleigh Dickinson University Press, Rutherford, NJ, 1982), 47.

12 Clandestine marriages were legally binding marriages conducted ostensibly by a clergyman but outside canon law and irregular in format. As clandestine marriages lacked the formalities of regular marriages they were also much less expensive for those involved. See Lawrence Stone, *Road to Divorce: England 1530–1987* (Oxford University Press, Oxford, 1990), chapter IV and p. 126.

13 H.S.Q. Henriques, *Jewish Marriage and English Law* (Jewish Historical Society of England, Oxford, 1909), 21.

14 As quoted in ibid., 24.

15 Parliament of New South Wales, 'An Act to Prevent Clandestine Marriages and to Provide for the Issuing of Licenses', 1836.

16 Parliament of Victoria, 'An Act to Amend and Consolidate the Laws Affecting the Solemnization of Marriage', 1859.

17 Henriques, *Jewish Marriage and English Law*, 49.

18 Kaplan, *The Making of the Jewish Middle Class*, 115.

19 For those unions of European partners, the data is unclear on whether these fall into occupational or familial relationships as well.

20 'Jewish Marriages. A Bill for Removing Doubts Respecting the Validity of Certain Marriages among Persons Professing the Jewish Religion', in House of Commons Parliamentary Papers, 1837.

21 The House of Commons, *Journals of the House of Commons*, vol. 92 (By Order of the House of Commons, London, 1837), 573–4.

22 Old Bailey Trials Online, Trial of David Langley 14 January 1830, <t18300114-135>.

23 Dubin, 'Jewish Women, Marriage Law and Emancipation', 68.

24 Marion A. Kaplan, 'For Love or Money: The Marriage Strategies of Jews in Imperial Germany', in Marion A. Kaplan (ed.), *The Marriage Bargain: Women and Dowries in European History* (Hanworth Press, New York, 1985), 124.

25 ChaeRan Y. Freeze, 'Making and Unmaking the Jewish Family: Marriage and Divorce in Imperial Russia 1850–1914' (PhD thesis, Near Eastern and Judaic Studies, Brandeis University, 1997), 53.

26 Kaplan, 'For Love or Money', 126; Kaplan, *The Making of the Jewish Middle Class*, 88.

27 Will of Isaac Levi, Public Record Office of Victoria, Index to Wills, Probate and Administration Records 1841–2009, VPRS 28 P02 250. Later documents show that Levi's daughter Rose married the non-Jewish Frederick James Field, and upon her death the surviving siblings applied to have a portion of the estate distributed to her daughter. Public Record Office Victoria, VPRS 7591 P02 141.

28 Geoffrey Kaye, 'Alfred Kaye: A Study in Adaptation' (unpublished manuscript, 1969), 32.

29 Gershon David Hundert, 'Jewish Children and Childhood in Early Modern East Central Europe', in David Kraemer (ed.), *The Jewish Family: Metaphor and Memory* (Oxford University Press, Oxford, 1989), 85.

30 Immanuel Etkes, 'Marriage and Torah Study among the Lomdim in Lithuania in the Nineteenth Century', in David Kraemer (ed.), *The Jewish Family: Metaphor and Memory* (Oxford University Press, Oxford, 1989), 156.

31 Manfred Jehle, '"Relocations" in South Prussia and New East Prussia: Prussia's Demographic Policy towards the Jews in Occupied Poland 1772–1806' in *Leo Baeck Institute Year Book*, 52 (2007), 38.

32 E.A. Wrigley and R.S. Schofield, *The Population History of England, 1541–1871: A Reconstruction* (Edward Arnold for the Cambridge Group for the History of Population and Social Structure, London, 1981), 255. This gives the average age at marriage for men in England in 1800–49 as 25.3 years. Average age at marriage in Victoria has not been determined. Statistical analysis is based on census returns and

analyses proportions married in specific age ranges. See Peter F. McDonald, *Marriage in Australia; Age at First Marriage and Proportions Marrying, 1860–1971*, Australian Family Formation Project Monograph (Dept. of Demography, Institute of Advanced Studies, Australian National University, Canberra, 1974).

33   Between the late eighteenth and mid nineteenth centuries British grooms were on average 4.3 years older than their wives. The middle class expanded this differential: Leonore Davidoff and Catherine Hall, *Family Fortunes: Men and Women of the English Middle Class, 1780–1850* (Hutchinson, London, 1987), 323. Analysis of census data of American Jewish families in 1880 shows large regional variations ranging from four to ten years, age difference: Lee Shai Weissbach, *Jewish Life in Small-Town America: A History* (Yale University Press, New Haven, 2005), 142. Variations were also widespread in Germany: Steven M. Lowenstein, 'Ashkenazic Jewry and the European Marriage Pattern: A Preliminary Survey of Jewish Marriage Age', *Jewish History* 8, nos 1–2 (1994), 157–8.

34   Hyman, 'The Modern Jewish Family', 185. Average age at marriage for women in England in 1800–49 was 23.4, older than for Victorian brides. As the century progressed the age of women marrying rose: Wrigley and Schofield, *The Population History of England, 1541–1871*, 255, 437.

35   E.A. Wrigley, *English Population History from Family Reconstitution, 1580–1837*, Cambridge Studies in Population, Economy, and Society in Past Time (Cambridge University Press, Cambridge, 1997), 123.

36   *Launceston Examiner*, 19 March 1868, 3.

37   Ava F. Kahn, 'Roaming the Rim, How Rabbis, Convicts and Fortune Seekers Shaped Pacific Coast Jewry', in Ava F. Kahn and Adam Mendelsohn (eds), *Transnational Traditions, New Perspectives on American Jewish History* (Wayne State University, Detroit, 2014), 50.

38   Barbara Falk, *No Other Home: An Anglo-Jewish Story 1833–1987* (Penguin, Ringwood, 1988), 22; New Zealand Government, 'Births, Deaths and Marriage Records' (2014).

39   *Hebrew Standard of Australasia*, 5 July 1945, 4.

40   Divorce case files, Melbourne, *Lobascher vs Lobascher* 1894, Public Record Office Victoria PROV VPRS 283 P0000 80.

41   *Argus*, 23 November 1863, 6.

42   Morris Goldman, *The Jews in Victoria in the Nineteenth Century* (self-published, Melburne, 1954), 181.

43   Minutes of the Melbourne Jewish Philanthropic Society, Australian Jewish Historical Society, State Library of Victoria, 6 February 1860.

44   This definition is based on the comment made by Goldman concerning the establishment of the East Melbourne Congregation: 'it attracted about 30 members of the old Synagogue and the foreign element who always looked with suspicion upon their reserved English brethren': Goldman, *The Jews in Victoria in the Nineteenth Century*, 133.

45   Simone A. Wegge, as quoted in Ran Abramitzky, Leah Platt Boustan and Katherine Eriksson, 'Europe's Tired, Poor, Huddled Masses: Self-Selection and Economic Outcomes in the Age of Mass Migration', *American Economic Review* 102, no. 5 (2012), 1837.

46   This is similar to the population as a whole, which dropped from 52 per cent in 1861 to 18 per cent by 1911: Marjory Harper and Stephen Constantine, *Migration and Empire*, The Oxford History of the British Empire Companion Series (Oxford University Press, Oxford, 2010), 3.

47   E.G. Ravenstein, 'The Laws of Migration', *Journal of the Royal Statistical Society* 52,

no. 2 (1889), 249, 259.

48 Hundert, *Jews in Poland-Lithuania in the Eighteenth Century*, 25.

49 Artur Eisenbach, *The Emancipation of the Jews in Poland, 1780–1870* (Basil Blackwell in association with the Institute for Polish-Jewish Studies, Oxford, 1991), 32.

50 Ravenstein, 'The Laws of Migration', 248.

51 Eliezer Sariel, '"In the East Lie My Roots; My Branches in the West". The Distinctiveness of the Jews of Posen in the First Half of the Nineteenth Century' *Leo Baeck Institute Year Book*, 58 (2013), 184.

52 *Australian Israelite*, 13 October 1873, 2; *Australian Israelite*, 20 October 1873, 2.

53 This is very different to the Irish community, where evaluation of marriage records for 1886 indicates that 75 per cent of Irish women married Irish men. Chris McConville, 'Emigrant Irish and Suburban Catholics: Faith and Nation in Melbourne and Sydney 1851–1933' (PhD thesis, University of Melbourne, 1984), 286.

54 Frank Fletcher, 'The Victorian Jewish Community 1891–1901: Its Relationship with the Majority Gentile Society', *Australian Jewish Historical Society* 8, no. 5 (1978), 228.

55 Sariel argues for a separate Posen identity, distinct from German or Polish. Sariel, 'In the East Lie My Roots', 178. Khan, however, argues that Posen Jews were culturally different from Germans, but perceived a German identity as culturally prestigious. See Fred Rosenbaum, *Jewish Voices of the California Gold Rush: A Documentary History, 1849–1880* (Wayne State University, Detroit, 2002), 38.

56 Isaiah M. Gafni, 'The Institution of Marriage in Rabbinic Times', in David Kraemer (ed.), *The Jewish Family: Metaphor and Memory* (Oxford University Press, Oxford, 1989), 15.

57 Although under Jewish law men hold the prerogative to initiate divorce against the will of the wife, this practice has generally been frowned upon: Rachel Biale, *Women and Jewish Law: An Exploration of Women's Issues in Halakhic Sources* (Schocken Books, New York, 1984), 6.

58 Irwin H. Haut, *Divorce in Jewish Law and Life*, Studies in Jewish Jurisprudence (Sepher-Hermon Press, New York, 1983), 25.

59 Stone, *Road to Divorce*, 2.

60 Isabel V. Hull, *Sexuality, State, and Civil Society in Germany, 1700–1815* (Cornell University Press, Ithaca, NY, 1996), 4.

61 Zvi Jonathan Kaplan, 'A Marital Dilemma: French Courts, Foreign Jews and the Secularization of Marriage', *Journal of Jewish Studies* 64, no. 2 (2013), 367; Zvi Jonathan Kaplan, 'The Thorny Area of Marriage: Rabbinic Efforts to Harmonize Jewish and French Law in Nineteenth-Century France', *Jewish Social Studies* 13, no. 3 (2007), 61, 69.

62 Henriques, *Jewish Marriage and English Law*, 58.

63 Henry Finlay, *To Have but Not to Hold: A History of Attitudes to Marriage and Divorce in Australia 1858–1975* (Federation Press, Sydney, 2005), 30. For the experience of wives attempting to migrate with their transported husbands see Perry McIntyre, *Free Passage: The Reunion of Irish Convicts and Their Families in Australia, 1788–1852* (Irish Abroad Academic Press, Dublin, 2011).

64 Synagogue Scribes, *Solomon, Joseph*, 19 November 2014, <http://synagoguescribes. com/blog/person-details/?value=1687>.

65 *The Times*, 21 October 1819, 3.

66 See Anne Rand, 'Temple House and the Judah Solomon Family', in Peter Elias and Elias Ann (eds), *A Few from Afar: Jewish Lives in Tasmania from 1804* (The Hobart Hebrew Congregation, Hobart, 2003); Hamish Maxwell-Stewart, 'Land of Sorrow, Land of Honey: Aspects of the Life of Judah Solomon (c. 1777–1856)', in Elias and

Elias (eds), *A Few from Afar*; David F. Solomon, 'From Convict to Colonist–Joseph Solomon of Evandale (c. 1780–1851)', in Elias and Elias (eds) *A Few from Afar*.

67   Abraham Abrahams, also convicted with them was not so lucky, being executed the day after sentencing: *The Times*, 26 August 1819, 3.

68   John S. Levi, *These Are the Names: Jewish Lives in Australia, 1788–1850* (Miegunyah Press, Carlton, 2006), 797–8.

69   Maxwell-Stewart, 'Land of Sorrow, Land of Honey', 17.

70   Levi, *These Are the Names*, 808.

71   L. Goldman, 'The History of the Hobart Hebrew Congregation, Part 1', in Peter Elias and Ann Elias (eds), *A Few from Afar: Jewish Lives in Tasmania from 1804* (Hobart Hebrew Congregation, Hobart, 2003), 37.

72   *Courier*, 21 September 1844, 2.

73   Jeremy Pfeffer, *'From One End of the Earth to the Other': The London Bet Din, 1805–1855, and the Jewish Convicts Transported to Australia* (Sussex Academic Press, Brighton, 2008), 298.

74   *Courier*, 6 January 1847, 2.

75   Levi, *These Are the Names*, 809.

76   Len Fox, *E. Phillips Fox and His Family* (Len Fox, Sydney, 1985), 13. An English-born Alexander Fox, photographer, appears in the 1880 Census Records for Salt Lake City, Utah, 'married' to Amelia Fox: United States Census, 'Salt Lake City, Salt Lake, Utah' (1880).

77   *Riverine Herald*, 25 March 1895, 2.

78   Margaret James, 'Not Bread but a Stone: Women and Divorce in Colonial Victoria', in Patricia Grimshaw, Chris McConville and Ellen McEwen (eds), *Families in Colonial Australia* (George Allen & Unwin, Sydney, 1985), 43.

79   'An Act to Amend the Law Relating to Divorce and Matrimonial Causes', in *Victoriae Reginæ, no. XXV* (1861).

80   Parliament of Victoria, 'An Act to Amend the Laws Relating to Children and Wives and to Divorce and Matrimonial Causes', 1884.

81   Freeze, 'Making and Unmaking the Jewish Family', 224.

82   Divorce case files, Melbourne, *Levy vs Levy* 1895, Public Record Office Victoria, VPRS 283 P0000 92.

83   Divorce case files, Melbourne, *Lobascher vs Lobascher* 1894, Public Record Office Victoria, VPRS 283 P0000 80.

Chapter 4

Migration and Connection

The French barque Alexandrine cleared out on Saturday for the Auckland Isles, with the German expedition for the observation of the transit of Venus on board. The German Consul General, Mr Brahe with some of his friends, and Mr S De Beer, as agent for the vessel, went on board during the afternoon to wish the party farewell and success in their undertaking.
—*Australasian*, 10 October 1874, 19

The waves of settlers who streamed into Melbourne and onto the goldfields sought the necessities of life, food and clothing; picks and mining equipment; housing and shelter. This rapidly expanding mercantile economy, distant from its intercolonial or international markets, was reliant on shipping to provide stock to its shopkeepers and to export the produce of its pastoralists. Letters, journals, circulars, newspapers, trade publications and other correspondence that fostered Melbourne's social and business life depended on reliable shipping for the spread of news and ideas. As the colony gained a more stable equilibrium, the population sought a greater array of home comforts, furniture and furnishings, clothing, books, sewing machines and imported foodstuffs, while imported raw materials supplied nascent manufacturing.

News was required for all aspects of trade, and vital for the maintenance of the economy. Analysis and information was provided for more than thirty years by the Emden-born shipping agent Samuel de Beer in his monthly Shipping Report, the importance of which saw it circulated and republished in the colonial press. De Beer's agency further connected Melbourne internationally through the ships that serviced the routes between Melbourne, New Zealand, Asia, Africa and America. Married in Melbourne to an American-born wife, active in philanthropy in the Jewish and wider community, and connected through the marriage of his son to the international Hallenstein family, de Beer forged a business and personal life based on a complex web of connections.

The hundreds of thousands of settlers who journeyed to the colony in mid century were drawn from Britain and many other parts of the globe. For adventurous Jews, the colony offered social and political freedom, coupled with an opportunity for economic success, unhindered by repressive restrictions. Jews were a formative part of the establishment of the Australian colonies, and as a community expressed the diversity of the Jewish diaspora. In Melbourne, this settlement occurred as Anglo-Jewry instituted its final push for complete emancipation. Those European Jews who arrived following the discovery of gold carried with them the experience of the changes that occurred following the 1848 upheavals.

Jewish identity is that of a diaspora rather than that of a specific political or geographic locality and this complexity produced new networks connecting Jewish settlers in the empire and beyond. Many Britons had multiple geographic or ethnic identities, and this was no different for the Anglo-Jewish community, for whom Englishness and Jewishness coexisted, but as Jews they also conceived of themselves as being connected to a wider Jewish diaspora.

No Jewish community has operated in isolation, cut off from the rest of the world. Rather, they functioned within the political, social and economic climate of the society in which they inhabited, forces that shaped their perspective and their world view. As with others, settlement did not sever their ties with family, community and business; rather, these were maintained through the expanded opportunities available in the colonies. Without restrictions and with limited overt anti-Semitism, the distinctive class structures and culture produced in Victoria permitted a level of acceptance for the community that was far greater than in Europe or the Caribbean, where many had originated. Their international connections facilitated trade and encouraged the flow of ideas, connecting the community to world events. This was a community influential as makers of public policy, as politicians, and as community and local government leaders.

Outside nation-states, Jews used language and a shared cultural experience to define identity, even as they moved in an increasingly globalised world. Language is often seen as a marker of cultural identity and nation building, and for Jews, the transnational languages of Ladino and Yiddish facilitated communication across national and empire boundaries, thus creating a new intellectual community broader than that of any one nation.[1] These languages also had the advantage of privacy, excluding 'outsiders' unable to read Hebrew.[2]

Anglo-Jewry's complete adoption of English has sometimes been seen as a repudiation of a unique and viable Jewish cultural alternative.[3] Yet English afforded this community a wider world view, enabling interconnectedness with a new diaspora linked through the political and economic connections of the British Empire and the New World. This interconnectedness was facilitated through the spread of ideas and the experiences of individuals. High levels of literacy assisted this process, and of the 1400 brides and grooms married in Melbourne synagogues up to 1890, only thirteen could not sign their names in English, while a significant number were literate in several languages.

Migration

As the economies of the New World colonies developed in the nineteenth century, improved communications and transport encouraged 50 million Europeans to migrate, seeking a new life. In Australia, these advances, particularly the demand for labour, were motivating factors for the estimated 1.6 million who came from Britain.[4] Included in these numbers are the several thousand Jews who relocated to Victoria, arriving as single men, families, sibling groups and occasionally as single women.

Jewish communities were able to maintain relationships transnationally as well as locally, through familial, business, religious and travel networks. This was particularly important as families were vital in societies in which there was little state assistance. Families could offer fundamental social welfare support unavailable elsewhere. Anglo-Jewry had already witnessed modifications in family ties through the waves of post-readmission immigration, reforming and creating new connections without necessarily severing previous relationships. To ensure a functioning society required individual wellbeing and communal survival and thus the Melbourne Jewish community fashioned and replicated a number of social welfare organisations to support its members and to create a cohesive community.

Although by the mid nineteenth century changes were taking place in London, and the community was beginning to leave its confines in the east of the city, census data reveals that the majority of those Londoners settling in Melbourne originated in the small area around Houndsditch, bound by tight endogamy and business networks. Even conviction and transportation did not break all of these bonds. Ellis Casper, previously a watchmaker, at the time living in prosperous Finsbury Square, was convicted with his son Lewin of the 1839 'Great Gold Dust Robbery', where father and son had attempted to steal £4640 worth of gold dust. His wife, Elizabeth Nathan, and eight children followed him to Van Diemen's Land and afterwards settled with Ellis in Melbourne.[5]

The Casper family seems to have favoured watchmaking as a profession, with Ellis and at least two of his brothers and a nephew engaged in this line of work. Prior to their 1841 transportation, the family's connectivity appears to have been strong, with several generations of brothers, nephews and nieces living in the small thoroughfare, Bury Street, St Mary Axe, beside the Bevis Marks Synagogue. As with many families, they not only lived in close proximity to each other but also married within a small circle, with several members over two generations marrying into the family of the distinguished Rabbi Solomon (Zalman) Ansell, one of the first members of the English Beth Din. Close relationships were ensured with the consecutive marriage of two of Ellis's sisters, Rebecca and Hannah, to the same man, Jacob Wolffson. Family ties were maintained. Ellis not only lived with his daughter Grace and her husband, Henry Wolff, but the two men were partners in a business somewhat ironically exporting small quantities of gold and importing groceries, which they sold in their stores in Geelong and Melbourne.[6]

Australia was not an easy destination to get to; the costs were high and travel arduous. Costs fluctuated with demand, particularly during the gold rush when steerage rates rose from £10 in 1851 to £21 by 1853.[7] For comfortable travel on technologically advanced ships such as the Great Britain, fares varied between £70 for salon class to £32 for the lower cabin.[8] To support the burgeoning economies of the Australian colonies, a labour force was required. To assist immigration, subsidised schemes were introduced, particularly aimed at securing agricultural labour and domestic servants. Approximately one-quarter of those leaving Britain in the nineteenth century were beneficiaries of some sort of assistance, in the form of a subsidised passage or a land grant.[9] Jews, whose religious requirements made living in other households difficult and as a community that came from urban areas, remained largely ineligible for these schemes.

Even for beneficiaries of assisted immigration, direct and indirect costs were significant. A financial outlay was required to meet the cost of internal transportation to the port of embarkation, as well as for outfitting for the voyage or contributions to the cost of bedding and utensils, expenses that could exceed the cost of a passage to America.[10] The indirect costs involved risk: initially the perils associated with long-distance ocean voyages, the loss of income on the voyage and then establishment costs in a new location.[11]

English newspapers supplied information for prospective immigrants to Victoria, with the *Jewish Chronicle* facilitating Jewish emigration to the goldfields through a number of high-profile articles. In August 1852 the paper cautioned young men about expecting to make a speedy fortune on the goldfields:

The recent discoveries of gold have tempted many young men to leave the land of their birth and depart in pursuit of fortune. Among their ranks the young Hebrew has gone also to seek an independence by frugal habits, industrious pursuits, and the sweat of his brow; but especially since the discovery of gold in Australia, numbers of our active young men have been drawn to the golden shores by the glowing accounts they have heard, and have started full of anticipatory hopes reaping a speedy self-sufficiency. Now, we are not of that number who are lead away with the idea that a fortune may be realised there in a few months, for if some have indeed been enriched in a short time, we believe them exceptions, not the rule.[12]

The demographic problems associated with Australian settlement were particularly acute for the Jewish population, which did not see equal numbers of men and women in the community until the twentieth century. As Judaism is transferred matrilineally, this was an ongoing problem for the colonial communities across Australia and New Zealand. At the height of the gold rush, the 1857 census records indicate that there were more than twice as many Jewish men in Victoria as women. To ensure a functioning community to which families and single women would want to migrate required the evolution of communal organisations that created an environment conducive to family life. In response to the potential problems that the lack of Jewish women generated for men who had migrated, the *Jewish Chronicle* published a number of articles encouraging female immigration, and requesting support from rabbis around the country:

yet by reason of the fast increasing population of the gold colonies, he will see that the acquisition of gain must of necessity become the work of time … He will want to settle down … because yearning for companionship, and, finding no damsels of his creed near, he became friendly with the stranger … To allay this evil the clergy must strain every nerve, and we doubt not that when pointed out, they will use every endeavour within their power. The best remedy will be to preach from their pulpit the necessity of 'female emigration', for though a large number of men have left us, scarcely one female has followed, although there is here such a preponderance of Hebrew females over males.[13]

The paper also reflected the prevailing notions of loyalty expected of the community. Five months later, when the paper again raised the issue, it stressed the virtues of Australia in comparison to the Californian gold rush:

> There gold is not a blessing but a curse … crime of the darkest
> form is rampant; neither property nor life is safe. Australia is a
> British colony, and that speaks its praise, the sovereignty of the
> crown is there acknowledged by the loyal community … in
> Australia the population have attained a high social and commer-
> cial position under a constitutional legislature; and beyond all
> these distinctions in its favour, the most important is, that whilst
> California has no wealth besides her gold, that Australia, indepen-
> dently of gold, is unlimited.[14]

The British Jewish community had sought ways throughout the nineteenth
century to raise the economic position of Jewry. Emigration afforded an opportunity to reduce the financial burden of relief, but as Jews did not fit the criteria
for many other schemes it was recognised that assistance was required if people
were to emigrate. In 1853 the Jewish Ladies Benevolent Loan and Visiting
Society expanded its scope, creating an auxiliary Emigration Committee chaired
by Nathaniel Montefiore, to provide assistance for migration to America and to
the Australian colonies. This assistance was in the form of loans financed
through subscriptions. The scheme was widely promoted, and this publicity
allowed the committee to give credence to its endeavours through the financial
endorsement and participation of high-profile individuals.

The issue was also taken up by the *Jewish Chronicle*, which responded to
the shortage of women in the colonies by promoting female immigration and
the advantages for women in emigrating:

> Young women who contemplate emigrating should, however
> remember that the settlers require industrious domesticated wives;
> and that they are sufficiently acute not to take any other … for
> the introduction of industrious, unpretending girls, whether as
> wives or servants, there is scarcely any limit … Female emigrants
> of the Jewish persuasion would have all the advantages and few of
> the disadvantages of other people. There is a bond of union among
> them so strong, that although some threads may be unravelled, its
> main strength remains unimpaired. As soon as a new emigrant
> arrives among them, they sally forth to welcome her, give a hospi-
> table reception, emulate each other in the desire of making her
> comfortable and seek employment for her that may prove ulti-
> mately advantageous.[15]

Although many women and the community at large were concerned about
the immigration experience, some care was taken for female protection, with

the Colonial Office overseeing strict segregation on board ships. These fears were also expressed by the Jewish community. Almost as soon as the Emigration Committee launched its scheme to assist female immigration to Australia, concern was voiced as to the suitability of sending single women to the colonies. Anxieties were raised about the dangers for the women and for the impact that marriage would have on the economic prospects of the male settlers. Initially the committee sought to utilise government ships, which led to 'Lily' penning the following in alarm:

> Your correspondent N shews his good taste and feeling when he advises those noble ladies who have taken up the cause of emigration to ponder well—before they consign the fair daughters of Judah to a fate worse than that of poverty and privation at home. Government ships are the very worst kind for Jewesses, who ... are generally nurtured and brought up in a modest privacy unknown among Christian females.[16]

A letter from the son of Abraham Harris to his father was even more strident:

> Respectable Jewish single girls, I should think, could get better situations as cooks or servants in England, without coming out here; and to come out on spec of marrying is, I fear, a very bad spec, as one-half of the Jewish young men are not getting more than a living for themselves much less for a wife, and the old standards can very well get married ... without waiting for an importation from home; and to send young girls to this colony where the house-rent is not to be had, and where the necessities of life are so exceedingly dear, ought to be argued by right minded persons, as, instead of doing a great good, they may do a great evil.[17]

An editorial continued in this vein:

> we have reason to fear that if indiscriminate emigration prevails, as at present, its effect on the moral and intellectual progress of Australia will be deplorable ... discourage the idea of unmarried females venturing out for the present ... Australia is yet drunken with success, and the civilising influence of women is not yet felt ... Women unprotected is not yet safe in the gold regions of Australia.[18]

For Jewish women, fear was compounded by the difficulty of cultural maintenance, particularly the lack of kosher food on the voyage, further restricting
Jewish participation in migration schemes. To assist as many migrants as
possible, the Emigration Committee endeavoured to negotiate with the
government over the provision of kosher meat on voyages, but this proved
problematic. The committee argued that the provision of suitable food on
emigrant ships was disadvantaging the Jewish community as a 'portion of Her
Majesty's subjects'. The British government placed various economic obstacles
in the way, although it allowed the provision of kosher meat at the individual's
own expense, without any equivalent reduction in the fare.[19]

As the Emigration Committee advanced its activities throughout 1853, it
sought the advice and services of Caroline Chisholm, the champion of female
migration. Chisholm argued strongly for a system of loans to prospective
migrants; as she considered this a more suitable way of attracting the desired
type of immigrant than those recruited through assistance schemes.[20] To allay
fears of the suitability of the venture, a reader from the Bristol Synagogue, Mr
Benjamin, and his wife were initially contracted to escort a group, but the
couple apparently withdrew due to ill health.

In order to protect 'vulnerable' women, the committee imposed two
criteria; prospective migrants were required to have friends in Australia and to
contribute towards the cost of their outfitting and passage.[21] Three months
later the committee reported that it had selected only 'persons whose characters and trades or occupations would enable them by industry and perseverance,
to gain an honest livelihood in Australia'.[22] The venture culminated in 1854
with the landing of the *Ballarat* in Melbourne and disembarkation of eighteen
single Jewish women and fifteen Jewish families assisted by the committee.

Although only a small number of single females migrated, the plight of
those for whom this was a negative experience is hard to uncover. Analysis of
the immigration patterns indicates that most immigrants settled in family
groups, although a significant number appear to be families headed by women.
This did not stop public concern and by 1858 the Emigration Society was
compelled to report publicly on its work, claiming that it 'refutes all calumnies,
and scatters to the winds all the innuendos which for some time floated about
in the atmosphere of communal opinion, and establishes beyond doubt the
usefulness of the charity'. It added that 'The cases of individual misconduct of
some female emigrants, so severely and so justly animadverted upon by our
Australian co-religionists, were those of persons who found their way into the
colonies of their own accord, sometimes against the advice of the society—at
all times without assistance.'[23]

The Emigration Committee reported in 1854 that they had assisted a
total of 130 individuals at a cost of £1366, of whom 85 had come to Australia.

It was expected that these individuals possessed such trade or domestic skills as would allow them to find occupation and to repay the Committee in instalments for their passage.[24] By February 1858 this number had risen to 388, of whom 210 had gone to the United States and 108 to Melbourne. In outlining the objectives for assistance, the committee stated that it hoped immigration would secure livelihoods for those who had previously depended on the community for charity. Their objectives for single women included furnishing suitable marriage partners for men in the colony.

The success of this program provided an additional and unexpected benefit: a number of recipients secured sufficient resources to contribute to remittances for others to fund their journey to the colonies. In the committee's reports, the issue of single female immigration was so contentious that they felt compelled to report the circumstances of those who had arrived with Caroline Chisolm on the *Ballarat*. As these were essentially privately funded ventures, the beneficiaries who arrived in family groups do not appear in the assisted immigration listing, and so are difficult to identify. The committee reported that it funded greater numbers of married women than married men. By implication these women were either travelling to reunite with husbands who had previously left for the colonies, or were widows (or divorcees) starting a new life away from Britain. Single women travelling alone appear rarely in shipping lists; rather, single women generally accompanied other extended family groups or married siblings. The Crownson family is an exception to this pattern, with sisters Rachel, Elizabeth and Phoebe migrating separately from London between 1864 and 1872.[25]

Chain Migration

The strong sense of family and extensive familial intermarriage is illustrated in the migration patterns of the Melbourne Jewish community. Not only did families offer financial and practical support in the migration process, but family connections in the colonies also provided paths for immigrants to follow. These could be transnational, with several branches of a family or interconnected families from various locations settling in Melbourne. In Sydney in 1848 a group of gentlemen convened a meeting to 'Promote Emigration to Australia'.[26] Among these were members of the Henriques and Montefiore families, which both had transnational migration patterns and a tantalising link to a large chain migration from Jamaica to Melbourne in the following few years.[27]

These were Sephardi families that maintained their connections to the West Indies through marriages to other Sephardi families from the Caribbean. The largest of these migrations to Melbourne is that of the interconnected Henriques, Lopez, de Leon and Belinfante families. The first in this family group to arrive was Joseph Henriques, who went first to Adelaide, where he married Judith Georgina Barrow Montefiore, while Judith's sister Emily Barrow Montefiore married in Adelaide the widowed Moses Benjamin Henriques, assumed to be Joseph's brother.[28] Joseph established the firm A Q Henriques & Co, in Melbourne with another brother, Abraham Quixano Henriques. Their parents, Benjamin Henriques and Abigail Mosquita and several siblings followed them to Victoria, arriving from 1853.

Another sister, Rachel, also initially settled in Adelaide with her husband Dr Solomon Iffla, and arrived in Melbourne in 1853. Another Henriques cousin, Joseph Augustus and his wife, Louisa Lopez, left Jamaica, successfully establishing themselves as merchants in New York, where the 1870 census listed the valuation of their personal and real estate at $105,000. They too later migrated to Melbourne permanently.[29] Louisa's sister, Rebecca Lopez, migrated to Victoria with her husband, David de Leon, and five of their children in 1858. Included in this extended family grouping was their married daughter Ada de Leon and her husband, Solomon Belinfante, whose occupation is listed variously as merchant and accountant. In Melbourne this couple produced a family of at least twelve children.

The pre-emancipation treatment of Jews in Jamaica had been restrictive. Coupled with the depressed conditions of the post-slavery economy, this influenced the decision of many to leave. The compensation payments made to slave owners provide an indication of the individual families' position there. Families such as the Montefiores had significant enterprises in Barbados, and Joseph and Jacob Montefiore received compensation for twenty slaves each, while most of the other families that arrived from the Caribbean had also held slaves. Numbers varied from a single slave to the thirteen slaves owned by Isaac Lopez, the father of Rebecca and Louisa Lopez, and thirty-one slaves owned by Abigail de Leon, the mother of Joseph Augustus Henriques.[30]

The settlement patterns of other families reflect different social and economic circumstances. Clara Isaacs arrived in Victoria in 1848, apparently as an independent traveller. In 1856 her brother Barnett Isaacs immigrated on the *Moorcroft* with his wife, Alice (Alsey) Hart, son, Woolf Barnett Isaacs, and unmarried sister-in-law, Agnes Hart, establishing himself in Melbourne as a successful publican. His sister-in-law, Agnes, subsequently married Jacob Andrade Isaacs, also a publican but no relation to Barnett. In 1877, upon the unfortunate death of both their spouses, Agnes and Barnett married, again reflecting the Jewish tradition outside English law, but allowable under changes to Victorian law enacted in 1873.[31]

Clara Isaacs' only child, Caroline, was a newborn when her mother left for Melbourne, and was left in London to live with relatives. In the 1860s she was sent to the New Zealand gold town of Hokitika, where she had extended family networks, prior to moving to Melbourne and marrying in 1872. Her marriage certificate lists her address as that of her uncle, Barnett Isaacs, in Burlington Terrace, East Melbourne. Although both Isaacs siblings settled in Melbourne, little trace can be found of Clara. Family notices published by Barnett, such as those in 1869 to notify the death in London of his mother, Elizabeth Barnett, and brother-in-law, Michael Myers, make no mention of his sister, but it appears that Barnett provided a home for his niece Caroline on her arrival in Melbourne.

Onward Migration

Of the millions who left Europe in the nineteenth century for the Americas, Australia, New Zealand and South Africa, an estimated 40 per cent returned to their country of birth.[32] Many others 'tried their luck' in a variety of destinations. 'No two British communities were entirely alike, although all offered opportunities for transformation, if not advancement, and all offered too, the routine dangers of over-reach, failure or quiet mediocrity.'[33] For Jews, their diasporic outlook extended opportunities: Europe, England and the various Australian colonies afforded triangular routes of communication, residence and return, while the Caribbean, America and South Africa provided other alternatives.

For many families New Zealand became a 'horizontal connection', providing spouses for those looking for marriage partners and linking families and businesses across the Tasman.[34] Jews were unlikely to send their children 'home' to be educated, while business and family connections resulted in some spending a peripatetic life in several continents or, for those with a sufficient fortune, retiring to London. Some, like the family of Moss Davis, amassed sufficient capital through breweries in the colonies to retire to Park Lane, where his children married into the English establishment, while two of his sons received titles for their services to business and politics in New Zealand.

Moss Davis's in-laws, the Jacobs family, exhibit the availability of chain migration and onward migration. Prussian-born Elias Rypinski Jacobs and his wife, Henriette Leishershonn, eloped to Manchester in about 1834, before moving back to Graudenz, Prussia, where a number of their children were born. The family returned to England, and in 1847 their daughter Leah was born in Liverpool. They moved again, this time to Manchester, where their final two children were born. Here Elias found work as a glazier, a classic itinerant immigrant job, requiring only a rough diamond and a few panes of glass. His economic fortunes temporarily improved and in 1861 he is listed in the census as a looking glass and picture dealer, unfortunately being declared bankrupt the following year.[35] He subsequently managed to establish himself as one of a new breed of Jewish entrepreneurs, opening a small factory, coating vulcanised rubber on cloth, in a process previously developed by Charles McIntosh.[36]

Elias Jacobs returned to Graudenz sometime before his death in 1874. Notification was sent to his sons Isaac and Lesser in Melbourne by their brother-in-law Isidore Gross, himself in Graudenz at the time.[37] The first member of the family to migrate to Victoria was the eldest son, Isaac, who arrived in 1852 as a representative of the Manchester firm Falk & Company. By 1878, all but one of the siblings as well as their widowed mother had made their way to Victoria, although only Isaac and his sisters Jane and Augusta settled permanently there. The others moved between Victoria, Sydney, New Zealand, America, Canada and London. The only sibling not to come to Australia was the eldest daughter, Betsy, who married in Manchester in 1856 and migrated with her husband to Baltimore.

The Jacobs family, Manchester, c. 1852. Augusta is holding a photograph of her brother Isaac, who was already in Victoria, Private Collection

Rebecca Jacobs' peripatetic life epitomises the difficulties settlement and onward migration could pose. After Rebecca married Isaac Herman in Melbourne in 1862, the couple moved to Christchurch, New Zealand, where they had eleven children. In 1887 Isaac Herman was declared bankrupt and sentenced to one month's prison for poor account-keeping, and the family's possessions were sold at public auction.[38] The Hermans then migrated to Vancouver, Canada, before Rebecca relocated to California (and her sixth country of residence) and all trace of her vanishes.[39] The younger brother, Lesser Jacobs, like many Prussian-British immigrants, worked for a countryman, a wholesale jeweller operating as Feldheim and Co. Lesser married in Sydney and eventually returned to London with his family. The youngest sister, Sophia, married Solomon de Beer in New Zealand before she too finally settled in Melbourne.

Female Employment

In Britain, emigration was seen as a solution to the plight of 'superfluous' women unable to find a husband, and an answer for women in need of improved financial status.[40] The selection was undertaken with care, ensuring those chosen had a level of education, had suitable skills and were considered respectable. Industrialisation expanded female employment opportunities, providing work in factories, but domestic service remained the dominant female employment. Female migration was aimed primarily at providing domestic servants for Australia, an occupation that local women were disinclined to undertake. Although the Jewish community recognised the financial benefits of immigration, the defining factor in attempts at organised female immigration was that of community preservation.

It would appear that whereas many of the non-Jewish female migrants were travelling in anticipation of a position in domestic service, this was rarely the case for their Jewish sisters. Of the 105 Jewish women for whom an occupation can be established, nine can be identified as servants and two as housekeepers (for family members). The majority of working women were employed in clothing manufacturing, as tailoresses, dressmakers, cap makers, feather dressers, milliners and furriers. A further eleven were employed in various retail industries, in positions such as storekeepers, pawnbrokers and general dealers; six in education as teachers or governesses, and three as publicans, while the remainder included a hawker and a machinist.[41]

The Victorian goldfields and the economy of nineteenth-century Melbourne provided opportunities for the enterprising. At a time when the education of Jewish girls in England was limited and the middle class was unable to find suitable Jewish governesses, at least five female teachers migrated to Victoria.[42] A Jewish education was important, even to families living in isolated rural communities. Although not an immigrant, the experience of Fitzroy-born Louisa Fredman is indicative of those who sought employment in this field. Louisa was a gifted student, winning prizes for Hebrew and General Achievement at the Melbourne Hebrew School.[43]

With few opportunities for employment as a middle-class woman but with some education, she obtained work in the isolated community of

Branxholme in Victoria's Western District as governess to the Silberberg family. Her achievements did not go unnoticed and were extolled in the description of Montefiore Silberberg's bar mitzvah at the Ballarat Synagogue in 1895. The *Jewish Herald* reported: 'In the course of an excellent address to the Bar Mitzvah the Reverend I.M. Goldreich paid a graceful compliment to Miss Louisa Fredman, of St. Kilda (governess in Cr. Silberberg's family), for the able and correct manner she had prepared the young gentleman for his confirmation.' After complimenting the boy on his achievement, the paper noted: 'Much sympathy was felt for the talented young lady when Mr. Goldreich explained that, owing to the recent bereavement she had sustained by the death of her father, she was unable to be present and enjoy the practical result of her labour.'[44]

A woman's working life often ended upon her marriage, but her skills could prove beneficial in establishing opportunities to support a family in uncertain times. Leah Fonseca is listed in the 1851 English Census as a furrier, living with her parents in Goulston Street, London. In June that year she married Danish-born Henry (Samuel Isaac) Cohn, also employed in the fur trade. The couple migrated to Bendigo, where Cohn joined his brothers, who had previously established a successful brewery.[45] Returning to Melbourne, Henry entered the hospitality sector, running hotels and the refreshment rooms at railway stations before being declared insolvent in 1870, citing 'falling off of business, loss of trade, high rents and heavy expenses' as the cause of his commercial failure.[46]

He returned to his initial occupation as a furrier in West Melbourne, but this also appears to have been unsuccessful. In 1874 Cohn committed suicide, leaving debts of more than £374 to suppliers and individuals.[47] Following Henry's death, his widow, Leah, re-established herself in Melbourne, opening as a wholesale furrier on the corner of Collins and Queen streets. The advice pages of the *Australasian* frequently quoted Mrs Cohn as an expert and directed enquiries to her, referring to her as 'the best furrier I know'.[48] On her death in 1902 she had not only weathered the depression but left an estate valued for probate at £780.[49]

Communications

Advances in technology and communications were vital to the empire, enabling the dissemination of ideas and knowledge through the English-speaking and wider Jewish world. Newspapers, letters, pamphlets and circulars became a means by which Jewish communities connected to local issues and those affecting their brethren around the globe. This enabled reciprocity of information, as Melbourne-based correspondents reported for the British and

European press, and British and European papers were reported locally, while papers were imported into the colony attached to correspondence from home and by subscription. Such publications were important during the gold rush, when published accounts, guides and articles, aimed at middle-class audiences, were widely circulated.[50]

The Jewish press played a unifying and consolidating role for Jewish solidarity and identity, 'embracing the imperatives of emancipation, which required the loyalty of Jews to the countries in which they lived', while maintaining interest in international Jewish affairs.[51] A Jewish press was developed during the nineteenth century and widely circulated; papers included the *Allgemeine Zeitung des Judenthums* in Leipzig, first published in 1837; the *Archives israélites* founded in Paris in 1840; the London-based *Jewish Chronicle*, begun in 1841; and the *Voice of Jacob* of 1841–48. This paper endeavoured to produce an Australian edition in Sydney, but ran for only three issues, entitled the *Voice of Jacob or the Hebrew Monthly Miscellany*. The time lag in communications meant that English, European and Australian papers reported information that was weeks or months old and this was the case for the Australian edition of the *Voice of Jacob*, which was largely culled from the home paper. The *Voice of Jacob* was especially directed at promoting Jewish education and scholarship, comprising opinion pieces encouraging Anglo-Jewish intellectual advance and reports on the newly developing English Jewish schools, as well as carrying international news of interest to readers.

The *Australian Israelite* was the first regular Jewish newspaper in Australia, produced from 1871 by Solomon Joseph, chairman of the Melbourne Jewish Literary and Debating Society. This was followed in 1879 by the *Jewish Herald*, edited by Reverend Blaubaum of the St Kilda Hebrew Congregation, assisted by the architect Nahum Barnet and the solicitor Maurice Benjamin. The *Jewish Herald* carried reports of Jewish political and cultural life from Europe, the Middle East, the Americas as well as Australia. The locally edited and the imported publications supplied Melbourne Jewry with a wider appreciation and a sense of connectedness to issues affecting the Jewish diaspora. They connected readers to political, religious and social changes, resulting in a transformation from 'intangible conceptions of the "community of Israel" (*Knesset Yisrael*) into the tangible reality of international Jewish organization'.[52]

The Jewish press was not the only source of information concerning Jewish affairs. The general press carried articles on local and international Jewish political issues, as well as reporting on Jewish philanthropy both at home and abroad, reprinting the minutes of a variety of Jewish philanthropic organisations. Wider Jewish philanthropic activities were promoted through the publication of lists of subscribers to local and international charitable activities. The integrated nature of the community can be gleaned from the frequent reporting of Jewish weddings, not only in *Table Talk* but also the city and local newspapers.

Knowledge of colonial society was promoted in England, with the *Jewish Chronicle* reporting on the Melbourne community as early as December 1844, at a time when only eleven Jewish families had settled in the town, and later encouraging migration to the colonies.[53] The British Jewish press marketed itself as spanning the empire, listing subscribers from across Britain and the colonies.[54] Australian contributions to the *Jewish Chronicle* were interspersed with those of local English communities, often giving greater detail on community activities and communal politics than for the English regional counterparts. The paper also contained articles culled from the colonial papers as well as commenting on articles from the colonial non-Jewish press. The *Jewish Chronicle* was widely circulated in Australia. In 1864 a letter from a non-Jewish reader described how he often read this 'valuable and intelligent paper' at his local Mechanics Institute.

The same correspondent reported on the case of a non-Jewish child undergoing a medical circumcision performed by Reverend Rintel, who had been recommended to undertake the procedure due to his proficiency, in contrast to that of local doctors.[55] The Melbourne Hebrew Congregation utilised the international Jewish press to assist with the recruitment of its rabbinical leaders, advertising internationally in the *Jewish Chronicle*, the Prussian *HaMagid*, the New York *Jewish Messenger* and the French *Archives israélites*.[56] Communication was not one way. Ballarat-based Newman Friedel Spielvogel, a scholar with an international reputation in Jewish learning and philosophy, was a frequent contributor not only to the Australian Jewish press but also to the East Prussian Hebrew language weekly *HaMagid*.[57] Through its readership and wide-ranging articles, *HaMagid* produced reports and information on political and mercantile themes that fostered connections at a local and international level and between the Jewish and non-Jewish worlds.[58]

Personal letters seek to diminish geographical space and to reduce imagined difference. For many in Melbourne, this was more complex. Victoria was a secondary destination for those who came from Europe via England, so maintenance of these transnational connections was important for family and business. Letters could thus be written from many 'homes' and in more than one language; even for English-born children, they were sometimes composed in their parents' mother tongue. The letters from the Posen-born but Sheffield-based Michael Levinson to his family in Victoria in 1860–61, written almost entirely in English, included many references to newspapers in the correspondence. The return letters went on to Posen and the family there. In a letter dated 24 October 1861, Michael wrote:

Not to you Dear Hyman complain of not getting letters from Posen after you know they never are so punctual in writing to us. I enclose the letters I received from there. You will find it is a טוֹב מַזְל (Mazel Tov) and that they are much pleased to hear good news from you.[59]

For those who had settled in Victoria from Britain and elsewhere, connection to family and place of origin was maintained through the improved communications offered by the efficient mail services and railways. From the 1850s voyage times were reduced, initially through the technological advances of steam-propelled ships, while the opening of the Suez Canal in 1862 provided a direct route, reducing time at sea.[60] Settlers such as Nathaniel Levi kept scrapbooks, recording not only his own achievements, but also those of his family in Liverpool and Coventry as well as issues pertaining to wider Anglo-Jewry.

The books contain annual reports for the Coventry Philanthropic Institution, of which the Coventry-born and Liverpool-resident father Joseph Levi was a founder. Also contained in the scrapbooks are cuttings relating to the New Synagogue, Liverpool, for which his brother Godfrey was a secretary; material relating to its sister congregation, the Liverpool Old Hebrew Congregation; an 1879 obituary for the Reverend Professor D.M. Isaacs, minister of the Old Synagogue, Manchester; and a pamphlet supporting the cause of Jewish political emancipation.[61]

The family notice section of the London-based *Jewish Chronicle* and the Victorian papers regularly listed lifecycle events captioned 'Australian papers please copy' or 'home papers please copy'. Australian notices were published in the *Jewish Chronicle*. Such was the case on the death of Alice Hart, wife of Barnett Isaacs, in 1856. In a similar vein, the death of parents in England was formalised in Melbourne through the posting of death notices and the holding of commemorative *minyanim*. Following the deaths in Lambeth, England, of Sarah Green and subsequently her husband, John Nathan, the *Argus* carried numerous notices over several days, posted by their four Victorian-based sons Abraham, David, Benjamin and Samuel Nathan, noting that the information had been received via cable and listing their *minyan* at Wavetree, Lonsdale Street, Melbourne.

The Jewish World

In establishing formal communal structures, the Melbourne Jewish community did not do so independently; rather, they followed the pattern of Ashkenazi England, placing themselves under the auspices of the chief rabbi of the British Empire and perpetuating their connections to Anglo-Judaism.[62]

Without any formal necessity for religious affiliation or communal representation, there was no requirement for an overarching structure covering the Ashkenazi communities of either England or Victoria. The role of the chief rabbi was a particularly European post-emancipation development in an otherwise non-hierarchical and independent religion. During the nineteenth century, a number of congregations in the English provinces and in London voluntarily accepted the religious and legal pre-eminence of the Great Synagogue's rabbi, who had previously been referred to as the chief rabbi. The formal institution of chief rabbi was created with the 1842 election by twenty-six congregations of Rabbi Nathan Marcus Adler to the post.[63] Adler oversaw all religious questions of the Ashkenazi community within the British Empire, with local religious leaders and communities appealing to his authority and seeking his guidance on a range of matters, including the appointment of rabbis, the vexed issues of conversion and the recognition of children's Jewish identity, and detailed matters such as the repair of *Siphrei Torah*.

Other congregations in the British Empire were not legally bound by the chief rabbi's jurisdiction, yet many, particularly those in Australia, willingly recognised his authority and supported it both financially and as a tie to the 'mother country'. In 1848 the Melbourne Hebrew Congregation accepted the rules and regulations circulated by the chief rabbi for its guidance.[64] The difficulty that distance created for colonial negotiations with the Office of the Chief Rabbi resulted in the ultimate independence of local Jewry, a position with greater autonomy than that of similar congregations in Britain.

Whereas for Christians, ministers and priests could receive education and training in Britain and Ireland, comparative formal instruction did not exist for the Jewish community and there was no rabbinic training available in any English-speaking country. Instead, Australian (and British) congregations relied on informally educated British-born religious functionaries, or imported European rabbis with various degrees of skill and learning.[65] Those serving the Melbourne communities all had connections to a variety of congregations, universities and communities in England, Europe, the Americas and South Africa as well as to the other Australian colonies.

However, until the appointment of Rabbi Dr Joseph Abrahams in 1882, none of those acting in rabbinic roles in Victoria were trained rabbis. Isaac Pulver arrived in Victoria in 1854, having previously held positions in Cheltenham, England and Cape Town, South Africa. Prior to his retirement to Hobart in 1871, Pulver acted as a member of the Melbourne Beth Din as well as *shochet* for the Melbourne community. The Reverend Moses Rintel, a Scottish-born and educated son of a Polish Rabbi, migrated to Sydney in the early 1840s, where he served the Sydney Congregation in the roles of *mohel*, *shochet* and principal of the Hebrew School. In 1849 he accepted an appointment in Melbourne as reader for the newly formed Melbourne Hebrew Congregation, eventually resigning and forming the East Melbourne Congregation in 1857.[66] The (ultimately) controversial Dr Dattner Jacobson held a doctorate from the University of Vienna and had been previously employed in a number of Austro-Hungarian congregations as a *chazan*, *mohel* and *ba'al kore*, prior to journeying to the United States and on to Melbourne.[67]

Important Jewish religious thinkers, particularly in the English-speaking world, were reported widely in the Jewish press. Isaac Lesser, a Philadelphia-based Jewish lay minister, author, translator, editor and publisher, was a frequent contributor to the Anglo-Jewish press and his writings were widely quoted, particularly in debates on divorce.[68] The young Harriet Levien corresponded with Lesser on issues of Jewish law. She also read the works of other American Jewish philosophers and founded a Hebrew Sunday School in Geelong based on a Philadelphian model established by Rebecca Gratz.[69] Levien came from a family with vast international connections. Her mother, Elizabeth Lindo, was the daughter of a wealthy Jamaican family of traders, privateers and planters and her grandmother Henrietta Salomons was the daughter of Yehiel Prager, head of a multinational trading empire. No doubt these connections formed part of Levien's expansive correspondence.

From the 1870s Australian Jewry was also connected to the Jewish world through the Anglo-Jewish Association, established initially in England, with a remit to promote the welfare of Jews in the Middle East, North Africa and eastern Europe by 'the removal of the disabilities of the Jews, their social, moral and intellectual progress, the granting of aid to those who may suffer through being members of the Jewish race and to promote the production of works calculated to advance these objects'.[70] The Anglo-Jewish Association was modelled on the French *Alliance Israélite Universelle*, founded a decade earlier with similar goals of advancing the status of Jews in the Middle East and North Africa.

The Anglo-Jewish Association not only sought to alleviate distress, but saw structural change as vital to the advancement of Jewish communities, particularly the acculturation of these communities through education, language and dress. They believed that Jewish emancipation was a two-way responsibility, requiring a more outward engagement by Jewish communities. The association considered that Anglo-Jewry's acculturation and subsequent rise in social position had been achieved through education. At a public meeting in London in 1875, the Reverend Professor D.W. Marks spoke:

> ... I look back ... and think what forty years have wrought, I am
> constrained to be thankful and to take courage. At that time there
> was scarcely a boy who was old enough to sell an orange or a

pencil in the street that ever was sent to school; and when I think that at the present time there is not an adult here who has not at his command the stepping-stones to all improvement, the common branches of education, reading and writing, and when I think you have done more than all the grandees of your people would have done by cultivating that education to raise the Jewish people, I stand awed at the contrast which presents itself, a contrast brought upon entirely by education ... We wish our brethren abroad to understand this: that if they want to be considered citizens of the country in which they live, they must do like we do; they must identify themselves with the interests and advantages of that country. They may be as strict in the observance of the precepts of their religion as they like, but in this country a man finds that he can be a Jew and dress like an Englishman, speak English like an Englishman; he can be a Jew and yet be ready to stand up whenever his arm is called for and defend the liberties of his county, aye, and if necessary, to bleach his bones in common with his non-Jewish subjects in defence of their altars and hearths![71]

The Anglo-Jewish Association linked Orthodox and reforming Jews into an institution that 'could share in the formal and visible management of British Jewish Affairs'.[72] This connection between the reforming and the Orthodox was followed in Melbourne, where for several years the agitator for religious reform, Isaac Jacobs, chaired the Melbourne branch of the Anglo-Jewish Association. The meetings and campaigns of the organisation were widely reported in the general press and across the Jewish world. In Melbourne, the *Argus* reported these under a 'Summary of Europe', recognising the international reach of the organisation. With the formation of committees in Melbourne, Bendigo and Ballarat, the association's first action was to support a petition from the English branch addressed to the Shah of Persia requesting protection for the Jews in his realm.[73] A year later the *Argus* reported on the success of the Anglo-Jewish Association in procuring an agreement from the Sultan of Morocco to improve the conditions of Jews in that country.[74]

International Business Connections

Antipodean Jewry traded widely across the colonies, the Pacific and traditional trade routes to Britain, America and Europe. But they also used their networks and family ties to develop trading opportunities. This is not the only side of the Nathan family's interconnected business enterprise. Their roots in Australia begin with Nathan Lyon Nathan, transported on the Third Fleet as a sixteen-year-old, for the crime of stealing a bundle of clothing.[75] Nathan completed his sentence and returned to England, where on 11 November 1807 he married his cousin Sarah Nathan. This marriage produced nine children, all of whom migrated to the Australian and New Zealand colonies.

Rosetta Nathan c.1845 and Moses Joseph c.1845, A. M. Rosenblum
Jewish Museum, The Great Synagogue, Sydney

The first was their daughter Rosetta, who arrived in Sydney in 1831 in order to marry her cousin Moses Joseph. Theirs was to be Australia's first Jewish wedding, conducted under a *chuppah*, performed by P.J. Cohen 'by authority of the Reverend Solomon Hershell, Chief Rabbi of the Jews in London'.[76] Moses Joseph had been transported for theft in 1826, but upon arrival had been assigned to the firm of successful colonial merchants Cooper & Levey, where he was able to develop his business skills. He received a ticket of leave and in 1848 the governor granted him an absolute pardon, allowing him to become involved in communal and business affairs in Sydney.

Joseph initially invested in a tobacco shop, but this quickly gave way to warehousing and the provision of ships, before the construction of his own fleet of fourteen vessels.[77] His wealth enabled him to purchase Mahratta, a pastoral run in the Monaro district of New South Wales, and 100,000 acres of freehold land in New England, and in 1841 land in New Zealand's first land sale, before he turned his attention to the opportunities offered by the discovery of gold. By 1855 Moses Joseph was the largest licensed gold buyer in New South Wales, and in a single year transferred 1000 ounces of the precious metal to London.[78] Moses Joseph died in London in 1889, leaving an estate valued at £300,000 in England and £185,499 in Australia, despite having lost another £250,000 investing in the Confederate States of America.[79]

The Nathan family was one of the most extensive of Jewish business families, spanning several generations and extensive chain migration. This family illustrates the advantages and support that significant chain migration can bring. It also shows how fortunes could be developed through familial sharing of financial resources. As the children of Nathan and Sarah Nathan settled in the various colonies of Australia, they were helped by their bene-factor and uncle, Henry Moses, proprietor of a wholesale clothing warehouse and married to Esther Nathan, Sarah's sister. It appears that Henry Moses provided £100 capital for many of the Nathan family to emigrate.

The first was Rosetta's brother, Louis Nathan, married to Henry Moses' daughter Harriette, who settled in Hobart and established a firm trading in China and the South Seas, as well as an extensive fleet of whaling boats. They were followed by Harriette's brother, Samuel Moses, a trained *mohel* who arrived with an 'Order of Service for Circumcision' inscribed in vellum. Samuel Moses and Louis Nathan established Nathan & Moses, one of Tasmania's largest importing and exporting business. Moses was also president of the Hobart Hebrew Congregation before all three returned to England on their retirement.[80]

Other Nathan siblings sponsored by uncle Henry settled in Launceston, Adelaide and Sydney. Two sisters also migrated: Miriam to Melbourne, where she married the early settler and successful businessman Solomon Benjamin before also retiring to London; and Rachel to Sydney, where she married the businessman and politician Samuel Cohen. Establishing themselves as traders in the port towns of the Australian colonies, the interconnected Nathan and Joseph families could utilise the merchant fleet built up by Moses and Rosetta Joseph to service their businesses.

Meanwhile across the Tasman, the New Zealand-based firm Glaxo's origins lie in the partnership established between Joseph Edward Nathan and his partner and brother-in-law Jacob Joseph. Following his mother's death, Joseph Nathan was lured by the opportunities of the Victorian goldfields. In 1853, on his way to the goldfields, Nathan met a police warden who warned him that his chances of making his fortune by prospecting were very slim, but indicated that supplies for the miners were in demand.[81] Like many Jewish settlers, Nathan followed this advice and established a store. Returning to Melbourne in 1857, Nathan married a cousin, Dinah Marks.

Two years earlier, Nathan's sister Catherine had married another cousin, Jacob Joseph, a London-born but New Zealand-based merchant, who was visiting his homeland from New South Wales where he had initially immigrated with his parents in 1834. Although blind as a result of an accident as a child, Jacob Joseph had vast entrepreneurial vision and was not afraid to take risks, establishing a successful warehousing venture in New Zealand before expanding his business with the help of his brother-in-law. In 1857 Joseph wished to make a return visit to England and asked his brother-in-law to assist in the management in his absence. This led to the formation of a partnership, as Jacob Joseph & Co, exporting wool and importing groceries, stationery, medical supplies, ironmongery and drapery.[82]

In 1873 Nathan established the independent trading business Joseph Nathan and Co., erecting Wellington's largest building, a warehouse measuring 13 x 21 metres and 17 metres high, complete with a hydraulic lift.[83] The 1890s saw improved transport from Britain reducing the need for the style of warehousing offered by Nathan. This coincided with the growth in mass consumption, providing a market for foodstuffs and products that could be produced in the temperate regions of Australia and New Zealand and distributed in Britain and across the empire.[84]

With his sons, Nathan diversified into one of New Zealand's chief agricultural products, butter. In 1903 on a visit to England, Nathan saw the potential for expansion of his dairy-based business into powdered milk. He formed a partnership with Debenham's in London to exploit the recently developed American 'Just-Hatmaker' processing, which he registered in 1907 under the name Glaxo, a euphemism for 'Lacto'.[85] On Joseph Nathan's retirement to London, his sons continued to manage the business internationally from bases in England and New Zealand.

Another of the successful and long-surviving companies were those of the extended Michaelis Hallenstein family, benefiting from the experiences of various family members in Germany and Manchester, honed through skills learned importing in Melbourne and culminating in their international tannery business. They expanded their business across the Australian colonies to New Zealand, London and Hong Kong, eventually returning to their place of birth with branches in Germany itself. The business commenced with the goldfields partnership between Hermann Buttner and Bendix and Isaac Hallenstein, who jointly operated a store in Daylesford.

Isaac Hallenstein had come to Victoria from Germany via California, where he had learned skills in tanning, as well as being tempted to try his luck on the goldfields. On his marriage in 1863, Bendix left Daylesford and migrated to New Zealand, where he built an empire in the clothing industry, leather, drugs and insurance as well as establishing a public profile through his involvement in local and provincial politics.[86] In 1864, still in partnership with Buttner, Isaac Hallenstein purchased a small tanning business in Footscray, trading as Isaac Hallenstein & Co, shortly after including his brother Moritz

Hallenstein in the business. Buttner subsequently sold his share of the business to the Hallensteins' uncle, Moritz Michaelis.

Moritz Michaelis had arrived in Melbourne as a representative of his Manchester employer Sampson & Leppoc, with Adolphus Boyd as his business partner. Later the two established an independent partnership as importers and auctioneers, at one stage turning over £25,000 in a single auction.[87] Despite embezzlement by an employee, the business thrived until the importation of faulty elastic-sided boots from America caused its insolvency. Agreeing to pay his creditors an initial amount of 14 shillings in the pound, he too bought into the partnership with his nephew and in 1883 was able to pay off his remaining creditors.[88]

As Michaelis Hallenstein, the business thrived, increasing production from 120–150 hides per week to 480. The business model was complex, with various family members as partners in each other's enterprises, proffering advice as required. Michaelis Hallenstein expanded first to Sydney in 1875 as Farleigh, Nettheim & Co., bringing Cosman Nettheim from Germany to train and manage this end of the business; Bendix had input in New Zealand as Hallenstein & Farquhar from 1879; and Moritz Hallenstein was sent to London to negotiate the European markets, while two of Moritz Michaelis's sons returned to Germany where they too opened branches of the family business.[89]

Hallenstein and Buttner's Store, Daylesford, Private Collection

Before refrigerated cargos, several Australian companies endeavoured to preserve and export Australian meat using a variety of new technologies. One of Moses Joseph's many enterprises was the Patent Preserved Meat Manufactory at Camperdown, New South Wales, established in 1846 to manufacture and export canned meat. In Victoria two enterprising brothers not only exported meat to Britain, but attempted to export for the Jewish poor by producing low-cost kosher preserved meats.

The brothers Daniel and Samuel David Tallerman had settled in gold-rush Victoria. The younger brother, Daniel, first tried his hand in California before becoming a successful storekeeper, hotelier and provider of entertainments in rural Victoria. He made and lost a fortune before settling in Ararat and subsequently Melbourne. By 1870 the brothers, as partners in the Victorian Meat Preservation Company, were exporting canned and preserved meats to England and France. They specialised in an innovative preserving process, packing rolled meat in tallow for transportation. This was more popular with British housewives than canned meat, as it more closely resembled fresh butcher's meat.[90] The brothers returned to Britain, where they established Tallerman's Australian Meats, importing a range of preserved meats and profiling their business through regular public dinners at which their produce was served.[91] Further developing international markets, they provided meat to the French army and represented Australia at the London International Exhibition of 1873.[92]

Recognising the prohibitive cost of kosher meat for the English poor, the brothers tried to export this from Australia, but the success of this enterprise was hampered by the refusal of the chief rabbi to certify the meat kosher.[93] This issue seemed to intrigue not only the Jewish press but also the Australian regional papers, many of which carried commentary on the issue:

> If there be any enactment in the Judaic code which forbids such beneficial innovation as Mr Tallerman purposes, surely it would be easy to cite book, chapter and verse in justification of the judgement. Until such be done one cannot help having a lingering belief that caprice rather than law dictates the veto.[94]

In 1880, when refrigeration further improved the ability to export meat, the *Jewish Herald* reprinted an angry comment from the *Jewish Chronicle*:

> Will our Jewish working men be allowed to profit by this new achievement in science? We are afraid not. Medieval Rabbis ... have, in their anxiety to protect Israel from the heinous transgressions of the law ... unwittingly placed an obstacle in the way,

which we are afraid, orthodox rabbis of our days will not have the moral courage to remove.[95]

Trade between the islands of the Pacific, New Zealand and Australian provided another source of wealth for entrepreneurial settlers. And this became the one area where Jews spearheaded colonisation, with merchants as importers, wholesalers, auctioneers, sugar producers and ship owners. The Melbourne-born brothers Edward Asher and Leopold Emanuel Benjamin built a mercantile business, both as partners and in partnership with Melbourne-born Henry Marks, importing and exporting to the Fijian markets and as merchants in Suva. The brothers were resident in the islands for many years, where they were engaged politically, socially and through the local Freemasons branch.[96]

International trade could be risky also, vessels sank, businesses collapsed and frauds occurred. In 1895 Moses Rosenfeld, Samuel Davis, Percy Benjamin and John Saxton were convicted, fined and imposed for claiming excess duties on imported goods.[97]

Freemasons

As predominantly self-funded settlers rather than impoverished immigrants, many of the Jewish community arrived in Victoria with financial resources and English at their command. Although pockets of anti-Semitism existed, Jews were largely accepted in civil society, participating in a range of private clubs and associations. Membership of such bodies expanded their connections and broadened business, personal and cultural life. They offered a space for Jews to develop greater levels of intimacy with their non-Jewish peers, and created an outlet for aspirational men wanting to connect with the wider community.

Freemasonry is based on the principle of universalism and belief in a Supreme Being, a conviction that does not differentiate between differing faiths and aims to transcend particular religious beliefs. The Masons' core values include personal self-development, charity and support of the community, obedience to national laws and a responsibility to safeguard the reputation of the fraternity. Internationally, Freemasonry maintained values of universalism and cosmopolitism, while simultaneously considering the nation as 'a site where virtue and merit should be rewarded'.[98] It promoted a 'form of cosmopolitanism ... a supernational identity, a mode of seeing oneself as being connected to communities that extended beyond the British nation'.[99]

The religious neutrality of the Masons afforded intellectual, spiritual and social connections, offering opportunities to connect locally and internationally to those in the city and more widely through its international network.

For the traveller, Freemasonry facilitated contacts and opportunities through fraternities of Masons across the globe. Connections were maintained by reciprocal rights at lodges and through publications that linked members internationally, identifying lodges across the world, promoting renowned local members and at times providing practical information such as coach times and fare prices.[100]

There were costs associated with membership and the activities of Freemasonry and it attracted prominent members of society. For Jews, the fraternity afforded an entrée, connections and acceptance that might not otherwise have been possible. Jews had been Freemasons since the early eighteenth century, participating in general lodges as well as developing predominantly Jewish ones. These provided a social circle for their members, and Jews established their own, enabling the more observant to maintain their strict dietary laws, while participation in other lodges supported broader networks in the city.

The Old Testament symbolism of the Masons was also familiar to Jewish participants, and the prayers contained nothing at variance with Jewish traditions.[101] Melbourne's Jewish community engaged with Freemasonry at all levels. The oldest lodge in Melbourne, the Lodge of Australia Felix, was established in Melbourne in 1840. By the 1860s it was constituted almost entirely of Jewish members. Members of the community officiated at the highest levels of the management of the organisation, allowing Moses Rintel to preside as grand chaplain, in which ceremonial role he laid the foundation stone for both the Benevolent Asylum (1851) and the Freemasons Alms House (1867).[102]

The connections between Freemasonry and the empire were strong. Freemasonry assisted in the transformation of a new and strange place into a recognisable outpost of British society; and the Masonic hall was often the first building erected in a new colony, providing a focal point for recreational, civic and business gatherings.[103] The international appeal of Freemasonry included social and business networks for those Jews who utilised the empire to expand their careers. In 1910 two Jews were elected mayor in Fiji, Melbourne-born Gabriel Jacob Marks in Suva and New Zealand-born David Jaffa Solomon in Levuka.[104]

Gabriel's brother Henry Marks arrived in Fiji five years after the islands ceded sovereignty to Britain, and four years before his younger brother Gabriel. While in Fiji, Gabriel became actively involved in the range of secular, religious and philanthropic institutions available to a colonist, not only as mayor of Suva but also as master of the lodge of Fiji. While on a world tour, Marks and his wife drowned in the sinking of the *Empress of Ireland* off the coast of Canada. Such was their connection to the community in Fiji that their bodies were taken there en route to Melbourne, where they were to receive a formal Jewish funeral. In a major public event in Suva, the Fijian Masons held a preliminary Masonic service over the bodies, and then the staff of Henry Marks & Co transported them to the wharf for the trip to Melbourne. The ecumenical nature of the day was captured by the press:

> As the procession left the Hall, the bell of the Church of England was tolled by the vicar. The coffins were followed by a large crowd ... All the stores closed at 4 pm for the remainder of the day, and flags were flown at half-mast. The 'Last Post' was played by a bugler and the coffins were taken aboard the ship, and the scene at this, the most affecting stage of all, was both sad and impressive.[105]

Gabriel Marks and Marion Alexander at home in Suva, Private Collection

Gabriel Marks's parents had settled in Melbourne from England, where his father established a pawnbroking business, and as with many who are successful in this trade, eventually moved to the more respectable title of financier. In Fiji the brothers' enterprise, Henry Marks & Co., specialised in the maritime trade, copra production, land ownership and shipping between Australia, Fiji and its neighbours, becoming the most extensive commercial enterprise in the western Pacific.

Henry Marks also sought political office, joining the legislature of the islands as soon as Europeans were permitted, becoming commissioner of currency and also mayor of Suva. Following the outbreak of the First World War, Marks gained permission from the secretary of state to recruit, train and provision 100 Fijians to enlist in the imperial army. This was half-funded by his company and the other half he provided himself. His wide participation in the civic life of Fiji earned him the title 'Honourable' and in 1933 he was knighted for his services to his adopted country.[106]

Fiji and the south Pacific became one of the first forays of Jewry taking an active role in the very act of colonisation. This role can be seen in the erecting in 1918 of a statue in memory of Gabriel and Marion Marks, at a site previously chosen for an unfulfilled memorial in honour of Edward VII.[107]

Notes

1   Benedict Anderson, *Imagined Communities: Reflections on the Origins and Spread of Nationalism* (Verso, London, 1983), 47.
2   Werner E. Mosse, 'Judaism, Jews and Capitalism Weber, Sombart and Beyond', *The Leo Baeck Institute Year Book* 24, no. 1 (1979), 13.
3   For a discussion of language as a creator of a cultural and national identity see Anderson, *Imagined Communities*.
4   Eric Richards, *Poor Australian Immigrants in the Nineteenth Century: Visible Immigrants: Two* (Division of Historical Studies and Centre for Immigration and Multicultural Studies, Research School of Social Sciences, Australian National University, Canberra, 1991), 7, 2.
5   Sue Silberberg, 'Middle-Class Mobility: Jewish Convicts in Australia', *History Australia* 15, no. 2 (2018), 10–13.
6   *Argus*, 22 September 1852, 4; *Argus*, 22 August 1856, 2; *Geelong Advertiser*, 23 March 1852, 1.
7   *Jewish Chronicle*, 12 August 1853, 358.
8   *Jewish Chronicle*, 24 June 1853, 304.
9   Gary Bryan Magee and Andrew S. Thompson, *Empire and Globalisation: Networks of People, Goods and Capital in the British World, c. 1850–1914* (Cambridge University Press, Cambridge, 2010), 73.
10   Andrew Hassam, *Sailing to Australia: Shipboard Diaries by Nineteenth-Century British Emigrants* (Manchester University Press, Manchester, 1994), 9.
11   Simone A. Wegge, 'Chain Migration and Information Networks: Evidence from Nineteenth Century Hesse-Cassel', *Journal of Economic History* 58, no. 4 (1998), 961.
12   *Jewish Chronicle*, 27 August 1852, 359.
13   ibid.
14   *Jewish Chronicle*, 14 January 1853, 113.
15   ibid.
16   *Jewish Chronicle*, 10 June 1853, 285.
17   *Jewish Chronicle*, 11 November 1853, 44, other incidents and negative comments were reported in the 10 February 1853 and 18 March 1853 issues.
18   *Jewish Chronicle*, 10 February 1853, 1.
19   *Jewish Chronicle*, 14 January 1853, 2.
20   *Jewish Chronicle*, 12 August 1853, 358.
21   *Jewish Chronicle*, 24 June 1853, 304.
22   *Jewish Chronicle*, 9 September 1853, 391.
23   *Jewish Chronicle*, 5 March 1858, 92.

24   *South Australian Register*, 4 September 1854, 2.

25   Public Record Office Victoria, Index to Unassisted Passenger Indexes to Victoria 1852–1923.

26   *Argus*, 18 April 1848, 4.

27   The precise interconnectedness of some of these families cannot be determined, although the names often imply linkages that the records do not clarify, such as that between Alexander Lindo Henriques (c. 1839–1869) and Elizabeth Lindo (c. 1804–1887).

28   Marriage Register of the Adelaide Hebrew Congregation.

29   United States Census, 1870.

30   University College London Department of History, 'Legacies of British Slave-Ownership', (University College London, 2015), 21 May 2015, <https://www.ucl.ac.uk/lbs/search/>.

31   Parliament of Victoria, 'An Act to Make Valid the Marriage of a Man with the Sister of His Deceased Wife', Melbourne, 1873.

32   Gary B. Magee and Andrew S. Thompson, '"Migrapounds": Remittance Flows within the British World, c. 1875–1913', in Kate Darian-Smith, Patricia Grimshaw and Stuart Macintyre (eds), *Britishness Abroad: Transnational Movements and Imperial Cultures* (Melbourne University Press, Melbourne, 2007), 53. It is estimated that 50 per cent of those migrating to the United States returned.

33   Robert A. Bickers, *Settlers and Expatriates: Britons over the Seas*, The Oxford History of the British Empire Companion Series (Oxford University Press, Oxford, 2010), 5.

34   Tony Ballantyne, *Webs of Empire: Locating New Zealand's Colonial Past* (UBC Press, Vancouver, 2014), 16.

35   1851 English Census; 1861 English Census; 'The Bankruptcy Act, 1861. Notice of Adjudications and First Meeting of Creditors', in *London Gazette*, National Archives, London (1862).

36   Bill Williams, *The Making of Manchester Jewry, 1740–1875* (Manchester University Press, Manchester, 1976), 179.

37   Letter from Isidore Gross to Isaac and Lesser Jacobs, dated 13 April 1874, private collection.

38   *Otago Daily Times*, 31 March 1887; *Ashburton Guardian*, 31 March 1887; *Wanganui Chronicle*, 31 March 1887; *Press*, 17 December 1886, 4.

39   Philip Acland Jacobs, 'The Family Tree', private collection, 6.

40   Chilton, Lisa, 'A New Class of Women for the Colonies: The Imperial Colonist and the Construction of Empire', *Journal of Imperial and Commonwealth History* 31, no. 2 (2003), 36–56.

41   Marriage registers for the Melbourne Hebrew Congregation, East Melbourne Hebrew Congregation and St Kilda Hebrew Congregation. It is not uncommon for women's employment to be left blank in marriage registers: Andrew Miles, *Social Mobility in Nineteenth and Early Twentieth-Century England* (St Martin's Press, New York, 1999), 146.

42   Harold Pollins, *Economic History of the Jews in England* (Fairleigh Dickinson University Press, Rutherford, 1982), 89.

43   *Argus*, 13 March 1876, 7; *Argus*, 1 February 1875, 6.

44   *Jewish Herald*, 16 September 1895, 6.

45   Bill Schwartz, '"Shivering in the Noonday Sun": The British World and the Dynamics of "Nativisation"', in Kate Darian-Smith, Patricia Grimshaw and Stuart Macintyre (eds), *Britishness Abroad: Transnational Movements and Imperial Cultures* (Melbourne University Press, Melbourne, 2007), 89.

46   *Argus*, 24 September 1870, 5.

47 *Argus*, 16 March 1874, 6; Will of Henry Cohn, Public Record Office Victoria, Index to Wills, Probate and Administration Records 1841–2009, VPRS 28 0002 26.
48 *Australasian*, 25 July 1885, 5.
49 Will of Leah Cohn, Public Record Office Victoria, Index to Wills, Probate and Administration Records 1841–2009, VPRS 28 0002 625.
50 Keith D. Lilley, '"One Immense Gold Field!" British Imaginings of the Australian Gold Rushes 1851–1859', *Landscape Research* 27, no. 1 (2002), 69.
51 David Cesarani, *The Jewish Chronicle and Anglo-Jewry, 1841–1991* (Cambridge University Press, Cambridge, 1994), 31.
52 Lloyd P. Gartner, *History of the Jews in Modern Times* (Oxford University Press, Oxford, 2001), 147.
53 *Jewish Chronicle*, 6 December 1844.
54 *Voice of Jacob*, 24 June 1842.
55 *Jewish Chronicle and Hebrew Observer*, 2 September 1864, 7.
56 Joseph Aron and Judy Arndt, *The Enduring Remnant: The First 150 Years of the Melbourne Hebrew Congregation 1841–1991* (Melbourne University Press, Carlton, 1992), 47.
57 Alan David Crown, 'The Jewish Press, Community and Jewish Publishing in Australia', in David Kessler and Alan David Crown (eds), *Noblesse Oblige: Essays in Honour of David Kessler Obe* (Vallentine Mitchell, London, 1998), 39.
58 Newman H. Rosenthal, *Formula for Survival: The Saga of the Ballarat Hebrew Congregation* (Hawthorn Press, Melbourne, 1979), 26.
59 Letter from Michael Levinson, 24 October 1861, private collection.
60 Eric Richards, *Britannia's Children: Emigration from England, Scotland, Wales and Ireland since 1600* (Hambledon & London, London, 2004), 177.
61 Private collection.
62 For a discussion on the role of religion and other social institutions for the dissemination of Britishness see Schwartz, 'Shivering in the Noonday Sun', 23.
63 Todd M. Endelman, *The Jews of Britain, 1656 to 2000* (University of California Press, Berkeley, 2002), 52.
64 ibid., 58.
65 In 1960 Rabbi Dr John Levi became the first Australian-born ordained rabbi.
66 Aron and Arndt, *The Enduring Remnant*, 28, 29, 32.
67 Lazarus M. Goldman, *The Jews in Victoria in the Nineteenth Century* (Self-published, Melbourne, 1954), 246.
68 *South Australian Advertiser*, 7 May 1886.
69 Adam Mendelsohn, 'Tongue Ties: The Emergence of the Anglophone Jewish Diaspora in the Mid-Nineteenth Century', *American Jewish History* 93, no. 2 (2007), 178; and Jewish Women's Archives, 'Hebrew Sunday School, Rebecca Gratz, 1781–1869', <http://jwa.org/womenofvalor/gratz/hebrew-sunday-school>.
70 *Argus*, 16 July 1872, 1.
71 *Jewish Chronicle*, 29 January 1875, 702–3.
72 Eugene Charlton Black, *The Social Politics of Anglo-Jewry, 1880–1920* (Basil Blackwell, Oxford, 1988), 45.
73 *Illustrated Australian News for Home Readers*, 15 July 1874, 111.
74 *Argus*, 26 September 1874, 4.
75 Old Bailey Proceedings Online, Trial of Nathan Nathan alias Nathaniel Newton, 4 December 1799, <t17991204-46>.
76 John S. Levi and G.F.J. Bergman, *Australian Genesis: Jewish Convicts and Settlers, 1788–1860* (Melbourne University Press, Carlton, 2002), 158–9.
77 Howard T. Nathan, 'Rosetta Joseph: The Bell, Her Husband and His Money',

Australian Jewish Historical Society XVII, no. 1 (2003), 6.

78   Howard T. Nathan, 'The Benefits of a Conviction', *Australian Jewish Historical Society* XIII, no. 1 (1995), 11.

79   John S. Levi, *These Are the Names: Jewish Lives in Australia, 1788–1850* (Miegunyah Press, Carlton, 2006), 396.

80   ibid., 571.

81   R.P.T. Davenport-Hines and Judy Slinn, *Glaxo: A History to 1962* (Cambridge University Press, Cambridge, 1992), 6.

82   Magee and Thompson, *Empire and Globalisation*, 135.

83   Sir Henry Jephcott, *The First Fifty Years: An account of the Early Life of Joseph Edward Nathan and the First Fifty Years of His Merchandise Business That Became Glaxo* (W.S. Cowell, Ipswich, 1969), 37–8.

84   E.J. Hobsbawn, *The Age of Empire 1875–1914* (Weidenfeld & Nicolson, London, 1987), 64.

85   Davenport-Hines and Slinn, *Glaxo*, 19–20, 27.

86   Charles Brasch and C.R Nicholson, *Hallensteins—the First Century 1873–1973* (Hallenstein Bros Ltd, Dunedin, 1973), 13.

87   Moritz Michaelis, *Chapters from the Story of My Life* (Norman Brothers, Melbourne, 1899), 82.

88   J. Ann Hone, 'Moritz Michaelis (1820–1902)', in *Australian Dictionary of Biography* (National Centre for Biography, Australian National University, Canberra, 1974).

89   'Obituary, the Late Mr Moritz Michaelis', *Australian Leather Journal*, 15 December 1902, 562.

90   Keith Farrer, *To Feed a Nation: A History of Australian Food Science and Technology* (CSIRO Publishing, Melbourne, 2005), 38.

91   *Sydney Morning Herald*, 19 January 1875, 7.

92   *Maitland Mercury and Hunter River General Advertiser*, 19 May 1874, 4.

93   *Jewish Chronicle*, 21 January 1876 and 21 July 1876, 246.

94   *Sydney Morning Herald*, 15 January 1876, 7; and regional papers such as *Capricornian*, 5 May 1876, 95, and *Rockhampton Bulletin*, 31 January 1876, 3.

95   *Jewish Herald*, 13 February 1880, 8.

96   *Riverina Times, Hay Standard and Journal of Water Conservation*, 30 September 1901, 1; *Sydney Morning Herald*, 14 June 1912, 10; *Jewish Herald*, 7 June 1912, 13.

97   *Wagga Wagga Advertiser*, 1 August 1895, 2.

98   Margaret C. Jacob, *The Origins of Freemasonry: Facts & Fictions* (University of Pennsylvania Press, Philadelphia, 2006), 22.

99   Jessica Harland-Jacobs, *Builders of Empire: Freemasons and British Imperialism, 1717–1927* (University of North Carolina Press, Chapel Hill, 2007), 64.

100 Jacob, *The Origins of Freemasonry*, 38.

101 Jacob Katz, *Jews and Freemasons in Europe 1723–1939* (Harvard University Press, Cambridge, 1970), 16–17.

102 H. Morin Humphreys, *Men of the Time in Australia: Victorian Series* (McCarron Bird & Co, Melbourne, 1882), 176; *Telegraph, St Kilda, Prahran and South Yarra Guardian*, 22 June 1867, 3.

103 Harland-Jacobs, *Builders of Empire*, 53.

104 *West Australian*, 6 April 1910, 7.

105 *Jewish Herald*, 14 August 1914, 11.

106 *Jewish Herald*, 4 May 1917, 13.

107 *Jewish Herald*, 12 July 1918, 10.

Chapter 5

Building a City

I charge Mr John Batman with leaving out the name of one of the partners joined with him in the land buying speculation, and this very man, who is Mr John Batman's particular friend, then was, or lately had been, a convict, viz, Joseph Solomon of Launceston. The supposed reason which actuated Mr John Batman in suppressing his partner's name, was that of Solomon being a prisoner of the Crown.
   —Letter from John Pascoe Fawkner to Lord Glenelg, 20 July 1837[1]

A friend before whom the claim was once made that there was a building designed by Mr Barnet in every street and thoroughfare in Melbourne promptly challenged it with the nomination of Carpentaria place, a byway without a building … 'You are wrong', replied Mr Barnet 'You have overlooked the cabmen's shelter, the gift of an anonymous donor. I built that.'
   —*Argus*, 2 September 1931, 5

Excluded from property ownership and with restricted employment opportunities, Jews have historically been inhabitants of urban centres. Although the ghetto was a physically restrictive place and a sign of subjugation, cities have been considered conducive to Jewish life, providing opportunities for education and culture unavailable in smaller centres.[2] The freedoms brought by emancipation intensified this response and Jews flocked to European capitals, taking advantage of their social, political and economic opportunities.

Here the spatial conditions of industrialisation, urbanisation, Enlightenment ideas and secular culture were elements in the forging of a new Jewish identity, 'ripe with the *promise* of modernity'.[3] Jews identified with the specific cultures of their chosen city, forging an identity shaped in response to the perceived uniqueness of these places. In central Europe, in cities such as Vienna and Berlin, the Jewish community's contribution to the urban fabric and cultural production is widely acknowledged. A parallel attribution has not been considered for Melbourne.

As settlers to Melbourne, these experienced urban dwellers carried with them a positive perception of urbanism. This is in contrast to their non-Jewish British contemporaries, for whom urbanism was fundamentally shaped by the dichotomy of the city as 'an integral part of national life' but one in which 'they shared an age-old aversion to urban living'.[4] This conceptualisation sees a linear migratory narrative, with urban living in Melbourne as the final stage in a progress from a rural birth in Britain to a temporary residence in a large English city.[5] As a new settler society, Melbourne does not reflect a single national spatial framework. Consideration of the diversity of experience brought by the Jewish settlers, their values and sense of place therefore enables us to determine more clearly how Melbourne developed its unique form. Building on this conceptual framework, the chapter will explore three interrelated themes—places, people and religious space—to establish how Jewish ideas, Jewish capital and Jewish social values were influential in shaping the city.

The nineteenth century witnessed the rapid urbanisation of Old and New World cities. London expanded from 1.1 million to 7.3 million, Manchester from 75,000 to 714,000 and Paris from 547,000 to 2.9 million, while in New York the population rose eighty-fold, from 60,000 to 4.8 million. Immigration rather than natural growth drove this expansion, in Europe stemming from internal migration and in the New World through transnational migration.[6] The discovery of gold fuelled the remarkable and rapid growth experienced in Melbourne, as settlers flocked to Victoria, seeking the riches offered. In the decade after 1851, the population rose from 77,345 to 540,322 and Melbourne developed into an 'instant city', in the process maturing

> from an unknown pioneer settlement into a proud metropolis. In London, Hamburg, Boston and Canton, Melbourne became the name synonymous with fame and fortune, and at the peak of its meteoric rise in 1852 and 1853 more British emigrants bought tickets to Melbourne than to any other destination in the world.[7]

This evolution shares many parallels with other nineteenth-century Pacific rim cities, which rapidly advanced as commercial and economic centres for their hinterlands. These have been styled 'instant cities' where, unlike the organic growth of Old World cities, the whirlwind of urbanisation and industrialisation came into intense focus.[8] The speed of development of gold-rush cities such as San Francisco and Melbourne left them devoid of a strong agricultural or manufacturing base, while they also lacked a developed communications or transport infrastructure connecting them to the world. These were cities stretched by their meteoric success, unable adequately to develop infrastructure to keep pace with growth.[9]

Melbourne was founded for commercial opportunity, with an economy reliant on raw material—wool and gold—and fuelled by immigration. As a consumption economy dependent on importation rather than production, this provided possibilities for enterprising merchants to gamble, not on digging for mineral wealth but on supplying the new markets with consumer goods. From barely fifty merchants and commission agents operating in the city prior to the gold rush, the number exploded to more than 300 of them employing 7687 people by 1854.[10] Jewish businessmen, who had honed their skills in other cities or were enterprising enough to see potential scope in the new markets, could prosper by meeting the demands of this voracious new economy.

The laying out of Melbourne's grid by Robert Hoddle reflects a philosophical, commercial and aesthetic sensibility employed in many New World cities. Structurally the grid was a manifestation of an imperial dialogue, defining the polarity between chaos and civilisation through a recognisable and familiar authority based on eighteenth-century classical principles of social order, defining and manipulating the quality of space. In the imperial context, grids delineated colonisation through the inclusion and exclusion of land ownership, excluding indigenous people from such a right.[11]

Colonisation was also defined by creating 'placelessness' and a 'place of equalised parts', applying structural uniformity to the 'elimination of viewpoints ... and indeed history ... Located against the imaginary grid, the blankness of unexplored country was translatable into a blueprint for colonization: it could be divided up into blocks, the blocks numbered and the land auctioned, without the purchasers ever leaving their London offices.'[12] The grid brought rationality and order to space, defining the boundaries of private property in this speculative venture and producing a spatial design that reflected the investors' ambition and expectation of the city's future.[13]

The implementation of this rigid structure in a society hungry for speculation, not only overrode existing topography, but resulted in an emphasis on private ownership over urban planning, developing a homogeneous urban form, unrelieved by squares or open space. As most investors were at some distance from the site, urban amenity was not their primary concern. Thus a grid produced an expedient uniformity of blocks, suitable to those seeking the opportunities offered by speculation. These were land gambles by men largely uncommitted to personal settlement, their colonial experiment undertaken in the hope of making a fortune and 'going home'.

Following the first land sales in 1837, the most desirable blocks were those bordering the future business centre, nearest the wharf at the junction of William Street with Flinders and Collins streets, while the churches at the eastern end of Collins Street required parishioners to go 'bush' for worship. By the 1860s the business centre had repositioned north to the corner of Elizabeth and Collins streets, the General Post Office at the corner of Bourke and Elizabeth streets became Melbourne's symbolic centre, while Collins Street was acknowledged as the primary street in the city. The various streets were recognised for their specialities: 'Bourke Street for palatial hotels, grand restaurants, Cobb's coaches, theatres and concert rooms—pretty barmaids to the east, horses to the west; Collins Street for fashion "at the longest credit and … the highest price"—doctors to the east, bankers to the west'.[14]

The plan whereby the deep rectilinear allotments were designed with their short side to the street inevitably led to the subdivision of blocks and the creation of small rights-of-way to service them. Before the advent of mass public transport in Melbourne, like other contemporary cities, workplace and residence were combined, located in the most advantageous position for undertaking the specific occupation. The back streets became the location for workshops and noxious industries while stratification was manifest in the wealthy who occupied the main streets, with the poor in the less desirable smaller streets and laneways behind. Thus the Amsterdam-born optician Moses Kasner and his family lived above the business premises of Kasner and Moss at 17 Collins Street, while the family of the illiterate hawker and general dealer Solomon Isaacs lived in Foundry Lane off Little Lonsdale Street, along with a number of other poorer Jewish families.

Establishing Melbourne
First Settlement

As with the settlement of Australia, Jews were at the very beginning of the formation of what would become the Colony of Victoria and at the foundation of its new capital, Melbourne. The initial settlement was not sanctioned by the British Government or either of the colonial administrations of New South Wales or Van Diemen's Land. The outpost was technically illegal and spearheaded by a cohort of Tasmanian businessmen and land speculators. Among these were the convict Joseph Solomon and his extended family. From the first land sale of 1837 and in subsequent sales, Solomon was one of a number of intercolonial speculators purchasing parcels of land. Solomon's acquisition was initially made under stealth and auspiced by Batman, but by the second sale of 1 November 1837 he acquired property in his own right, paying £39 for lot number 7 in Bourke Street between Elizabeth and Queen streets.[15]

Following the 1837 sale, auctions were moved to Sydney, affording financial opportunities for a broad array of investors. Those purchasing land at these sales were not settlers bound for Melbourne; rather, they possessed sufficient capital to speculate across the colonies, recognising the potential of new colonial outposts. Apart from Joseph Solomon, others acquiring land in the first five land sales were Joseph Barrow Montefiore, the brothers David and Solomon Benjamin, purchasing as individuals and in partnership, as well as another brother, Samuel Benjamin, and his business partner and brother-in-law Elias Moses. Following his immigration in 1843, their fourth brother, Moses Benjamin, also became a substantial landowner in Melbourne.

This initial cohort displayed shrewd business skills and prospered in Australia, with all but Elias Moses and Moses Benjamin returning to London after making a colonial fortune. Joseph Barrow Montefiore arrived with already established wealth and connections, commanding significant capital and colonial networks through the family's West Indies and London enterprises. His career was launched in 1826, when as a nineteen-year-old he was admitted to the London stock exchange, paying £1500 for the privilege of being one of only twelve 'Jew Brokers' allowed to trade. Three years later, lured by the experience of another Jewish former London stock broker, Lionel Samson, he applied for a grant in New South Wales, sailing for Sydney with his wife, Rebecca Mocatta, two daughters, his brother-in-law George Mocatta and David Rebeiro Furtado and his wife, Sarah Egras, forming the nucleus of Jewish free settlement to the colony.[16] Montefiore arrived with £10,000 to invest and a recommendation from the treasury describing him as 'most respectable'. His request for a land grant stated:

> I am now desirous of removing there with my family to establish myself as an agriculturalist I respectfully solicit a grant of five thousand acres of land my means are entirely adequate I propose taking with me an experienced agriculturalist in all its branches and as I have resided many years in the West Indies I anticipate being able to develop the cultivation of drugs, marino [*sic*] sheep, breeding of horses and cattle.[17]

Montefiore was granted land at Wellington, and by 1838 he had amassed 5000 hectares by grant or purchase, as well as further land at Maitland in partnership with David Rebeiro Furtado and Philip Joseph Cohen. Although processing significant pastoral holdings, his agricultural ambitions were not his prime focus. Rather, perceiving opportunities for expansion into newly opening markets, he invested in the Port Phillip District, purchasing land in Williamstown, Geelong and Portland. While Furtado also made his way to

Melbourne, where by 1847 he appears in the directories as a merchant with property in Richmond and Flinders Lane, he too eventually left the Australian colonies and died in France.[18]

The Montefiores were active in public, cultural, political and commercial spheres and this activity shaped the structure and institutions of a number of the Australian colonies. Significantly, Joseph's Barbados-born brother, Jacob Barrow Montefiore, was one of the eleven commissioners of the South Australian Colonisation Commission, appointed by King William IV to plan and administer that colony, praised for being 'indefatigable in his efforts for the advancement' of South Australia.[19]

Together the brothers formed a partnership as J.B. Montefiore & Co., invested in real estate and were instrumental in the foundation of the Bank of Australasia, a conduit through which English capital contributed to the pastoral expansion and speculative boom of the late 1830s.[20] Although bankruptcy during the downturn of the 1840s saw Joseph temporarily retreat to England and Jacob to Madras, this did not halt their colonial ambitions.[21] Jacob settled in Melbourne as a financial agent of the Rothschilds, and as Jacob Montefiore & Co., acting as a gold buyer and trading in a variety of products across the gold-fields. Joseph Montefiore later settled in Adelaide, where he became active in politics and established a new mercantile firm of importers and shipping agents in partnership with his Barbados-born nephew and son-in-law Eliezer Levi Montefiore, husband of his daughter Esther Hannah Barrow Montefiore.

Eliezer was active in three of the colonies, beginning in the fledgling Adelaide Jewish community, where he was a trustee for the Jewish section of the cemetery and a founder of the Adelaide Synagogue. In 1849 his partnership with Joseph brought him to Melbourne, and he was later engaged as a director of the Australian Fire and Life Insurance Company of Melbourne and the Pacific Fire and Marine Insurance Company of Sydney. But it is in the intellectual sphere that he made his greatest contribution. An artist of note, he became trustee of the Public Library, a member of the establishment council of the Victorian Artists Society, a magistrate, and an agent for Victoria at the Inter-Colonial Exhibition of 1875. His most notable cultural achievement occurred following his relocation to Sydney in 1870, as a board member and the first director of the National Art Gallery (now the Art Gallery of New South Wales).[22]

Intimately involved in the shaping of Melbourne over two generations was another Sephardi family, the Benjamins. As some of the earliest investors in Melbourne, they purchased land in the 1839 and 1840 sales. Samuel, the eldest brother, had arrived in Sydney on the *Anna* in 1833. This ship contained a number of Jewish settlers, including his brother-in-law Elias Moses.[23] As business partners, Samuel and Elias established commercial ventures in Sydney,

Goulburn and Windsor, also purchasing property in each location.[24] Shifting their attention to Port Phillip, they acquired land in Melbourne 1839 and two years later in Williamstown and Portland. As further settlements were established they expanded their portfolio, purchasing in Brisbane in 1842.[25]

Following Samuel Benjamin, his brothers David and Solomon arrived in 1838 on the *Henry*, already prepared for their future business, with luggage comprising '21 cases (of clothing) and 6 bales of slops'. The pair moved to Launceston where they opened Tamar House with the slogan 'Small profits quick returns'.[26] Expanding to Melbourne in March 1839, they launched a second store, Cheapside House in Collins Street, initially in David Benjamin's name, but a year later amending the partnership to D & S Benjamin.[27]

David Benjamin's house, Collins Street, 1849, designed by Charles Laing

In 1843 Moses Benjamin, his wife and six children also reached Melbourne, likewise opening a drapery business at Albert House, 7 Collins Street, where Benjamin advertised that his shop had 'no connections with any other house in Port Phillip'.[28] He eventually reconciled with his brothers, joining them in Cheapside House, and in 1847 diversified from a retail focus, advertising to 'Trade, Hawkers and Up-Country Storekeepers' that they would instead be importers of 'British and Foreign Merchandise'.[29] It was in the Benjamins' Cheapside House that Melbourne's first Jewish services were held for the New Year and Day of Atonement 1840 (5601).[30]

In 1849 tenders were announced for a house designed by Charles Laing in Collins Street, for David Benjamin. This was an elegant and austere ten-room villa, with a rusticated base and an entrance flanked by Doric columns.[31] Moses Benjamin, the only brother to remain in Melbourne, became a significant landowner and the most prosperous of the family. At his death in 1885, his estate was valued at £201,504, including several residential, commercial and retail properties in Bourke Street, Collins Street, Little Collins Street, Spencer Street, Flinders Lane, Victoria Parade, William Street, East Melbourne, North Melbourne, South Melbourne, Williamstown, six acres of land in Prahran and 126 acres in Derrimut and further land in Geelong.[32] His home was a nine-room villa at the eastern end of Collins Street, where he also owned the four contiguous properties, which were leased to doctors, politicians and a professor of languages.

By the mid 1840s land was changing hands so quickly that 'buyers and sellers found it difficult to know to which category they belonged'.[33] Due to uncertainty of title, building was hampered by the reluctance of banks to provide loans. This was alleviated somewhat by the introduction of deed registration in 1851, but it wasn't until the late 1850s and early 1860s that the Torrens system of registration provided greater certainty and accurate information on property ownership.[34] Yet this headlong development was hampered by the paucity of available tradesmen to construct suitable dwellings for the rapidly expanding population. Although the impact of the discovery of gold took nearly a year to affect population growth, the economic dislocation was swift.[35]

In 1852 only forty-one buildings were erected in the city, although the following year construction was somewhat normalised with 1027 built in the first six months alone.[36] Although during the 1850s 'permanent' dwellings increased from 10,935 to 78,336, this was not enough to keep pace with population expansion. The housing shortage continued, resulting in high rents.[37] This is clear in the 1861 census, where in each small residence of less than three rooms, occupation density was two people. Almost one-third of the Victorian population was living in huts and tents, primarily on the goldfields, but also in Melbourne. Here the government agreed to allow a 'tent city' on the south bank of the Yarra, providing temporary accommodation at 5 shillings per week.[38]

Forewarned and enterprising settlers such as Siacob Silberberg and his wife Golda Messenger took a proactive approach, arriving with prefabricated housing (in this case from France), which could be erected on landing.[39] As with land speculation, this laissez-faire response to the city's growth reflected the short-term thinking of the many, whose intention was to reap the rewards of the colony and return 'home' in comfort.[40] For Jewish settlers, Melbourne offered freedom and stability, and the majority stayed.

Australia has historically been a country of urban dwellers. As early as 1850, 40 per cent of the Australian population resided in cities, a density that continued to increase. By the end of the century the figure had risen to 70 per cent, comparable to England, and markedly higher than in the United States, where 6 per cent of the population could be considered urban. At the same time, Melbourne's rateable value was surpassed only by that of London.[41] This preference for urban living was often at odds with the expectations of those promoting immigration, who imagined settlers would be hoping to escape the evils of the big cities and were amazed to discover that these were re-created.[42]

New immigrants arriving in the 1850s initially settled in Melbourne before fanning out to the mining districts, lured by the prospect of gold.[43] The mining centres did not provide a long-term place of residence for the majority of Jewish families. Mining created unattractive environments and Melbourne was a more appealing location.[44] From the 1860s there was a steady drift of families back to the metropolis. Although religious law defined the distance a person could travel on the Sabbath and therefore the distance from a syna-gogue, the size of the mid-century city was such that walking was feasible in all areas. In this predominantly Anglo-Jewish community, families lived in close proximity to each other, either in suburbs such as St Kilda, Fitzroy, Emerald Hill, Carlton or East Melbourne, or even in the same street or terrace complex.

As the city developed, so too did the spread of the community. Although pockets of residential space founded on occupation, social status, family or business connections can be discerned, their variability parallels the social and economic aspirations of the wider community. In Melbourne the specific densities of Jewish residence contemporaneously formed the urban fabric, adapting it for the specific cultural, social and political needs of the commu-nity. By undertaking an examination of this phenomenon a clearer understanding of Melbourne's structure and development is revealed.

East Melbourne

East Melbourne, immediately to the north-east of the city, became a favoured location for a number of Melbourne's affluent Jews. The Jewish presence was established with the initial land sales of 1852–54, when Jews became the leading property investors. Solomon Benjamin acquired twelve parcels of land and his brothers another five, while the next most significant purchases were by Morton Moss, who bought three in his own name and another seven in partnership with Barnett Isaacs.[45] Moss, a Tasmanian emancipist and future father-in-law of Sir John Monash, was a major Melbourne property investor, while Isaacs was a gold buyer, importer and publican.[46] In 1857–63 Moss secured at least another forty-six parcels of land, particularly in Carlton, Fitzroy, Northcote and Emerald Hill.[47]

For Moss and Isaacs their purchase in East Melbourne must have been a quick speculative venture, as by 1858 neither is listed as owning any property in this suburb. Moss lived in Alfred Place, Carlton, while Isaac commissioned the architects Crouch and Wilson to design a house for him on St Kilda Road. Notwithstanding Moss and Isaacs's sale of their East Melbourne holdings, Jewish investment in the suburb continued and in 1858 the Benjamin family, Michael Cashmore and the Henriques family owned substantial property in the suburb. In 1847, prior to the first land sales in East Melbourne, land on Eastern Hill had been granted to the Catholic Church and in 1858 William Wardell was commissioned to design a cathedral for the site. The subdivision of East Melbourne set aside land for the various Christian denominations, although not all built upon their allocations.

The 1858 Horrell map shows land around the parliamentary precinct for the Church of England including St Peter's Church, the Lutheran and Unitarian churches, a Presbyterian church, a Free church and St Patrick's Cathedral. A number of other religious and philanthropic institutions spanned either side of Victoria Parade, including St Vincent's Hospital, a Congregational church and a number of denominational schools such as St Patrick's College, Scotch College and the Presbyterian Ladies College (the latter two became popular educational establishments for local Jewish children). With a grant to the Church of England for the establishment of an episcopal residence, Bishopscourt, in Clarendon Street, the cachet of the suburb rose further.

Victoria Parade and Albert Street became areas particularly favoured by Jewish residents, both as landowners and tenants. In Victoria Parade, the western end from Nicholson to Regent streets was initially owned by the pastoralist Josh Bear, who in the 1850s subdivided and auctioned it as ten titles, which were purchased mainly by the extended Benjamin family and tenanted by Jewish residents. These included the London-born merchant Henry Horwitz; Samuel Levy, who was later a resident in Hugh Glass's Brunswick Street development; Benjamin Nathan, whose son, another Benjamin, was born there and would later own Rippon Lea; while Abraham Emanuel, a professor of music, tenanted a timber house owned by Josh Bear.[48]

The Benjamins' commitment to East Melbourne was not only financial but also as long-term residents. In 1870 Moses' son Benjamin Benjamin moved from Victoria Parade to Canally, a twelve-room mansion designed by Reed and Barnes on the corner of George and Powlett streets, and named after a cattle station jointly owned by Benjamin and his brother-in-law Edward Cohen.

Melbourne's fourth Jewish marriage was that of Isaac Hart to Rachel Benjamin, the daughter of Moses Benjamin. This family was to become the long-term occupants of Walmer House, a substantial ten-room house, erected in 1853 for Sir Thomas A'Beckett and purchased by Hart in the mid 1860s. This was one of the most extensive properties on Victoria Parade, occupying a large allotment with a frontage of 19 metres and a depth of nearly 90 metres, with an entrance to Mason Street at its rear.[49] The two-storey rendered house was symmetrical around a recessed central arched doorway, with five upper and four lower square windows and flanked on its east–west axis by tall chimneys.

Throughout this period a number of Jewish investors, financiers and architects helped shape Melbourne's urban fabric through the creation of a range of commercial and residential buildings, and their impact requires some consideration. An early example is Burlington Terrace, designed by Charles Webb, a row of sixteen, eight-room houses elegantly curving around the corner of Albert and Lansdowne streets, and built for the London-born developer Henry Philip Harris in 1866.[50]

As would be typical for Melbourne, the population was always mixed, with an average of just over half of the houses leased to Jewish occupants. The non-Jewish residents included several ministers of religion, two police superintendents and the Italian consul, while the Jewish residents ranged from Barnett Isaacs, the financier and clothier Lawrence Benjamin, the furniture manufacturers brothers Louis and Saul Solomon to the Reverend Ornstein of the Melbourne Hebrew Congregation and the journalist Maurice Brodzky.[51]

The Jewish presence in Victoria Parade was consolidated with the building of a number of mansions for Jewish clients. Many of these were designed by the architectural firm of Crouch and Wilson, including Ensor in 1875 for Joseph Levy, later the home of Benjamin Fink. Flanking Ensor and also designed by Crouch and Wilson, Rosenau was erected by Lawrence Benjamin in 1881. A few doors up Alfred Kursteiner designed a house for James Simeon Raphael. Kursteiner had been employed as the architect for a house on the corner of George Street occupied by Raphael's brother Henry as well as the more reserved Linden in Acland Street, St Kilda, for Moritz Michaelis and his wife, Rachel Gotthelp.

Victoria Buildings

Although by the 1860s Melbourne's demographic centre had shifted north towards the corner of Collins and Elizabeth streets, the area around A'Beckett Street was still considered on the periphery. Victoria Buildings was erected by the owner-builder James Lawrence in the 1860s and faced Queen Street, spanning the block between A'Beckett and Franklin streets, just south of the market, and became another population concentration of Jewish residents. The terrace may have been built in two sections, as the rate books reveal that houses 1–4 were of seven rooms with stables and 5–8 were of five rooms with a kitchen.[52]

The building includes a curiously numbered 5A or sometimes 5 1/2, and a surviving photograph shows a row of double-storey bluestone terraces with timber detailing to their balconies, broken by a lighter coloured double-storey premises flush to the street.[53] Throughout the 1860s and 1870s half the residents of this terrace were Jewish, and it was home to many small business people including jewellers, outfitters, importers and other merchants, although none appear to have stayed long in this location.

Victoria Buildings, c.1863, Queen Street

In the 1850s the suburbs immediately surrounding Melbourne were a rural-urban fringe, developing to absorb new arrivals as the population increased.[54] The neighbourhood, which became Collingwood and Fitzroy, was not initially intended for dense residential development, but apportioned into large rural parcels of 40–90 hectares. These land parcels subsequently changed hands and were subdivided many times before they evolved into their present configuration. The outcome of this was a street pattern designed by individual developers rather than planned as an overall coherent strategy. In the mid century a concentration of Jewish residents occurred in King William Street.

This street was initially a part of parcel 71 and sold in the 1838–39 land sales and was not further subdivided until 1850–51, at which time a number of small wooden stores and dwellings were erected.[55] The street was rebuilt in the 1860s when these flimsy structures were replaced by more substantial brick and stone dwellings, and it was at this time that the Jewish community took up residence. In particular favour was Carlton Terrace, a building or group of buildings that appears to have been under construction throughout the 1860s, until it covered almost the entire south block from Nicholson to Fitzroy streets.[56]

A number of owners and occupiers of this block shared the surname Levy or Levi and their exact relationships cannot be unravelled. Henry Levy owned at least half a dozen properties in the 1860s and many were leased to Jewish tenants, including Lewis Levy, a commercial traveller, and the tobacconist Joseph Benjamin.[57] One interconnected family was that of Nathaniel Levi and John Levy. A merchant and magistrate, John had settled in Melbourne by 1841 and became father-in-law to his cousin on the marriage of his daughter Sarah to Nathaniel in 1855. Also neighbours in King William Street were another of John's daughters, Esther, and her husband, Devon-born Fitzroy city councillor Simeon Cohen, at the time a partner in John Levy and Sons and owner of both 10 King William Street and 3 Carlton Terrace.

Another extended family group living in King William Street was the Phillips family. London-born Solomon David Phillips and his wife, Caroline Solomon, were residents in King William Street by 1854. Solomon and Caroline Phillips immigrated to Sydney in 1833 where Solomon accepted the position as the assistant Jewish minister for the Bridge Street Synagogue, later moving to a new congregation in Parramatta. In 1849 Phillips applied for the position of reader for the Melbourne Hebrew Congregation, but he was judged 'not qualified to fulfil all the duties required'.[58] The high regard to which the Sydney community held him is reflected in the presentations made to him on his departure for Melbourne two years later, when he was presented with a silver cup engraved in Hebrew and English and a 'suburb purse' bestowed in expression of their esteem for his services.[59]

The creation of a Jewish environment was important to Phillips, and he was one of those who sought to establish a Jewish school in Melbourne in 1855.[60] Although a number of questions were raised about Phillips's religious practices, two years later the *Argus* reported a public presentation from the Melbourne Hebrew Congregation, commending Phillips publicly for his role as reader, *mohel* and committee member.[61] By the 1860s the extended Phillips family were also settled in King William Street. Hannah and Angel Ellis lived at number 56, while at number 41 resided Hannah's sister Rosetta and her London-born photographer husband, Alexander Fox.

Fitzroy became a favoured location for 'city gentlemen' seeking to live outside the central business district in townhouses on its gentle slopes and expansive thoroughfares.[62] Aside from central Melbourne, this suburb acquired more buildings by prominent architects than any other place in Victoria.[63] Of those, two designed by Charles Laing for the developer Hugh Glass abut each other on the corner of Gertrude and Brunswick streets. Glass Terrace, facing Gertrude Street, was built in two sections in 1854–56, the later stage designed by Laing and the earlier by David Ross, beside the grander unnamed terrace built in 1856 at 39–49 Brunswick Street.[64] Many Jewish tenants progressed from one Jewish enclave to another and 45 Brunswick Street demonstrates this social mobility. In 1870 Morris Cohen relocated from this address to the more fashionable Burlington Terrace, in parallel with a change in occupation from furniture broker to financier. His house was then occupied for the succeeding five years by Joseph Benjamin, formerly of King William Street, and before the family returned to London where Benjamin operated as a colonial merchant.

Whereas English suburban development has been described as 'a convergence of aristocratic preference and middle-class needs', in Australia, suburbia became an intersection of democratic political values and Chartist sympathies, in a less rigidly defined class system.[65] This produced a society of 'proprietorship and respectability' allowing for a diversity of suburban expansion.[66] Glass's two developments display the heterogeneous nature and social fluidity of mid-century Melbourne. Glass Terrace has been described as the home of professionals, especially doctors and those of the upper middle class.[67]

The rapid social mobility of gold-rush society can be seen in two interconnected convict families, the children of those convicted for the Great Gold Dust Robbery. The two families had swindled each other in the process of the crime, but now their descendants became neighbours (and *mishpacha*) in Glass's two properties. At number 58 Glass Terrace lived Grace Casper and her husband, Henry Wolff. Wolff had arrived in New South Wales as a seventeen-year-old free settler in 1840, but was almost immediate convicted of larceny and imprisoned. On his second conviction he was transported to Van Diemen's Land, where he met Grace, the daughter of emancipist Ellis Casper. By 1857 he was wealthy enough to make a return trip to England with his family. Unfortunately he died within weeks of returning, and his widow remained at the property until her second marriage.

Also resident in Glass Terrace was Rachel Moses, the daughter of Emanuel 'Money' Moses, the co-accused of Ellis Casper, and her husband, Samuel Levy, a London-born merchant who had previously resided at 7 Victoria Parade. Similar trajectories can be seen in the occupants of Glass's other speculative development adjacent in Brunswick Street, which by the 1870s was owned by Edmund Gleeson.[68] Residents here included Morris Joseph Cohen, prior to also moving to Burlington Terrace, and the draper Louis Abrahams and his family, who appear to have lived in two of these properties.

Carlton

Following the 1852 land sales, Carlton grew as a suburban extension of the city of Melbourne. Its initial conception was to resemble the formality of British developments, particularly London's Bloomsbury or Edinburgh's New Town, with prominent architects arguing for 'controlled and homogenous design' of terrace houses and squares. Although a number of squares were built, the housing was not designed or assembled as those in London or Edinburgh; rather, developers often constructed houses in sequence, creating terraces not necessarily of a uniform floorplan, often 'only welded into an architectural unit when the central pediment was finally added'.[69] Morton Moss and Mark Moss as financiers and developers were responsible for significant development in Carlton and Fitzroy as well as holding substantial rural and other urban property. Mark Moss operated principally as a financier, also entering into a partnership with Barnett Isaacs in 1865, as the Equitable Loan and Investment Company of Victoria Monte Pieta.[70]

Miles Lewis describes the southern end of Drummond Street as Carlton's 'architectural heartland' and it was here that the Jewish community concentrated in the block bounded by Victoria and Queensberry streets.[71] From the 1860s to the 1880s these terraces were owned by and rented to a large number of Jewish families of merchants, particularly those of European background. Such was Melbournia Terrace, built by Woolf Davis, in the mid 1870s. Like many, Davis and his wife Rachel Moses' migration story had started with a primary migration to England, where they married in 1853. They arrived in Victoria four years later on the *Eastern City* with two children.

Woolf Davis, a serious and orthodox Jew, followed Moses Rintel to his breakaway synagogue, where he became a board member, treasurer and subsequently president. He was described by the *Jewish Herald* as 'one of the best-known exponents of Jewish orthodoxy', and the East Melbourne Hebrew Congregation unsuccessfully nominated him to the chief rabbi as a suitably qualified candidate for the initial Beth Din.[72] By the 1880s Davis's concern for wider Jewish affairs saw him participate as a committee member of the Sabbath Observance Committee, the Jewish Philanthropic Society, the Jewish Orphans and Neglected Children's Society, the Anglo-Jewish Association and the Jewish Aid Society. His interest in Jewish philanthropy had an international view, and he was instrumental in raising funds for Jews in the Holy Land, personally funding the building of ten charity homes in Jerusalem.[73]

Davis retained his position as a board member of the East Melbourne Hebrew Congregation, while founding a *minyan* for newly arrived eastern Europeans who could not afford synagogue fees.[74] This eventually evolved into the Woolf Davis Chevra, which offered a pay-as-you-could-afford system, with all profits returning to support the poor of the Holy Land.[75] Davis died in 1902, leaving no will. At the time of his death his daughters Jane and Caroline were living with their husbands at Melbournia Terrace at numbers 3 and 11, while daughter Deborah lived in Elgin Street, Miriam in Sydney and Abraham, Rebecca and David in London. Each child inherited a house, with Jane, David and Caroline living for some time in their inherited properties.

In the 1870s, immediately to the north of Melbournia Terrace were a block of houses in Drummond Street favoured by Jewish landlords and residents. Next door to the Davis family was a ten-room brick house owned by another Polish-born resident, Marks Herman. Herman, like Davis, was also an inaugural member of the East Melbourne Hebrew Congregation, described as a 'strict observer of all ancient Jewish rites and ceremonies and was all things strictly orthodox'.[76] Herman's professional life progressed from tobacconist to draper, warehouseman and finally financier, and similarly he changed his place of residence from Drummond Street to Fairmount, 476 Albert Street, East Melbourne. Fairmount had been built in 1874 by George Browne, designed as a substantial pair of houses unified by their symmetrical facade, with a central carriageway providing access to the stables behind.

Two doors away, German-born Jacob Gerson owned Bodford Terrace, constructed in 1868, and tenanted by a number of Jews including the financier Abraham Goldberg, who also subsequently relocated to Albert Street, East Melbourne.

Rosaville by Nahum Barnet, 1883

Opposite are two villas of architectural significance which stand adjacent on the east side of Drummond Street. Rosaville, designed by the Jewish architect Nahum Barnet for Abraham Harris and his wife, Rose Davis, previous tenants of Victoria Buildings, was completed in 1883. This house is a striking amalgam of Boom-style architecture made exotic through mannerist details to the facade and an elaborate ornamental grill screening the two floors. In 1893, next door Leah Solomon commissioned Walter Scott Law to design the grander and more flamboyant Benvenuta, in high Victorian Baroque style. Leah Solomon was a pawnbroker and the widow of the small arms dealer and pawnbroker Henry Abrahams. Benvenuta contained a dining-room, drawing-room, billiard-room, six bedrooms and in light of her occupation, a purpose-built strong room.[77]

St Kilda

St Kilda was the home of the 'mercantile community', consisting of a core group of merchants who had established themselves in the early 1850s, consolidating their position over the following thirty years.[78] Among these were a large number of interconnected Jewish families, and their prominence led Marcus Clarke to refer to the area disparagingly as 'the second Canaan'.[79]

Again, Jews had been at the establishment of the area. In 1857 the architects Ohlfsen-Bagge, Spencer and Kursteiner designed a terrace in Barkly Street for German-born merchant Paul Joske, becoming the first terrace constructed east of the Melbourne Town reserve.[80] It can be assumed that Joske's land ran through to High Street (now St Kilda Road), as backing onto the terraces he subsequently developed a row of five shops, which by 1872 appear in his wife's name.[81]

Tolanda by Crouch and Wilson, 1868, National Trust of Australia (Victoria)

Jews were early residents as well as developers and in the 1850s the suburb was home to Samuel de Beer and his wife Louisa Hart at Park Terrace, a row of thirteen, six-room brick houses in Fitzroy Street; Casper Marks and his wife, Julia Isaacs; Gibraltar-born Henry Cohen Pirani; Moritz Michaelis and his family; as well as James Simeon and his wife, Eleanor Saunders. Eleanor was the niece of Judah Solomon's de facto wife Elizabeth Howell, whose son's birth had resulted in a meeting of the Melbourne Hebrew Congregation 'to consider the propriety of making *guersits*'. Unable to secure a conversion for his wife and children in Melbourne, Simeon and his family left for to Europe, where Eleanor and four children were converted in The Hague. On their return to Melbourne the couple were remarried under religious law in September 1854.[82]

Significant villas were owned by Moritz Michaelis and his nephew Isaac Hallenstein, David Rosenthal, Israel Bloomington, Nathaniel Levi, Isaac Jacobs and his brother-in-law Hyman Levinson, as well as the architect Nahum Barnet. Between 1864 and 1890, St Kilda was also a preferred address for forty-four architects, including the business partners and popular architects to the Jewish community, Thomas Crouch and Ralph Wilson, of Crouch and Wilson.[83] In St Kilda they built a number of substantial villas from 1868, including Toldara in Alma Road for the manufacturing jeweller David Rosenthal and Rondebosch in Chapel Street for Israel Bloomington. These houses share stylistic similarities, being double-storey neo-classical colonnaded buildings, while Rondebosch appears lighter due to the combination of wrought iron and solid columns on the upper floor, creating a delicacy lacking in the heavier Toldara with its symmetrical pairing of Doric columns on the lower colonnade with Corinthian on its upper.

The tight endogamy of the Jewish community is evident at Northampton Buildings, a row of terraces built by 1858, owned by Isaac Jacobs and Abraham Benjamin.[84] Manchester in the 1830s and 1840s had experienced the immigration of a number of German Jewish families fleeing political oppression, often from areas where the Jewish population was engaged with the radical sentiments that finally erupted in 1848. Among those who fled to Manchester at this time were a group who became prominent jewellers in the city, including Bromberg-born David Falk and his kinsman Louis Beaver.[85] By 1851 David Falk was running a business that employed another Prussian-born Mancunian, Isaac Jacobs. A year later, Jacobs arrived in Victoria representing Falk's firm and eventually formed a partnership with Phillip and Salis Falk as P & S Falk, general merchants, which they operated from Manchester, Melbourne, Adelaide and Sydney.

Meanwhile, another Manchester-based jeweller, Abraham Benjamin and his wife Theresa Falk, arrived in Melbourne aboard the *Somersetshire*. He too later formed a partnership with Phillip and Salis Falk as P Falk and Co, while a nephew, Salis Schank, operated the Adelaide side of the business. In 1870 Northampton Buildings hosted a double wedding, that of Salis Schank to Laura Beaver, the other couple being Laura's elder sister Evelyn who also married a German-born spouse, Julius Salenger. These family connections were further cemented with the employment of their brother Albert, a manager of Phillip Falk and Co.[86]

The establishment committee of the St Kilda Hebrew congregation represents a microcosm of the demographic makeup of the St Kilda community; of the ten members of this committee, five were born in Germany or Prussia, two in Australia and one in Wales. David Abraham was a money broker, while the other committee members were manufacturers and merchants in jewellery, tanners and in the tobacco industry. Moritz Michaelis and Isaac Hallenstein were uncle and nephew, Nelson Marks and Isaac Jacobs were brothers-in-law, while the honorary secretary, Hyman Hart, represented Melbourne's earliest settlement, the son of Edward and Isabella Hart, whose 1844 wedding was the first Jewish marriage to take place in Victoria. The establishment of the synagogue and its location further encouraged the community to congregate around this pocket of St Kilda.

Chatsworth, c. 1894, Private Collection

The Land Boom
The Developer

As the children of gold immigrants reached adulthood, the 1880s saw a second phase of rapid development in Melbourne, the city being again rebuilt, creating an urban fabric of extensive public buildings and modern infrastructure. Public and private growth was funded by substantial borrowings. Across Australia in the thirty years from 1860, gross residential investment represented one-third of capital formation.[87] This was underwritten by loans from Britain; in the four years from 1886 these were estimated to be worth £20 million annually, with considerably more than half flowing into Victoria. In the decade prior to 1891, this funding subsidised Melbourne's residential expansion, increasing Melbourne's dwellings by more than 40,000.[88] Public borrowing was supported by private borrowing and the influence of the private 'financiers' and large-scale pawnbrokers of Melbourne in supporting the book is unknown. By 1893, in one of the many insolvency trials undertaken in Melbourne, Alfred Deakin asked rhetorically, 'If wild, even reckless speculation is to be treated as a crime, who in Melbourne is to go free?'[89]

Benjamin Fink was one of the greatest speculators of the boom period, and his activities are described by Michael Cannon: 'Nobody else … started so many billowing companies, borrowed so heavily, speculated so widely, failed so disastrously, or left such a swathe of ruin and despair.'[90] At the same time Benjamin Fink epitomises the integrated nature of place-making of Victorian Jewry.[91] Born in Guernsey in 1847 to Prussian parents, Moses Fink and Gertrude Ascher, Benjamin Fink was educated on the island, before being sent to London to attend the Jews College.[92] The family migrated in 1861 to join his uncle Hirsch Fink in Geelong, and Moses took to the road as an itinerant hawker, but within a few years was describing himself as a 'merchant' and 'financier'.

At sixteen Benjamin Fink sailed to New Zealand to begin a career as a produce dealer. Returning to Victoria two years later, he accepted a position with Maurice Aron at the furniture firm Wallach Bros in Elizabeth Street, and quickly rose to be a partner. In 1880 he secured a loan of £60,000 to buy out his partner and expanded Wallach's to Sydney, where he opened two stores. At the height of the boom he spent £120,000 rebuilding Wallach's Melbourne emporium, expanding it to provide floor space of 10,000 square metres. The business was further enlarged by the purchase of Steinfeld Levinson & Company, a furniture-manufacturing firm owned by the brothers-in-law Emanuel Steinfeld and Hyman Levinson, as well as through the purchase of Steinfeld's warehouse in Elizabeth Street. Fink further expanded his business with the acquisition of another neighbouring furniture emporium, W.H. Rocke, the oldest furniture business in the city.[93]

Furniture was only one of the many enterprises Benjamin Fink undertook. He built a complex web of investments and speculations that created much, but ultimately left a trail of ruin. The 1880s saw him acquire interests in coalmines, goldmines and pastoral properties. He established a private bank—the Joint Stock Bank of Ballarat—which within twenty-four hours of establishment had '£100,000 of paid-up capital with a reserve fund of £12,500'.[94] He later merged this with the City of Melbourne Bank, thus creating the colony's largest gold-buying concern and providing him with credit to undertake further activity.

In 1883 Fink was elected to the Legislative Assembly, representing Maryborough and Talbot, the electorate in which his mining interests were located. This proved not to be a stellar career, and Fink was described by Leavitt as a 'silent member', but 'respected for his independence, truthfulness and utter incorruptibleness'.[95] The 1880s saw Fink turn his attention to speculation and he began a project to rebuild large parts of central Melbourne, erecting Fink's Building on the corner of Flinders and Elizabeth streets at a cost of £110,000, creating the Block Arcade as one of Melbourne's leading shopping hubs and rebuilding Georges Ltd. Other ventures included the purchase of Cole's Book Arcade at a cost of £40,000, Gresham's buildings for £52,000, and he successfully convinced the stock exchange to relocate and build on his land, reaping a further profit of £55,000.

Fink also converted a number of sites into shops and offices and invested in a series of Melbourne hotels, purchasing the Ballarat Star, Albion, Saracen's Head, Governor Arthur and the Rose and Crown. After purchasing McCracken's Brewery in 1888 for £250,000, he attempted a public float of £2 million. His biggest speculative venture was the Mercantile Finance Co. Ltd, which he formed in 1885, taking over the accountancy firm of Andrew Lyell and J.M. Howden and floating it on the stock exchange. There was little interest in this venture until it began returning investments of 40 and 50 per cent, in what turned out to be an elaborate Ponzi scheme and market manipulation.

Re-forming a partnership with Maurice Aron in the furniture trade, Benjamin Fink and Aron established three public companies as equal shareholders, Wallach & Co, W.H. Rocke Ltd and Maurice Aron & Co, incorporated with capital of £700,000, of which £350,000 was in shares in the names of Fink, Aron and their nominees. This attempt to monopolise the furniture trade may have succeeded, but coincided with a downturn in the economy, which was followed by depression.

The entire empire was funded through a complex network of cross-financing, which on collapsing was never fully untangled. At the time of his insolvency in 1892 Fink owed perhaps £1.5 million to £1.82 million, but it would appear that before his ruin he had transferred considerable property to his wife, Catherine Fink. Over the next fifteen years Catherine sold parts of the empire in her own name. The couple fled the country after claiming an assassination attempt and in 1901 they were living in the Russell Hotel, Bloomsbury.[96] It was in London that Benjamin died intestate in 1909.

Fink's Building by Twentyman and Askew, 1888,
Royal Historical Society of Victoria

The Reporter

Space can be physical and intellectual, and the society magazine *Table Talk*, established in 1885 by Maurice Brodzky, provided both. In the magazine's coverage of Melbourne's social life it fully integrated that of the Jewish community, reporting marriages, balls and other gatherings alongside those of Melbourne's non-Jewish society. Throughout the land boom, the magazine was particularly influential in its investigation and coverage of the speculative land developers. Articles alerted readers to the shady financial dealing that funded this surge of building and widely reported the subsequent economic crash in the early 1890s. This was achieved through Brodsky's close association with the Fink brothers, particularly Theodore Fink.

It has been speculated that Theodore, ironically an insolvency and company lawyer, politician and for nearly fifty years the owner of the influential Herald and Weekly Times group of newspapers, provided capital for the publication.[97] Theodore Fink also provided much of the insider information published, reflected in the oft-quoted phrase 'Information in the hands of Fink, Best and Phillips is understood'. From 1891 the magazine focused more on company manipulations and less on society gossip and cultural interests.[98] As investors sought to understand the machinations of the speculation occurring around them, the circulation of the magazine rose rapidly, but this was equally matched by a decrease in advertising revenue.

Brodzky's cosmopolitan education and career provided a level of depth and sophistication, which is reflected in the diversity of his output. His life reads something like an adventure story: apparently pulled from a burning house shortly after birth; educated in London, Vienna and Paris, he fought as a volunteer for France in the Franco-Prussian War; and on arrival in Victoria was shipwrecked.

Maurice Brodzky by Aby Alston, Private Collection

Noted as a Hebrew scholar, Brodzky began his career in Melbourne as a teacher of Hebrew, French and German. It was the English-speaking world that facilitated his multinational journalism career, which took him to Melbourne, Sydney, Queensland, London and New York.[99] His marriage in 1882 to Florence Leon brought him into the extended family of the Fink brothers. Florence Leon was their cousin, while her brother Samuel married his first cousin Theodora Fink, sister of Benjamin and Theodore. Brodzky's journalism career was launched through his initial employment at Theodore Fink's *Herald* newspaper, and in addition he was engaged as the Australian correspondent for the *Daily Telegraph* and as the Australian distributor for the Prussian magazine *HaMagid*, further developing his international connections.

While employed at the *Herald*, Brodzky also published two books with an Australian Jewish theme. The first, *Genius, Lunacy & Knavery: A Story of a Colonial Physician* (1876), was a life of Dr David Hailperin, a rabbi of Polish birth who in the 1850s claimed to be able to divine the location of gold, but proved to be a fraud. The second was *Historical Sketch of the Two Melbourne Synagogues* (1877).[100] Brodzky was twice declared insolvent, in both instances due to the loss of libel cases. The first, in 1885, just prior to the founding of *Table Talk*, was against the Reverend Elias Blaubaum of the St Kilda Hebrew Congregation. In 1902 he lost a second case, after claiming that the state labour leader was an accessory to a criminal act.[101] The outcome of this second insolvency was the forfeiting of the magazine. Yet again he was saved, inheriting £500,000 on the suicide of a wealthy nephew.[102] The family travelled to San Francisco, where they survived the 1906 earthquake before relocating to New York, where Brodzky died in 1919.

The Investor

A search of the Melbourne directories indicates the great fluidity and social mobility of the city's residents. Although many families appeared to be constantly moving house, this was not always due to economic necessity; rather, a number of wealthy individuals moved with great regularity. Among these is Lawrence Benjamin, who from the 1870s and especially in the heady 1880s, built a large portfolio of investment properties and dwellings. As a financier, he arranged many private mortgages for commercial and residential building projects and was responsible for the collection of rents for others.[103]

London-born Benjamin immigrated in 1852 on the *Cambridge*, marrying his first wife, Elizabeth Solomon, at the Melbourne Hebrew Congregations in 1856. Starting a family and in business as a clothier, he lived in the Victoria Buildings before moving to the more desirable Burlington Terrace. Two years later he again moved house, this time to Fontainebleau in Victoria Parade, before returning with his family to London where he was now sufficiently wealthy to occupy a house in Upper Bedford Place, Russell Square. On his return voyage in 1877, Elizabeth died on board ship and the bereft family settled again in Melbourne.

Engaging the architects Crouch and Wilson, Benjamin built Rosenau in Victoria Parade. Following his 1891 remarriage to Clara Benjamin he commissioned a new and grander house, Clarence, in Queens Road, designed by John Beswicke, and there he died seven years later.[104] Benjamin's probate lists a considerable fortune of £215,980 including a large property portfolio valued at £138,321, comprising his home in Queens Road; the Beehive Chambers; Wuhallow in St Kilda Road; Witherleigh in Evelina Road, Toorak; Roseau in Dalgety Street, St Kilda; another timber house in Brunswick Street, Fitzroy; brick warehouses in Flinders Lane; two shops in Elizabeth Street; two city hotels; vacant land in Moonee Ponds and South Melbourne; as well as four, two-storey buildings in North Melbourne and in Collins Street.[105]

Not all families survived the crash. In 1888 David Rosenthal's firm Rosenthal and Aronson had 100 employees.[106] In 1893 when he drafted his will he had substantial assets to distribute, but on his death seventeen years later he left no property and a personal estate valued at only £120.[107] Benjamin Benjamin lost the £60,000 inheritance from his father and was in turn declared insolvent, when he naively floated a bank with unscrupulous advisers and partners.[108] For those families who did survive the crash, consolidation of their property holdings could be achieved through intermarriage. This can be vividly observed in the fascinating collection of auction notices retained from the firm Sydney Arnold, Best & Co, held in the University of Melbourne Archives.

Although Lawrence Benjamin's son Randolph was his principal beneficiary, his daughter Jane and her financier husband Bernard Marks built upon Benjamin's legacy. The Marks portfolio at the time of their deaths included Nestlewood, a two-storey eleven-room residence at 187 George Street, East Melbourne; another family home of equal size, Branda, in Mitford Street, St Kilda; factories and warehouses in Niagara Lane, Little Bourke Street and Crossley Street, Melbourne; a row of shops in High Street, Malvern and other shops in South Melbourne and St Kilda; vacant land in St Kilda; and a hotel and warehouse complex in Lonsdale Street.[109] The marriage in 1900 of their daughter Lizzie Marks and Joseph Isaacs, the grandson of Elias Moses, saw the amalgamation of two dynasties of Melbourne property investors.

The Jewish Architect
From the middle ages, Jews had been excluded from guilds throughout Europe and thus training and practice in architecture and building were also barred to them, and further restricted by the necessity for articled pupillage. The first

modern English Jewish architect was David Mocatta, articled to Sir John Soane in 1821.[110] Architectural practice requires patronage by the client and this again has historically precluded Jewish involvement. In the nineteenth century only one Jewish architect practised in Victoria, and his career spanned the boom and its aftermath. He was perhaps the most influential Jewish creator of space. Nahum Barnet, born in Melbourne in 1855 and educated at Scotch College and the University of Melbourne, was a public figure, a frequent contributor to the press, writing on issues as diverse as building style, the provision of open space, public transport, public health, the provision of public art, Jewish ritual and practice and labour politics, and was involved in a number of Jewish cultural and charitable organisations.[111]

Paton Building by Nahum Barnet, 1905

As an architect, Barnet's interest was in buildings suitable for the Australian climate. This is particularly evident in his residential designs, where his preference was for materials that would maximise climate control, reinforced by designs that shielded interiors from harsh light.[112] In his attempts to design for

Australian conditions he evolved stylistically, moving from Gothic Revival and Romanesque to Classicism and Art Nouveau. This interest is evident in the incorporation of Australian motifs in schemes such as the capitals of the Allen's Building, which was designed with Terry & Oakden in Collins Street in 1887.[113]

Barnet's career was launched in 1883 when he won a competition to design the Working Men's College in partnership with the firm Terry & Oakden, with whom he had undertaken his articles.[114] As a prolific architect, designing everything from theatres to shops, synagogues, office buildings, houses, factories and warehouses, Barnet's vision and expertise shaped the fabric of Melbourne. Barnet designed the Paton Building in 1905 for the Paton Trustees, relocating his office to the top floor. His private clients included a number of Jewish families. In 1888 for Nathaniel Levi he designed the architecturally restrained Liverpool, Princes Street, St Kilda, named after Levi's place of birth. Projects for other Jewish clients included a factory for David Rosenthal in Lonsdale Street; a house in Hotham Street, East Melbourne, for David Benjamin; extensions and alterations to Theodore Fink's house in Walsh Street, South Yarra; and, as discussed below, his extension and rebuilding of the St Kilda Hebrew Congregation and the Melbourne Hebrew Congregation.

Barnet's career and public writing show him to have been a man of empire, simultaneously British and Australian, while being staunchly 'ethnically' Jewish. Although creating architecture that was self-consciously Australian, his allegiance to the British Empire was strong, witnessed in his presidency of the Anglo-Jewish Association, in his description of himself as a 'British' Australian, and in his assertion that Australian Jewry should maintain loyalty to Chief Rabbi Herman Adler. This duality is seen in his debates promoting adaptation of synagogue services and ritual to ensure contemporary Judaism remained relevant and engaging to the local community.[115]

Religious Space

As equal citizens in a free society, the Jews of Melbourne have claimed space and equality for their religious requirements. The stylistic choices and selection of architects for their public buildings and private dwellings were a public affirmation of the community as sophisticated and educated equals. This is particularly apparent in the synagogues created for and by the community. Synagogues have a three-fold purpose: as a place of congregational worship, as a space for study and as a centre for communal activities.

Being neither hierarchical nor centralised, Judaism is based around the congregation and each synagogue preserves the faith, laws and traditions of its community. Thus the synagogue's sanctity comes from the activity undertaken in it, rather than the building itself, and as has happened in Melbourne, synagogues can be sold or rebuilt if their purpose is no longer being fulfilled.[116]

The founding of the Melbourne Hebrew Congregation raised the one issue that challenged the equality of Jewish space—the recognition of Judaism under the Church Act. In the Australian colonies no official declaration or legal enactment defining the position of Jews was made, and this was assumed to be an indirect indication of equal rights. Thus, the deed of grant for the allotment of a synagogue in Melbourne explicitly accepts Judaism as an element in society:

> Know ye that in order to promote Religion and Education in our territory of New South Wales We of our Grace have granted ... all that piece of parcel of land ... for the erection thereon of a synagogue for the use of the Members of the Jewish Persuasion and for no other purpose whatsoever.[117]

Concern arose over the payment of religious leaders, which for the Christian communities were subsidised under the Church Act of 1836. The original drafting by Governor Bourke had 'granted assistance systematically to more than one Church ... a claim is given to assistance upon the same principal to every Congregation of Dissenters and of Jews'. But when the Act was passed, it had been weakened to provide 'for the advancement of the Christian religion', thus Jews were excluded.

This change arose from an attempt to include Catholics and Dissenters in the colony, at a time when the Jewish community of unorganised convicts was so small that the omission was not considered relevant. Although aid was granted through other acts and charters, the battle for equal recognition of Jewish interests simmered for the next thirty years, as concepts defining a Christian state within the framework of a disestablished church were debated. This issue was still unresolved in 1851 when Victoria separated from New South Wales. As members of society and as tax payers, the Jewish community asserted that they:

> considered themselves loyal subjects of the British crown, with the rest of their fellow-colonists and contributing alike with them towards the support of the State, deem themselves justly entitled to a share of the revenue raised in this colony, to assist them in maintaining their religious establishments.[118]

In a parliamentary debate on the matter, John Pascoe Fawkner summed up the favourable position of the community:

> The Jews were as quiet and orderly a class of men as any in the British dominions, and were entirely free from vagabonds and beggars. Our book of religion was received from the Jews, and if on that ground alone, we ought to admit them to equal privileges with ourselves. The Jews are very liberal with their charity even to those persons who were not of their own communities.[119]

Although the Victorian Parliament removed oaths of allegiance, supremacy and abjuration in 1856, it took until 1862 for aid to be granted to the Jewish community.[120]

In pre-emancipated communities, synagogues were generally externally discreet, and in many places were prohibited from possessing facades facing public streets, resulting in the sophistication of the architecture and richness saved for the privacy of their interiors. Emancipation allowed communities to utilise this public face, to communicate their cultural sophistication and social respectability, while simultaneously announcing their 'Jewishness'. Throughout Europe, Jewish communities initiated building projects that ensured synagogues became visible components of the urban landscape, proclaiming their presence through size, architectural distinctiveness, location, religious symbols and rituals.[121]

No one architectural style was developed to characterise synagogue architecture; rather, communities employed a variety of rival styles ranging from Classical to Romanesque, Greek to Egyptian to symbolise the cultural and political aspirations of their communities in the new post-emancipation world. Hobart Synagogue, erected in 1842 and the oldest surviving Australian synagogue, was built in an Egyptian Revival style, as were those of York Street, Sydney (1843); Launceston (1844) and Adelaide (1850).

Egyptian Revival was a style made fashionable by Napoleon's conquest of Egypt in 1798, reinforced through the symbols of Freemasonry, and particularly spread through the British colonies by architects who subscribed to Freemasonry. Others considered it to be the architecture of Solomon's Temple and therefore suitable for synagogue architecture. Egyptian Revival was deemed a suitable architectural style as an overt expression and identity statement in societies where Jews faced little discrimination.[122] Many Old and New World Ashkenazi synagogues chose a Moorish Revival style, reflecting the 'oriental' roots of Judaism and forging a link to the cultural esteem of Spanish Jewry and to the Muslim world. Moorish architecture had the added cachet of aristocratic flamboyance, as expressed in the Brighton Pavilion.[123]

Although a few Moorish Revival synagogues appeared in England, synagogue architecture there tended to be more restrained, conforming to the existing urban fabric, and internalising contemporary Victorian values of private display, which in synagogue design meant a restrained exterior but allowed for greater flourishes in interior decoration.[124] This was an architecture reflecting the level of acculturation of British Jewry in 'dimensional space, structure, form and style'.[125]

In a society where 'architectural tone and style' were considered to be indicative of the character of a community, the first two synagogues in Melbourne exhibited a particular Anglo restraint, an expression of the community's outward projection of decorum and good manners. In 1844 the first of these, the Melbourne Hebrew Congregation, received a land grant for a building in Bourke Street adjoining St Patrick's Hall.[126] Responding to the symbolic importance of design, the community commissioned all seven synagogue buildings from notable contemporary architects. This began in the 1840s, with the appointment of Charles Laing to design the first synagogue building. Laing not only designed the synagogue, but was also engaged by a number of Jewish developers, particularly Solomon and Moses Benjamin for their private schemes.[127]

By the 1850s the synagogue was already too small and for the High Holidays of 1852 the community was obliged to fit 100 members into a space initially designed for seventy and accommodate another seventy in the school room, set up as a temporary synagogue for the purpose.[128] The decision was taken to enlarge the synagogue. In 1853 the congregation established a building fund, and commissioned Charles Webb to be the architect. Webb designed a Greek Revival temple, graced by imposing double-height Doric columns supporting a pediment roof. Greek Revival was a style used by non-conformist Christians in Britain and unusual for synagogue architecture.[129] The building lacked any Jewish distinctiveness, which was left for the interior arrangement, as reported in the *Argus*:

> The interior of the synagogue is of a striking character—lofty, roomy, and richly ornamented. At the extremity opposite the entrance is the 'holy of holies', surrounded by gilded Corinthian pillars and foliated frieze work, and reached by a short flight of broad steps. An inscription in Hebrew signifying 'Remember before whom thou standest', is placed immediately over the ark or 'holy of holies', and above this appear twin tablets bearing the ten commandments. Inside the ark the sacred scrolls, enveloped in velvet wrappings and with silver bells and pointers attached, are deposited. The doors of the ark are concealed by a beautiful

curtain appropriately embroidered. On either side of the recess
containing the ark appear, respectively, Hebrew and English versions of the Jewish formula of prayer for the royal family ...

The ladies who attend the synagogue are provided with a
gallery for their especial behalf ... a common thing in English
synagogues to place a somewhat intricate iron railing in front of
the gallery, so that the fair occupants are almost concealed from
the view of their brethren below. Here, however, the committee
has had the good taste to omit this apparently grotesque and
unnecessary screen.[130]

After seceding from Melbourne, the East Melbourne Hebrew Congregation
initially operated from a hall in Lonsdale Street. Two years later the community also received a land grant for a property in Stephen Street (now Exhibition
Street), on the corner of Little Lonsdale Street, commissioning a design by
Knight & Kerr, architects of Parliament House. The Victorian Heritage
Register defines the architectural significance of this building 'as an interesting
example of the conservative Classical style, unusually applied to a synagogue,
and of the small scale work of Knight and Kerr. The conservative Classical
style was more commonly used by the Methodists and Baptists'. The citation
continues by comparing this small and restrained building to Knight and
Kerr's major and parallel commission, that of Parliament House.[131]

Also outgrowing this initial iteration, in 1877 the congregation moved
from the less desirable Stephen Street to a substantial new building in Albert
Street, East Melbourne, closer to its wealthy congregants. This location situates
the synagogue squarely in the middle of the religious and parliamentary
precinct of Melbourne, flanked by the Roman Catholic Cathedral, Parliament
House and a number of other important churches of various dominations.
This affiliation with the religious establishment was reinforced through the
selection of the architects for this project, Crouch and Wilson. Not only were
they fashionable architects of residential developments, but due to Thomas
Crouch's strong Wesleyan-Quaker background, the partners were particularly
noted for their ecclesiastical work, responsible for over forty churches in
Victoria and Tasmania.[132]

An outward expression of emancipation was a change in synagogue form,
with the community proudly proclaiming their presence in the architectural
significance and outward symbolism of their synagogue.[133] Although the East
Melbourne Hebrew Congregation is of neo-classical design flanked by squat
mansard towers, it projects overtly Jewish symbolism on its exterior, with a
Magen David in the middle of the pediment front and its Hebrew name
proudly emblazoned on the banding between the floors.

In his discussions of synagogues in an emancipatory environment, Lerner describes a new confidence in the public's imagination. For the synagogue '[t]he signifying power ... derived in a large part from its role in a larger story ... In the speeches of the community presidents and patriotic Rabbis, the story is often of Progress of Civilisation in which emancipation constitutes the key event, the proof of the gradual improvement of the lot of humankind.'[134] In a similar vein, the consecrations of Melbourne's synagogues other public Jewish institutions and major events were widely reported in the press, underpinning the integrated nature of the community, with particular attention drawn to the non-Jewish dignitaries in attendance.

Whereas many have observed that population growth in England and Europe was not matched by a growth in religious institutions, particularly churches, this was not the case for the Melbourne (or Victoria), where the Jewish community had established two synagogues by the 1850s expanding and rebuilding these and establishing a third by the 1870s.[135] Synagogues were also established in Bendigo, Ballarat and Geelong, with *Sefer Torah* being lent to smaller regional centres on the goldfields.

By the 1870s there was a Jewish population in St Kilda of sufficient size to warrant the creation of a third synagogue in the city. At a meeting at Israel Bloomington's home, Rondebosch, a committee chaired by Moritz Michaelis was formed to inaugurate a new community.[136] The significance of Jewish place-making was not lost on the community, with the *Australian Israelite* reporting that it 'will effectually remove the stigma of the Jews being the only sect in the suburb without a meeting place of Divine Worship'.[137]

As with its sister synagogues, the first services, for the High Holidays of 1871 (5632), were held in the local Town Hall, with a foundation stone and a new building being laid the following year. Again Crouch and Wilson were selected as architects, although their design was made architecturally more substantial with the addition of twin towers by Nahum Barnet in 1904.[138] By the 1920s this building in Charnwood Road was also considered too small and the site was sold and a new synagogue erected across the road, designed by Joseph Plottel and based on the model of a synagogue in Chicago.

As early as 1874 the committee of the Melbourne Hebrew Congregation had considered moving the synagogue to a more populous part of the city.[139] This was not achieved for another generation when, following the residential depopulation of central Melbourne, the synagogue moved to a socially prominent position just behind Melbourne's premier boulevard, St Kilda Road, and immediately behind the Anglican establishment's school Melbourne Grammar. This new building was designed by Nahum Barnet and, as with its sister congregation in St Kilda, in scale this new building was a 'cathedral', which through the incorporation of religiously neutral classical architecture echoed the monumental synagogues of post-emancipation Europe, particularly those of Berlin, Florence and Rome.[140]

As the Jewish community grew in tandem with the rest of the city, the land acquired by grant or purchase connected the community into Melbourne's social, cultural and political power structures. Not only were Jewish architects, developers and clients active creators of public and private architecture in the city, but through the location and siting for these buildings, the community was able to make a public and conscious decision to align itself with the powerful and the fashionable. While this influence is often subtle and reflects adaptability to social and cultural requirements, it is that of an independent and emancipated community continually shaping space to meet its contemporary demands.

Like their contemporaries, the community was dispersed throughout the city, settling in new areas as these were established. What can be observed is a preference to live in neighbourhoods connected by various forms of endogamy, in close proximity to their immediate families or business partners. This was not a ghetto formation; rather it reflected the interconnectedness of a community, at once prepared to engage with the opportunities the city offered while supporting and maintaining a minority community.

As a city grows and develops, its early form is lost and transformed. This applies equally to the Jewish presence in Melbourne, with synagogues growing and expanding to meet new demands, and as this organic growth occurred the first two synagogues were rebuilt or sold. In some cases the Jewish presence has been obliterated. What was initially Synagogue Lane had by 1868 become Little Queen Street (later renamed Bourke Lane). In other areas, the presence has been transformed; the Knight and Kerr synagogue in Exhibition Street is now a restaurant, and its statement of significance describes its progressive use as a venue for social welfare activities.[141]

William Westgarth, commenting on early Melbourne, suggested that new societies in a state of flux exhibited no cohesion and unity.[142] Observations gained from the Melbourne Jewish community and their patterns of residential location and architecture would seem to dispute this. This was a community expressing its pride and wealth through the built environment, while also maintaining tight family endogamy and shaping the city to its requirements.

Notes

1   Michael Cannon and Ian MacFarlane, *Historical Records of Victoria. Foundation Series* (Victoria Public Record Office, 1984), 12, 15.
2   Steven M. Lowenstein, 'Was Urbanization Harmful to Jewish Tradition and Identity in Germany?', in Ezra Mendelsohn (ed.), *People of the City: Jews and the Urban Challenge* (Oxford University Press, Oxford, 1999), 81.
3   Hillel J. Kieval, 'Neighbors, Strangers, Readers: The Village and the City in the

Jewish–Gentile Conflict at the Turn of the Nineteenth Century', *Jewish Studies Quarterly* 12 (2005), 61.

4   Gunther Paul Barth, *Instant Cities: Urbanization and the Rise of San Francisco and Denver*, (University of New Mexico Press, Albuquerque, 1988), 32.

5   Graeme Davison, 'Australia: The First Suburban Nation?', *Journal of Urban History* 22, no. 1 (1995), 52, 55; see also Eric Richards, *Britannia's Children: Emigration from England, Scotland, Wales and Ireland since 1600* (Hambledon & London, London, 2004), 162.

6   Andrew Lees, *Cities Perceived, Urban Society in European and American Thought, 1820–1940* (Manchester University Press, Manchester, 1985), 1–2.

7   Graeme Davison, 'Gold-Rush Melbourne', in Ian McCalman, Alexander Cook and Andrew Reeves (eds), *Gold: Forgotten Histories and Lost Objects of Australia* (Cambridge University Press, Cambridge, 2001), 53.

8   Barth, *Instant Cities*, 130–2.

9   Davison, 'Gold-Rush Melbourne', 52–3.

10   ibid., 54.

11   Andrew Brown-May, *The Itinerary of Our Days: The Historical Experience of the Street in Melbourne, 1837–1923* (Australian Scholarly Publishing, Melbourne, 1998), 15.

12   Paul Carter, *Road to Botany Bay: An Exploration of Landscape and History* (University of Minnesota Press, Minneapolis, 2010), 204.

13   Dell Upton, 'The Art and Mystery of Historical Archaeology', in James Deetz, Anne E. Yentsch, and Mary Carolyn Beaudry (eds), *The Art and Mystery of Historical Archaeology: Essays in Honor of James Deetz* (CRC Press, Boca Raton, 1992), 54–6; D.A. Hamer, *New Towns in the New World: Images and Perceptions of the Nineteenth-Century Urban Frontier* (Columbia University Press, New York, 1990), 181.

14   Brown-May, *The Itinerary of Our Days*, 23–4.

15   Cannon and MacFarlane, *Historical Records of Victoria*, 84–5.

16   Israel Getzler, 'Montefiore, Joseph Barrow (1803–1893)', *Australian Dictionary of Biography* (National Centre for Biography, Australian National University, Canberra, 1967), <http://adb.anu.edu.au/biography/montefiore-joseph-barrow-2472>.

17   John S. Levi, *These Are the Names: Jewish Lives in Australia, 1788–1850* (Miegunyah Press, Melbourne University Publishing, Carlton, 2006), 543; State Records Authority of New South Wales, 'New South Wales, Australia Historical Electoral Rolls 1842–1864'.

18   'New South Wales, Australia Historical Electoral Rolls 1842–1864'.

19   *Southern Australian*, Friday 2 June 1843, 2.

20   Getzler, 'Montefiore, Joseph Barrow (1803–1893)'.

21   Returning to Australia in 1846, Joseph's family now comprised nine children, while his baggage indicated some intention of permanence, as they arrived with a vast array of luggage including a harp, a piano and 300 packages.

22   Ruth Faerber, 'Eliezer Levi Montefiore', *Australian Jewish Historical Society* 8, no. 4 (1977), 186; *Sydney Morning Herald*, 23 October 1894, 5.

23   *Sydney Morning Herald*, 14 November 1833, 2.

24   *Sydney Monitor*, 13 February 1836, 2; *Sydney Gazette and New South Wales Advertiser*, 22 March 1836, 4; *Sydney Gazette*, 4 March 1837, 4; *Sydney Gazette*, 15 December 1840, 4.

25   *Sydney Gazette and New South Wales Advertiser*, 30 March 1841, 4; *Sydney Gazette*, 24 April 1841, 4; *Sydney Morning Herald*, 4 December 1842, 2.

26   *Port Phillip Gazette*, 23 February 1839, 1.

27   *Port Phillip Patriot and Melbourne Advertiser*, 6 May 1839, 5; and 26 March 1840, 6.

28   Levi, *These Are the Names*, 93.

29   *Geelong Advertiser and Squatters' Advocate*, 6 July 1847, 3.
30   Lazarus M. Goldman, *The Jews in Victoria in the Nineteenth Century* (self-published, Melbourne, 1954), 33.
31   *Argus*, 31 October 1849, 2.
32   Will of Moses Benjamin, Public Record Office Victoria, Index to Wills, Probate and Administration Records 1841–2009, VPRS 28 P0000 365.
33   Margaret Kiddle, *Men of Yesterday: A Social History of the Western District of Victoria, 1834–1890* (Melbourne University Press, Melbourne, 1962), 77.
34   David Merrett, 'Paying for It All', in Patrick Troy (ed.), *A History of European Housing in Australia* (Cambridge University Press, Cambridge, 2000), 243.
35   Ian W. McLean, *Why Australia Prospered: The Shifting Sources of Economic Growth* (Princeton University Press, Princeton, 2013), 84.
36   Miles Lewis, *Melbourne: The City's History and Development*, 2nd edn (City of Melbourne, Melbourne, 1995), 53.
37   N.G. Butlin, *Investment in Australian Economic Development, 1861–1900* (Dept. of Economic History, Research School of Social Sciences, Australian National University, Canberra, 1976), 215.
38   Geoffrey Serle, *The Golden Age: A History of the Colony of Victoria, 1851–1861* (Melbourne University Press, Melbourne, 1963), 68.
39   *Sydney Morning Herald*, 5 November 1929, 4.
40   Hamer, *New Towns in the New World*, 60.
41   Serle, *The Golden Age*, 370.
42   Hamer, *New Towns in the New World*, 155.
43   As a result, during the 1850s Melbourne's population represented only 23 per cent of the colony, the lowest in its history: Lionel Frost, 'The Urban History Literature of Australia and New Zealand', *Journal of Urban History* 22, no. 1 (1995), 278.
44   Hamer, *New Towns in the New World*, 158.
45   Winston H. Burchett, *East Melbourne, 1837–1977: People, Places, Problems* (Craftsman Press, Hawthorn, 1978), 31.
46   James Butterfield, *The Commercial, Squatters and Official Directory for 1854* (James Blundell & Co, Melbourne, 1854); John Needham, *Melbourne, Commercial, Professional and Legal Directory* (James Blundell & Co, Melbourne, 1856). Moss showed rapid social advancement after having been convicted in 1825 for stealing two bags of seeds valued at eight shillings. His brother George was also a convict, having been jailed for stealing a watch. George became a repeat escapee and was fatally shot after an attempted escape from Norfolk Island: Levi, *These Are the Names*, 620.
47   *Age*, 26 November 1857, 4; *Age*, 23 October 1857, 4; *Age*, 28 November 1857, 4; *Age*, 17 March 1860, 4; *Age*, 23 June 1863, 4; *Age*, 23 October 1863, 5; *Argus*, 29 September 1859, 6.
48   This relationship was cemented with the 1883 marriage of Moses' granddaughter Kate Hart to Henry's son Louis Howitz: Fitzroy City Council, Rate Books, 1864–69, Fitzroy Library.
49   Melbourne and Metropolitan Board of Works, 'City of Collingwood, Detailed Plan No 1208', MMBW, Melbourne, 1899.
50   Giselle Roberts, 'A Grand Vision: Henry Philip Harris and the History of Burlington Terrace', *Australian Jewish Historical Society Journal* XV, no. 1 (1999), 61.
51   Sands and McDougall Directories 1868–83.
52   Melbourne City Council, Rate Books, 1864–68, Public Record Office Victoria.
53   Casey et al, *Early Melbourne Architecture 1840 to 1888*, 66.
54   Bernard Barrett, *The Inner Suburbs: The Evolution of an Industrial Area* (Melbourne University Press, Carlton, 1971), 15.

55 Fitzroy City Council, Rate Books.
56 The extent of this 'Terrace' is difficult to determine, as the house of Nathaniel Levi at number 6 appears to have been one of the first to be built, while its auction notice of 1876 describes a cemented bluestone residence of five bedrooms with drawing room and dining room on a block 19'5" [19 feet, 5 inches] by 100': *Argus*, 8 December 1876, 2.
57 Fitzroy City Council, Rate Books.
58 Melbourne Hebrew Congregation, 'Minutes of the Melbourne Hebrew Congregation', 23 January 1849.
59 *Argus*, 17 June 1851, 2.
60 Also on the committee were the Reverend Rintel, Michael Cashmore, Elias Ellis, Isaac Lyons, Nathan Salmon, Dr Solomon Iffla, Isaac Hart, Eliezer Levi Montefiore and Simon Hamburger: *Argus*, 24 July 1855, 5.
61 *Argus*, 28 July 1857, 8.
62 Tony Birch, 'Fitzroy', in Andrew Brown-May and Shurlee Swain (eds), *The Encyclopaedia of Melbourne* (Cambridge University Press, Melbourne, 2005), 268.
63 Jacobs Lewis Vines Architects, Miles Lewis and Fitzroy Urban Planning Office, 'South Fitzroy Conservation Study' (Fitzroy City Council and the Historic Buildings Preservation Council, Fitzroy, 1979), 14.
64 Fitzroy City Council, *Glass Terrace, 64–78 Gertrude Street, Fitzroy, Victoria, 3065: A Report on its Architectural Significance and Historic Merit* (Sub-Committee of the Fitzroy City Council, Fitzroy, 1977), 12.
65 David Cannadine, 'Victorian Cities: How Different?', *Social History* 2, no. 4 (1977), 463.
66 Graeme Davison, 'Colonial Origin of the Australian Home', in Patrick Troy (ed.), *A History of European Housing in Australia* (Cambridge University Press, Melbourne, 2000), 12.
67 Fitzroy City Council, *Glass Terrace, 64–78 Gertrude Street*, 21.
68 Fitzroy City Council, Rate Books.
69 Miles Lewis, 'Terrace Houses and Gothic Splendour: The Architecture', in Peter Yule (ed.), *Carlton: A History* (Carlton Residents Association, Carlton, 2004), 446, 451, 452.
70 *Argus*, 22 April 1865, 7. Although a financier by occupation, Moss became insolvent in 1893, having previously transferred his house Rosebank, Clarendon Street, East Melbourne, to his wife and died intestate with assets valued at £20: *Table Talk*, 4 May 1894, 7; and Probate of Mark Moss, Public Record Office Victoria, Index to Wills, Probate and Administration Records 1841–2009, VPRS 28 03 1399.
71 Miles Lewis, 'Terrace Houses and Gothic Splendour: The Architecture', 454.
72 East Melbourne Hebrew Congregration, 'Minutes; December 1860 – October 1875', Australian Jewish Historical Society Collection, State Library of Victoria, 23 August 1863; *Jewish Herald*, 19 May 1893, 7.
73 *Jewish Herald*, 14 March 1902, 12.
74 Hilary L. Rubinstein and W.D. Rubenstein, *The Jews in Australia: A Thematic History* (William Heinemann Australia, Port Melbourne, 1991), 260.
75 *Jewish Herald*, 18 September 1908, 10.
76 *Hebrew Standard of Australasia*, 6 July 1923, 14.
77 Henry Abrahams was the son of Alice Abrahams and grandson of Emanuel 'Money' Moses of the Great Gold Dust Robbery.
78 Graeme Davison, *The Rise and Fall of Marvellous Melbourne* (Melbourne University Press, Carlton, 1981), 19.
79 As quoted in Rubinstein, *The Jews in Australia*, 262.
80 Howard Raggatt, 'A Study of the Development of St Kilda from its Beginning till

1873' (Undergraduate thesis, University of Melbourne, 1978), 47.

81 J.E.S.Vardy, Surveyor &c, 'Plan of the Borough of St. Kilda' (Hamel & Ferguson, Melbourne, 1872).

82 Interestingly Eleanor was not buried as a Jew: Levi, *These Are the Names*, 745.

83 Raggatt, 'A Study of the Development of St Kilda from Its Beginning till 1873', 77.

84 *Argus*, 26 June 1858, 3; Vardy, Surveyor &c. , 'Plan of the Borough of St. Kilda'.

85 Bill Williams, *The Making of Manchester Jewry, 1740–1875* (Manchester University Press, Manchester, 1976), 127.

86 *Argus*, 9 August 1867, 1, 3; *Argus*, 23 September 1870, 4; *Newcastle Morning Herald and Miners Advocate*, 26 March 1890, 5; *Jewish Herald*, 28 March 1890, 6; *Argus*, 2 April 1887, 5; *South Australian Register*, 29 July 1887, 8; Museum Victoria, 'S. Schlank & Co., Adelaide, South Australia', <http://museumvictoria.com.au/collections/themes/2437/s-schlank-co-adelaide-south-australia>; Paul de Serville, *Athenaeum Club, Melbourne: A New History of the Early Years 1868–1918* (Athenaeum Club, Melbourne, 2013), 223.

87 Butlin, *Investment in Australian Economic Development*, 211.

88 Asa Briggs, *Victorian Cities* (Penguin, Ringwood, 1971), 290.

89 *Argus*, 4 March 1893, 6.

90 Michael Cannon, *The Land Boomers: The Complete Illustrated History* (Heritage Publications, Melbourne, 1972), 281.

91 Arijit Sen and Lisa Silverman, 'Embodied Placemaking: An Important Category and Critical Analysis', in Arijit Sen and Lisa Silverman (eds), *Making Place: Space and Embodiment in the City* (Indiana University Press, Bloomington, 2013), 7.

92 Thad. W.H. Leavitt, *Australian Representative Men* (Wells & Leavitt, Melbourne, 1887), 217.

93 *Table Talk*, 10 March 1893, 11-12.

94 Leavitt, *Australian Representative Men*, 218.

95 ibid., 218.

96 Census for England and Wales, 1901.

97 Rubinstein, *The Jews in Australia: A Thematic History*, 390.

98 Cannon, *The Land Boomers*, 132–3.

99 *Jewish Herald*, 2 May 1919, 10; *Jewish Herald*, 13 June 1919, 11; *Table Talk*, 14 April 1919, 31.

100 Suzanne D. Rutland, *Edge of the Diaspora; Two Centuries of Jewish Settlement in Australia*, (Brandl & Schlesinger, Sydney, 1997), 128.

101 Michael Cannon, 'Fink, Benjamin Josman (1847–1909)', in *Australian Dictionary of Biography* (National Centre for Biography, Australian National University, Canberra, 1972).

102 *Jewish Herald*, 6 June 1913, 6.

103 Allan Willingham, 'The Mansion formerly "Clarence", the Residence of Lawrence and Clara Benjamin, 83 Queens Road St Kilda 3183: Assessment of Cultural Significance', report compiled for Interprop Investments, 1998, 3.6.

104 ibid., 3.7.

105 Will of Lawrence Benjamin, Public Record Office Victoria, Index to Wills, Probate and Administration Records 1841–2009, VPRS 28 P0000 906.

106 Ruth Dwyer, 'A Jewellery Manufactory in Melbourne: Rosenthal, Aronson and Company', *Journal of the Public Record Office Victoria* 7 (2008), <https://prov.vic.gov.au/publications/provenance/provenance2008/jewellery-manufactory>.

107 Will and Probate of David Rosenthal, Public Record Office Victoria, Index to Wills, Probate and Administration Records 1841–2009, VPRS 28 P0003 129 and VPRS 7591 P0002 447.

108 The case is laid out in detail in Cannon, *The Land Boomers*, chapter 28.

109 Sydney Arnold, Best & Co Collection, University of Melbourne Archives, 1968.0012 Unit 3.

110 Edward Jamilly, 'Patrons, Clients, Designers and Developers: The Jewish Contribution to Secular Building in England', *Jewish Historical Studies* 38 (2003), 93.

111 See for example *Argus*, 5 February 1885, 7; *Argus*, 26 December 1924, 11; *Argus*, 12 February 1889, 8; *Argus*, 9 May 1908, 19; *Argus*, 4 September 1890, 7.

112 *Argus*, 24 January 1908, 7.

113 Philip Goad and Julie Willis, *The Encyclopedia of Australian Architecture* (Cambridge University Press, Melbourne, 2012), 69.

114 *Argus*, 21 May 1883, 8.

115 *Jewish Herald*, 1 February 1901, 14; *Jewish Herald*, October 1910, 10; *Jewish Herald*, 20 January 1888, 7.

116 Carol Herselle Krinsky, *Synagogues of Europe: Architecture, History, Meaning* (Architectural History Foundation, New York, 1985), 8.

117 Israel Getzler, *Neither Toleration nor Favour: The Australian Chapter of Jewish Emancipation* (Melbourne University Press, Carlton, 1970), 83.

118 *Jewish Chronicle*, 25 April 1851, 230.

119 *Argus*, 11 September 1852, 4–5.

120 Getzler, *Neither Toleration nor Favour*, 107.

121 Saskia Coenen Snyder, *Building a Public Judaism: Synagogues and Jewish Identity in Nineteenth-Century Europe* (Harvard University Press, Cambridge, 2013), 4; Saskia Coenen Snyder 'A Narrative of Absence: Monumental Synagogue Architecture in Late Nineteenth-Century Amsterdam', *Jewish History* 25 (2010), 44.

122 Diana Muir Appelbaum, 'Jewish Identity and Egyptian Revival Architecture', *Journal of Jewish Identities* 5, no. 2 (2012), 2, 10–12.

123 Ivan Davidson Kalmar, 'Moorish Style: Orientalism, the Jews and Synagogue Architecture', *Jewish Social Studies* 7, no. 3 (2001), 70–7.

124 Snyder, *Building a Public Judaism*, 17.

125 Sharman Kadish, 'Constructing Identity: Anglo Jewry and Synagogue Architecture', *Architectural History* 45 (2002), 387.

126 Hamer, *New Towns in the New World*, 52.

127 Goad and Willis, *The Encyclopedia of Australian Architecture*, 396.

128 *Jewish Chronicle*, 21 January 1853, 127.

129 Kadish, 'Constructing Identity', 391.

130 *Argus*, 3 September 1858, 5.

131 Victorian Heritage Register, *Former Mickveh Yisrael Synagogue and School* (Heritage Council of Victoria, Melbourne, 2015).

132 Goad and Willis, *The Encyclopedia of Australian Architecture*, 183.

133 Geoffrey Wigoder, *The Story of the Synagogue: A Diaspora Museum Book* (Weidenfeld & Nicolson, London, 1986), 177.

134 L. Scott Lerner, 'The Narrating Architecture of Emancipation', *Jewish Social Studies* 6, no. 3 (2000), 4.

135 Lees, *Cities Perceived*, 29; Owen Chadwick, *The Secularization of the European Mind in the Nineteenth Century* (Cambridge University Press, Cambridge, 1977), 97.

136 *Hebrew Standard of Australasia*, 21 October 1921, 11.

137 *Australian Israelite*, 8 September 1871, 5

138 Newman H. Rosenthal, *Look Back with Pride: The St. Kilda Hebrew Congregation's First Century* (T. Nelson, Melbourne, 1971), 48.

139 *Jewish Chronicle*, 4 September 1874, 361.

140 For a discussion on the role of emancipation and synagogue building in the

nineteenth century see Lerner, 'The Narrating Architecture of Emancipation'; and L. Scott Lerner, 'Narrating over the Ghetto of Rome', *Jewish Social Studies* 8, nos 2–3 (2002).

141 Brown-May, *The Itinerary of Our Days*, 160; Victorian Heritage Register, 'Former Mickveh Yisrael Synagogue and School'.

142 Hamer, *New Towns in the New World*, 145.

Chapter 6

In Public Life

Foremost amongst the many privileges we enjoyed, that of civil and religious equality was the greatest.
—Sir George Verdon, Governor of Victoria, at a dinner for the
Melbourne Hebrew School, 1875[1]

The Jews have, as a matter of tacit understanding, not only full and free rights of political equality with the rest of their fellow-colonists, but they hold high— indeed a signally high—position.
—Jewish Chronicle, 20 October 1871, 8

In pre-emancipation societies, the political status of Jews was inseparable from their religious status. Although subject to similar political and economic frameworks, Jews and Christians operated in two distinct realms.[2] With no bar from political participation in the Australian colonies, there was a flowering of civic participation by the small Jewish community. For colonial development, their cosmopolitanism and their multifarious relationships delivered to these isolated communities a diverse intellectual and economic resource.

From the mid-nineteenth century Victorian Jewry engaged in active citizenship, volunteering their services and providing expertise in a range of civil, political and communal organisations. Internationally their skills and connections were also employed by governments in research and strategy, as advisers and members of royal commissions, as commissioners in the intercolonial and international exhibitions in Melbourne and as consuls representing foreign governments. For ambitious and socially aware Jews, participation brought not only social recognition but also an opportunity for meaningful influence over the shape of this new society and a concrete representation of the values of *Tikun Olam*.

Unlike in Europe, where political emancipation was slow and often non-linear, the process of colonisation and the establishment of representative government in the colonies offered a unique opportunity for Jewish civil participation. The colonies were settled and established during the final push for emancipation in Britain. This final stage was a religious-political issue revolving around the necessity to undertake the Oath of Abjuration, whereby office holders were required to swear as an Anglican or, following the Catholic Emancipation Act, as a Christian. The oath excluded Jews not only from holding office under the Crown, but also from any roles in civic government, parliament, or employment in the administration of justice.[3] This was an indirect form of exclusion, which Anglo-Jewry strove to overcome in other areas, partaking in social and economic life, demonstrating in a practical sense their integrated nature in British society.

Emancipation in England is considered to have been complete by 1858, when Lionel de Rothschild was able to take his seat in parliament, a seat he had won eleven years earlier, and to which he had been re-elected on several occasions. Until that year the restrictive nature of the oath had prevented him taking up his seat. With the establishment of the Australian colonies, English law was transferred, and then subsequently overwritten or adapted by colonial legislatures. This included the swearing of oaths of office.

Although application of these restrictions was applied as a form of social or class hegemony, they do not appear to have been strictly enforced in the Australian colonies, as Jews were not excluded from civic office. In Victoria, Jews stood as candidates for local government almost as soon as Melbourne was granted representative government in 1842, and David Ribeiro Furtado was elected auditor for the city of Melbourne (a role he refused) in 1852. Such appointments were technically not permitted until New South Wales and Victoria introduced acts officially removing the religious considerations for the swearing of oaths in 1857 and 1858 respectively. In Victoria the Act read:

> Whereas the civil and religious rights and liberties of all Her Majesty's subjects in Victoria are and ought to be absolutely equal irrespective of their faith or form of belief … it is expedient to provide and establish two uniform oaths or affirmations of allegiance and office respectively in lieu of the oaths and declarations now by law required in that behalf.[4]

Melbourne Jewry kept up a constant flow of information about communal affairs through reports to the London-based *Jewish Chronicle*. In the 1860s the correspondents were commenting on local conditions. 'All denominations being placed upon equal footing, Jews here could hold the highest office in the State.'[5] 'Every position a citizen can hold, is occupied by our co-religionists-magistrates, legislators, city and municipal councillors, and chairmen of municipalities.'[6]

Although the goldfields attracted numerous 'Chartists and continental revolutionaries', it cannot be established how many of the Jewish population had Chartist sympathies, and although some had arrived as a result of the revolutions of 1848 and the turbulence that followed, it is unclear whether any had participated in political change.[7] What is clear is that in a society without racially based enfranchisement, the Jewish community took up with alacrity the opportunities offered. By the mid 1850s, European-born Jewish merchants in the gold towns were eagerly taking up naturalisation, with bundles of inter-related applications submitted from across Victoria.

With naturalisation, these men could purchase property, becoming rate payers and be eligible to vote, a civic right unavailable in most parts of Europe. Some have asserted that commercial occupations were generally incompatible with political leadership, where 'the colonies were mere milch cows'.[8] This was not the case in Melbourne, where the Jewish community principally consisted of merchants and manufacturers; and it was merchants who dominated the political institutions of Melbourne.[9] Although Jews were excluded from some of the more establishment institutions such as the Melbourne Club, they could join their colleagues in active participation in civic affairs.

Local Government

Municipal government afforded another avenue for aspiring politicians and, as has been noted, the issue of oaths appears to have been overlooked, whereas in England it still presented an obstacle. In 1835 David Salomons was elected sheriff of London (although some opposition had been expressed on religious grounds) but unable to take up the position due to the requirements of the Oath of Office. To resolve this problem, parliament quickly passed the Sherriff's Declaration Act, allowing special provision for persons elected to this task. But this exception was uniquely defined to the sheriff's role and thus when Salomons was elected an alderman the following year; he was unable to assume office. It was not until 1845 with the introduction of the Jewish Disabilities Removal Act that municipal and judicial functions were open to Jews. In 1855, David Salomons was elected lord mayor of London, 'thereby setting the seal on the municipal emancipation of English Jews'.[10]

In Melbourne the trajectory was very different. With the establishment of the council of the City of Melbourne in 1842, Jewish participation occurred almost immediately, with the nomination of Asher Hymen Hart as a candidate, although he was unsuccessful in this and in a subsequent election of 1845. Michael Cashmore, representing the La Trobe Ward, became Melbourne's first Jewish councillor, before resigning in January 1848.[11] These initial attempts at representation were quickly followed by others across metropolitan Melbourne and regional centres, as Jewish men, and later women, were elected as councillors and as mayors.

In 1862 Edward Cohen became the first Jewish mayor of Melbourne, and twenty-five years later his brother-in-law Benjamin Benjamin, first elected for the Albert Ward in 1870, became the first Melbourne mayor to be knighted. Benjamin, as an observant Jew, ensured that the 1000 dignitaries at his inaugural banquet were served only kosher food.[12] Political participation was not restricted to men: Ada Marks, a long-term councillor for St Kilda, served on the council alongside her brother-in-law Henry Florin Barnet and acted as mayor when Barnet was unavailable.[13] For Solomon Iffla, accepting the mayoral robes of Emerald Hill in 1880 would have been inconceivable at the time of his birth in Jamaica, where the Jewish population was disenfranchised until after the abolition of slavery.

The Judiciary

Justice in Victoria was administered through appointed court officers who were formally selected by the monarch, while governors were responsible for the appointment of justices of the peace, coroners and constables of police.[14] Stipendiary magistrates, also called 'police magistrates', combined the functions of preservation of peace, detection of crime and apprehension of offenders, as well as the duties of sentencing and punishing.[15] These were paid officers, appointed by the governor-in-council and 'usually taken from the ranks of the existing civil service'.[16]

While the role of justice of the peace dates back to pre-Norman times, initially an appointment of the Crown to perform administrative and judicial duties, by the nineteenth-century justices of the peace provided judicial functions for the courts of Petty Sessions.[17] In England eligibility for appointment as justices of the peace required a property qualification, a further restriction on Jews where the legal status of Jewish property ownership was unclear. Again, in Victoria the situation was markedly different, as Jews were not restricted from property ownership, nor was this a prerequisite for office.

Here the role was honorary, but in reality only available to men of independent means, who were able to devote the requisite time to their duties. The title was also conferred on shire presidents, mayors of cities, towns and boroughs, indirectly leading to a greater diversity in those presiding over the lower courts.[18] From the mid nineteenth century dozens of Jewish men across Victoria were appointed justices of the peace. Those holding office were rarely lawyers and many appointees served a number of public functions in government, the judiciary and in consular roles. As a form of patronage, these duties not only carried the responsibility of office, but also conveyed social kudos.

The sense of security the Jewish community felt in Victoria allowed them to be involved in the shaping of Jewish communal life and in the shaping and development of the new colonial society. This brought into play their international connections for a two-way exchange of knowledge, promoting Victoria's interests and the development of the structures of society.

Henri John Hart was born in New York. His father, John Hart, had served in the Royal Navy at the Battle of Trafalgar before migrating to America, where he married Isabella Levy, (who according to Hart's obituary was the descendent of a 'revolutionary hero') and there the couple started a family.[19] Henri Hart's education was designed to lead to a legal career, and he attended the Grammar School attached to Colombia College and subsequently spent some time working in the office of the attorney-general, Hugh Maxwell. At the age of seventeen he left New York for London, but hearing 'romantic stories' about the Australian colonies, arrived in Sydney in December 1839, and by 1841 had established himself in Melbourne.

Hart recognised that the discovery of gold in New South Wales in 1851 posed an economic threat to the Victorian economy, so he took the proactive step of organising a public meeting in the Melbourne Mechanics Hall, the outcome of which was the establishment of the Gold Committee, with Hart as honorary secretary. The committee offered a £200 reward for the discovery of 'payable goldfields in Victoria, and also inducing search parties to visit localities where the most likely gold would be found'.[20]

Henri Hart returned to England in April 1852, bringing with him specimens of Victorian gold. By then, excitement at the promise of the Victorian gold rush was great, and Hart joined a committee of Australian colonists whose aim was to promote Victoria, providing useful information, advice and statistics regarding the colony. His prominence was such that during this visit he was elected an honorary corresponding member of the Society of Arts of England, under the patronage of Prince Albert. Returning to America, he married Philadelphian Sarah Jane Rowland, before returning to Australia in 1854, on a ship also carrying the governor, Charles Hotham.

Six months later he again returned to America, having been appointed a commissioner for the Supreme Court to exercise jurisdiction throughout the Americas. This trip also took him to England, where at a royal levée he was presented to the American ambassador, an introduction that eventually led to him being appointed acting consul for that country in 1866. His connections extended to Italy as well, and in 1879, following the death of the incumbent, Chevalier Maranucci, he was also appointed acting consul for this new nation. Between 1869 and 1875 he was annually elected one of the auditors for the City of Melbourne.

His early years in Melbourne saw Hart engage in a number of mercantile pursuits. He sold ale in Eastern Hill; in 1850 he was listed as the proprietor of the 'Temple of Fashion' in Collins Street, and was in partnership with his father John Hart in 'Uncle Tom's Pawnbrokers Shop', Lonsdale Street.[21] Tragedy struck the family in 1863 when his wife died at the age of twenty-eight, leaving Henri a widower with four children.

Deeply connected to the Jewish community, he initially joined the Melbourne Hebrew Congregation, where he acted as the honorary secretary.[22] Following the split in 1857 he accompanied his brother-in-law Moses Rintel, to East Melbourne. As a member of the Board of Advice under the Education Act for the District of West Melbourne, he assisted with the land grant for the Stephen Street premises, and was variously honorary secretary and president, laying the foundation stone for the Albert Street building.

Epergne presented to Henri Hart by the East Melbourne Hebrew Congregation,
Illustrated Australian News for Home Readers, *28 February 1870*

His standing saw him appointed a justice of the peace, a magistrate and a territorial magistrate for Victoria, New South Wales and Queensland. He was also intensely involved in many of the philanthropic organisations of

Melbourne. Henri John Hart sat on the boards of management of the Melbourne Hospital and the Lying in Hospital, he was vice-president of the Eye and Ear Hospital, and guardian of minors under the Marriage Act. He was also a founder and treasurer of the Discharged Prisoners Aid Society, assisted in the establishment of the Society for the Prevention of Cruelty to Animals and on the council of the Victorian Art Union. His international vision helped shape the Melbourne International Exhibition, to which, like a number of other Jewish residents, he was appointed a commissioner.[23]

The Public Service

Although the judicial roles and charitable engagement that many in the Jewish community were engaged in could broadly be termed 'public' activities, few Jews appear to have been employed in senior roles in the public service in Victoria. Whether this is a translation of the historical exclusion of Jews from the civil service to Victoria is unclear. A search of the parliamentary Blue Books indicates only one member of the community, Louis Ellis, listed in the senior ranks of the expanding public service.[24] Ellis was employed from at least 1856 until his retirement in the Sheriff's Office as deputy sheriff and later acting sheriff. Other Jews must have been employed in other areas, as the necessity of government employees working on Saturdays was raised as an issue by the Sabbath Observance Society.

Parliament and Politics

Having been excluded from parliament in Britain as elsewhere, Jews in Australia almost immediately followed Lionel de Rothschild's lead, standing for parliamentary election in Victoria and the other colonies. Between 1860, when Nathaniel Levi became the first Jew to sit in the Victorian Parliament, until the federation of the Australian colonies forty years later, Victoria had seventeen Jewish parliamentarians, representing the upper and lower houses, rural and metropolitan seats. This was a greater representation per capita than that in Britain, where from a Jewish population of up to 430,000, eighteen Jewish parliamentarians were elected in the thirty years following Lionel de Rothschild's accession to his seat.[25]

Unlike in Britain, these politicians were not from wealthy banking or legal dynasties, and while their British counterparts were noted for their lack of political accomplishments, many of those in Victoria were particularly vocal on a number of important issues.[26] This period saw the formation of a number of political dynasties, and this was equally true for the Jewish community, with half the Jewish politicians in the Victorian Parliament having brothers or brothers-in-law who were also sitting members. The place of birth of these parliamentarians is indicative of the community: ten were British-born, although five of these had settled as children and been educated in Australia, five had been born in Victoria and two were German. Two represented families whose presence in Australia was due to a family member being transported as a convict, both being families of Sephardi origin: Jonas Felix Australia Levien, the first Jewish child born in Victoria, and Edward Cohen, parliamentarian and mayor of Melbourne.

A property franchise defined suitability for office and thus this group represented individuals who had acquired wealth in the colony. For these men their motivation for participation was also the important symbolic expression of acceptance by the community who had elected them. In a society where Jews were not set apart from other citizens, 'Jewish solidarity' is more complex as individuals express themselves as citizens, articulating their interest in the social and communal activities of society. This becomes apparent when considering the three areas in which Jewish parliamentarians were prominent, those of public education, taxation reform and federation.

Education

Education proved to be one of the areas where Jewish politicians and the interest of the Jewish community had significant impact, but where this influence simultaneously created difficulties for the community itself. Education is a quintessential Jewish preoccupation and in emancipated societies, structuring an education to provide for secular and religious knowledge proved a complex problem.

As early as October 1835 it was recognised that an education system was required for the Port Phillip District, and a system based on that of Ireland, whereby children of different religious persuasions would be taught without distinction, was considered a suitable solution for providing education in a thinly dispersed population.[27] Although such a system was not introduced, it nevertheless prompted consideration of an education policy that would take more than thirty years to stabilise. Education was incorporated into the initial planning for Melbourne: land was not only set aside for the various Christian denominations, but for their schools as well.

Following separation in 1851, funding was made available for schools that gave at least four consecutive hours of daily secular education, with the stipulation of a minimum number of pupils. A system of inspectors to monitor performance was established,[28] and later reinforced in legislation. Initially churches had been the primary providers of education, but by 1861 it was recognised that only half the children of school age were literate and a new system was required.[29]

The maintenance of Judaism and the education of the younger generation were preoccupations for the community throughout the nineteenth century. As in other post-Enlightenment centres, it was recognised that education required a combination of secular and religious teachings for the education of the young. A view summed up in the *Jewish Chronicle*: 'There can be no doubt that no plan of education which does not embrace Hebrew in all its branches, can prove satisfactory to a Jew.'[30] As with the foundation of the St Kilda Hebrew Congregation a generation later, the initial consideration for the Melbourne Hebrew Congregation was to ensure that they could education their young.

Writing to the Sydney congregation to request help in identifying a suitable candidate for the rabbinical post in Melbourne, Asher Hyman Hart stressed how important it was that the individual be qualified to teach Hebrew and English, 'next he will be required to act as a reader'.[31] With a Jewish population in the entire colony numbering 100–200, in October 1847 the Melbourne Hebrew Congregation appointed Walter Lindenthal its first teacher and reader, with the hope that a successful school would be established. Lindenthal was then a resident of Sydney, where he had advertised as a professor of Hebrew and German, including placing advertisements in German in the Sydney papers.[32]

It was Lindenthal as acting reader who delivered the sermon at the consecration of the synagogue in March 1848.[33] By May 1848, the Victorian and Tasmanian papers reported that Jonas Lincoln, the son of Isaac Lazarus Lincoln, had completed his bar mitzvah. Noteworthy in the report was that Lincoln's Hebrew education had only commenced in the previous two months, following the arrival of Lindenthal as teacher.[34] Lindenthal left for Tasmania in September 1848, opening a school and holding public lectures in Hobart. By June 1849 he was advertising for a vessel to charter to Shanghai and Batavia, and by May he had been arrested in India, accused of debts in association with the purchase of antiquities for the firm of Moses, Levey and Co of London.[35]

In 1855, following the influx of immigrants to the gold rush, a committee consisting of Moses Rintel, Michael Cashmore, Elias Ellis, Isaac Hart, Eliezer Levi Montefiore, Nahum Salamon, Solomon Iffla, Solomon Phillips and Simon Hamburger advertised the opening of a school in Melbourne, to ensure that Jewish youth could 'not only obtain a liberal English education comprising all those branches taught in the highest establishments, but also instruction in the tenants and principles of the Jewish faith and a thorough knowledge of Hebrew'.[36] The Melbourne Hebrew Congregation, however, refused them the use of a room for the school. Under the education acts, clergy had the right to attend Common Schools to provide religious instruction and Moses Rintel and later his successor Emanuel Myers offered tuition to Jewish students at the Model School.[37]

With changes to the education acts and the founding of the denominational school boards, money was available for Jewish education and the West Melbourne Grammar School was founded under the auspices of the Melbourne Hebrew Congregation. In 1860 this became the Common School 1880 and, following the Education Act of 1862, it was placed in the same position as other denominations, receiving grants in aid from the government. Further, Jewish interests were recognised with the appointment of Isaac Hart as the Jewish representative on the Education Board, enabling him to oversee the community's interests.

This act required a minimum attendance of sixty students, and throughout the school's existence, the number waxed and waned, at times rising to nearly 200 while at others falling below the requirement, as the quality of education, competition from other educational establishments, its funding and the residential location of the community changed. Students were not exclusively Jewish and were drawn from afar a field as Carlton, Collingwood, Hotham, Emerald Hill, Fitzroy and Richmond.[38] The importance of Jewish education for the community was recognised, and the papers and community struggled to resolve the issue. Jewish education was offered in the Sabbath Schools of the two other metropolitan synagogues, while a number of private tutors were also teaching male and female students in their homes.

A number of the private schools also regularly advertised in the Jewish press, offering students specific Jewish subjects. In 1872 Scotch College catered for thirty Jewish boys, who were taught Hebrew (rather inadequately, it was reported) and were excused from New Testament classes, only studying the 'Hebrew Bible'.[39] Scotch was considered a suitable school for Jewish youth for its educational excellence, but primarily for its location in the heart of the wealthy Jewish neighbourhood of East Melbourne. A number of other schools also advertised Hebrew classes, with Maurice Brodzky teaching Hebrew in several, including the coeducational Fitzroy Secular Academy, which found no contradiction in offering such classes, and Turret House Commercial College, also in East Melbourne.

Julia Fama opened a school in Napier Street, Fitzroy for 'young ladies of the Jewish Faith' teaching among other subjects Hebrew and religion, while she also taught at the East Melbourne Hebrew Congregation's school. Wesley College and the Church of England Grammar School, which apparently did not cater specifically for Jewish students, still thought it worth their while to advertise in the Jewish press. Jewish literature, religious tracts, prayer books and Judaica could all be purchased in Melbourne from booksellers such as Joseph Jacobs, in Russell Street.

The issue of free secular and state education was one that occupied the attention of a number of Jewish politicians: Charles Dyte, whose focus was free education, with an emphasis on access to self-education through public libraries and who sat as a representative on the Royal Commission on Education; Emanuel Steinfeld, who was able to apply his international connections, undertaking research and providing advice as a member of a Royal Commission on Technical Education; and Edward Cohen, a passionate advocate for secular education.

London-born Cohen was a major figure in mid-century Melbourne. A city councillor and the first Jewish mayor of Melbourne while also holding a seat in state parliament, he maintained various business interests in banking, real estate, insurance and grazing. He had arrived in New South Wales following the transportation of his father, Henry Cohen.[40] Henry Cohen was an ostensibly prosperous clothing retailer from Paddington, London, who claimed a turnover of £4000–£5000 per annum. In 1833 Henry was convicted of passing forged promissory notes, his fourth such offence, and was sentenced to fourteen years transportation to New South Wales.[41]

Like many Jewish families, Henry's wife, Elizabeth Simmons, chose to join her husband, sailing with nine of their children and arriving on a separate ship the same year. The Cohen family prospered in New South Wales, developing shipping and retail enterprises. In 1842 their eldest son, Edward, seeing the possibilities of the newly settled district of Port Phillip, relocated to Melbourne, where he established a firm of auctioneers and tea merchants and soon became involved in politics. In 1871 the *Australian Israelite* would describe Cohen as 'the public Jew of Victoria, par excellence ... Genial in manner, of an affable disposition, and easily accessible to all persons of all creeds and climes, Mr Cohen as a public man, is the central figure around which our community revolves.'[42]

Implemented first in Victoria, free, compulsory and secular education became an important reform movement across the Australian colonies.[43] It was considered that universal literacy would solve a number of social issues: improving economic prospects for children; encouraging vocational training; and reducing crime. For those interested in furthering democracy, education was essential in the development of active citizenship, and the study of history formed a central element in this ideal. For a new and emerging society, it was recognised that an educated populace was important for efficient government, national prosperity and to alleviate child labour.[44] The expense of a passage to Victoria and the limited criteria for assisted immigration ensured that those settling in Victoria, generally had a basic level of education.

In 1867 a royal commission was established to examine alternatives for education reform and to assess the structural arrangements of the education system. The report recognised the advantage of the educational standard of the population, expressing the belief that as educated parents they would be conducive to educating their children. Concern was raised that without suitable and effective educational opportunities, subsequent generations would not have the same levels of literacy as their parents. 'The comparatively high degree of education of the present adult class', argued the royal commissioners in 1867, 'seems to make the adoption of such means less difficult than it would be in the mother country, or than it may yet become in this colony, if we do not speedily turn our present opportunities to account'.[45] To ensure efficient learning, stress was placed on regular attendance, but achievement of this goal was difficult to enforce.

Although the Jewish community aimed at a combined Jewish and secular education for its children, free and secular education was judged as a way of safeguarding basic learning. From a religious perspective, secular education without a syllabus dominated by Christianity provided a guarantee of independence, ensuring the recognition of the pluralism inherent in Victoria. In its research phase, the royal commission consulted the Jewish community, with the Reverend Ornstein of the Melbourne Hebrew Congregation acting as an expert witness. Ornstein had considerable experience as an educator, having previously held the positions of principal of the Birmingham Jewish School and assistant principal at the London Free School. He argued for a separation of secular and religious education, emphasising the importance of shared community values based on common ideals of morality. These were universal values, at variance with religious instruction, which was specific.

> Morality is the laws which govern us according to our duty to our fellow men; but religious instruction would teach us a different thing ... I think the same laws of morality hold good, whatever a man's religious belief may be. I think that this is the great point that should be observed. A pupil may be taught to be moral without having any sectarian differences imparted to him.[46]

Five years later the issue was still unsolved. Cohen was a vocal and keen supporter of secular education, as a social responsibility and as a pragmatic response to the alternative of an education system defined and controlled by religious partisanship. Regarding religious education as a private matter, he deemed education to be an issue of justice in a diverse community and as a way of protecting freedom of religion. As he asserted in a parliamentary debate:

> the state shall teach all those who require teaching, and who can't afford to pay for it, and it leaves those who want dogma, and can

afford to pay for it, to do so. All sections of the community will be able to go to the schools provided by the State, because those schools will be completely unsectarian. What religion would the honourable members have taught in schools? Who shall say which religion is right? Who shall say that this religion is truth, and that every other man's religion is in error? It is a subject which people can no more agree here than they can in any other country.[47]

In his role as an architect of public policy, Cohen openly used the historic perceptions of Judaism and Judaism's relationship to other parts of the community to influence his fellow parliamentarians, hoping to avoid the mistakes of the past in shaping a modern society:

I assert that, whenever a church has had power in any State, it has been persecuting and intolerant to all opposed to it. I can speak on this subject freely … I am descendant from a race that has been persecuted more than any other race under the sun. And for what reason? Because we chose to worship God after our own hearts, according to the laws of our fathers. This being a new and free country, let us leave behind us all the superstitious nonsense of the old world. Let us meet here on common ground.[48]

In a report of the debates over the Jewish School, Cohen is quoted at length elaborating on these views: 'It was quite proper for us, as Jews to wish for a distinct school, and it is quite proper that we should have it … we should put our hands in our pockets and pay for it ourselves.'[49] He asked rhetorically, 'were we not satisfied with some amount of liberty as was enjoyed by our fellow citizens, or did we wish to return to our ghettos?' He stated that he 'has no other home and had no desire for any other than Victoria' and that he considered it his duty to serve his co-religionists.[50] In Cohen's view, to protect the secular basis of the Victorian education system, the community assumed a monitoring role.

Henri J. Hart was appointed to the school board for the Bourke and Lonsdale wards, where he objected to the books issued for the Common Schools as being against the principles of secular education, arguing that 'it was unjust as well as a flagrant violation of the liberty of conscience to compel those who did not profess Christianity' to have to use the books prescribed.[51] The Reverend Ornstein similarly took a public stance, writing to the minister for education to draw attention to an inconsistency in the text books being used in Victorian schools, which he believed did not accord with this secular position.[52] The staunch beliefs and the active championing by a number of

Jewish politicians reveal a confidence of the community in exerting their needs and opinions, outside the Christian norm yet within the dominant Christian culture of colonial Victoria.

Following the introduction of the Education Act of 1872, the Common School was placed in a difficult position, the Jewish community having argued persuasively for free, secular and compulsory education. But if the Melbourne Hebrew Congregation wished its school to remain a denominational school, its grant aid would be lost, creating further destabilisation, or alternatively, the requirement that Hebrew should be taught as an extra fee-paying subject. In 1873 the school was forced to forego government support when it re-formed as the Melbourne Hebrew School, funded by a combination of fees, subscriptions and synagogue subsidies.[53]

Taxation Reform

Where Cohen was able to shape his society through education reform, the next generation of politicians were also actively engaged in contemporary political issues. The two German-born parliamentarians unfortunately did not live long after their respective elections, but each was influential outside elected office and brought new and innovative ideas from their place of birth.

Max Hirsch, Land Values Taxation in Practice, 1910, University of Melbourne Archives

Max Hirsch, perhaps the most internationally influential Victorian Jewish politician of the nineteenth century, is now largely forgotten. Hirsch held office only briefly when he was elected to the Victorian Parliament in 1902 for the rural seat of Mandurang. He resigned the following year to contest the seat of Wimmera in the federal election, at which he was defeated by 160 votes by another Jewish politician, the protectionist Pharez Phillips. But it was through his political activism and writings that Hirsch's local and international reputation was made.

Hirsch's Australian work was responsive to the social and political conditions of the 1890s. The speculation of the land boom had been funded through extensive and unsustainable borrowings, and the subsequent financial crash led to a severe depression, with Melbourne experiencing particularly high unemployment.[54] The separate colonies had been founded in different economic and social conditions and governed by separate legislatures, each with its own tax base. Land distribution was an issue in many of the colonies, with property having been initially deemed by grant or acquired by wealthy 'squatters' who secured vast tracks of arable land, leased at low rates from the crown, before purchasing it later in the century.

As a result, later settlers were largely excluded from land ownership in the most fertile parts of the colony. At an economic level, many considered that trade was hampered by the many taxes and tariffs due on goods shipped between the colonies. Taxation and its corollary protectionism became one of the principal debates surrounding Federation, although politicians such as Nathaniel Levi had argued as early as 1870 that tariff protection hindered trade.[55] Two factional issues characterised politics: the 'protectionist' landed and small industrial lobby on one side and, on the other, the more radical who considered taxation and land reform imperative to a fair and functioning society. As depression struck in the early 1890s, these issues came into stark relief.

Two organisations formed the most radical elements of these debates: the Free Trade League and the Single Tax League, which had similar but slightly differing reform agendas, both focused on taxation of land. The Free Trade League sought the removal of restrictive tariffs and duties, particularly those related to manufacturing and trade; abolition of special privileges accorded to landowners in the recovery of rents; reform of insolvency laws and the federation of the colonies.[56] The Single Tax League was more narrowly focused, takings its lead from the American single taxationist Henry George, seeing reform of society and the economy in the removal of all duties and tariffs and the introduction of a single tax on land. The Single Tax League perceived that the depression resulted from land speculation, which it blamed for an increase in property prices. The league was supportive of Australian federation, which it considered a 'triumph over protection'.[57] There was crossover not only of philosophical views between these two organisations, but of leadership as well. Cologne-born Max Hirsch headed the Single Tax League and was vice-president of the Free Trade League.

Hirsch had studied commerce at the University of Berlin before gaining a transnational perspective through his career as an international trader in Germany, England, Russia, Central Asia, North Africa, and Ceylon.[58] He first visited Australia in 1879, before settling in Melbourne in 1890, where he became passionately involved in radical taxation issues. Hirsch believed the benefits from single taxation included the elimination of land speculation, which would lead to full land utilisation; reduction in rent and building spec-ulation; increases in wages resulting from the expansion of effective demand; stimulation of production, and full employment; a decrease in class divisions; and the reform of working conditions. These changes would stem the flow of people from the country to the city and generally result in greater social justice, he argued.[59] In his book *Protection in Victoria*, Hirsch argued that protec-tionism decreased wealth by diminishing the purchasing power of wages, created debt and did nothing to dissuade emigration:[60]

> Protection obstructs the production of wealth and alters the dis-tribution of wealth unfavourably to the interests of the working classes ... But a system of free trade, the removal of the veil which hides from workers the fact that they pay the bulk of all taxes, will teach workers the true theory of taxation and will cause them to place taxation where it belongs on the rental value of land ... not created by any one individual, but by the community as a whole.[61]

Hirsch's political awakening has been attributed to his experience in Ceylon during the 1870s, where he was incensed by the unfairness of a 'paddy tax'.[62] On returning to England, and with assistance from the Cobden Club, Hirsch prompted a resolution in the House of Commons supporting the abolition of this tax.[63]

Contemporary newspaper coverage of Hirsch's many public speeches makes no mention of his Judaism, but he assumes Judaeo-Christian metaphors to convince his audience of his views. A report in a regional newspaper describes at length a speech Hirsch delivered:

> He was one of those who believed that God made the world; and had therefore to show them that God did not make the world and its luxuries and comforts for one class of men; that he did not intend that opportunity to live in contentment should be

monopolised by a few, while the many should toil in penury to supply those who did not work with opulence and wasteful luxury.[64]

Hirsch's writing was widely circulated during his lifetime and following his early death on a trip to Vladivostok. This stemmed from the number of his public addresses that were reported in the press, as a correspondent to the British Board of Trade, and through the Max Hirsch Commemoration Essay prize, established after his death as an annual honour to his legacy of economic thought. As an economic theorist his influence was extraordinary and the approximately twenty books he published in his short time in Victoria and in Germany were distributed in universities as far afield as Japan.[65]

Hirsch was not the only Victorian Jewish parliamentarian involved in these issues. By 1894 there were eight sitting Jewish Victorian parliamentarians, of whom six were identified by the single tax journal the *Beacon* as publically supporting free trade and taxation reform, and of these, four were further identified as supporting a land tax.[66] Single taxation has been described 'as a "ghetto" for Jewish radicalism'.[67] This interest could perhaps be better explained as the response of urban-based politicians, reflecting not just a pragmatic and nuanced response to the important economic and political issues of the day, but importantly, a response of urban Jews to an issue of social justice, taking a lead from the fundamental premise of *tsedakah* of social justice and charity.

Federation

Silesian-born Emanuel Steinfeld came from a family with an extended cosmopolitan perspective. He was a cousin of Emanuel Deutsch, an orientalist at the British Museum, and of Emin Pasher (Isaak Eduard Schnitzer), governor of the province of Equatoria on the upper Nile. As a nineteen-year-old, Steinfeld left home to work for a firm of German wine merchants in London, which in 1853 sent him to Victoria as a partner. He later established a substantial furniture-manufacturing and importing business in Melbourne and in the goldfields city of Ballarat, before entering the political arena.

Steinfeld displayed the complexity of identity that this community exhibited, simultaneously proudly German, British and Jewish, but above all an Australian patriot. Maintaining international personal, familial and commercial bonds, he travelled extensively in Europe, Britain and America. In 1872, on the eve of one such departure, the councillors of East Ballarat, where he had thrice been mayor, held a valedictory dinner in his honour. There he observed that as 'as an Australian ... [if] he could in any way benefit the colony ... this would be his aim, object and ambition'.[68] This political reception was followed by one at the synagogue, of which he had been a founder and board member, and a third by the German Liedertafel, a group of German choral singers.

Victorian Chamber of Manufactures, election material in support of Emanuel Steinfeld, 1887, Private Collection

The German Liedertafel … proceeded to the residence of Mr Emanuel Steinfeld, Victoria street, in order, to pay their musical regards previous to that gentleman's departure from Ballarat on his proposed European tour. The members of the Liedertafel, on arriving, entered the garden of the residence, and lighted their torches. Thereupon, they proceeded to sing several songs having reference to the nationality of the party, and the person honored. At the close of one of these songs Mr Steinfeld came forward and, in his native language, thanked the party for the honor done, and invited them to partake of what was prepared in an adjacent verandah … Considerable excitement occurred without, by reason of a large crowd which had assembled in consequence of a publicity having been given to the proceedings which the originators never desired.[69]

The Victorian Government made good use of Steinfeld's international connections and frequent travel by appointing him to research economic and educational issues and to advise on a diverse range of topics. These included technical education; German immigration; forest prevention and the effectiveness of Victoria's representation at the Vienna Exhibition. His views, opinions and observations were widely reported in the press.[70]

Although repeatedly asserting his loyalty to Britain and to Australia, Steinfeld maintained a strong German identity and stressed the close relationship between Britain and his homeland: 'There are a great many Germans in the colony, and it is pleasing for them to know that the mother of the future Emperor was the Crown Princess of England and he was sure he was right in saying that Queen Victoria had no more loyal subjects than the German colonists of Victoria.'[71]

Australian unification was to be Steinfeld's defining contribution, He presented his arguments publicly in his many reports and speeches, including during his brief parliamentary career, but principally through his presidency of the Chamber of Manufacturers. Over a twenty-year period he agitated for Federation, culminating in his instigation and chairing of a number of influential intercolonial free-trade conferences. Convinced of the advances that unification and economic development had brought to Germany, he presented this as an example that should be emulated in his new home. In his many speeches at these conferences, he argued for a German approach, with an Australian *Zollverein* model of customs union, consistently citing recent German history. In 1887 and in 1888 he compared recent German history to contemporary Australian politics to provide a framework for his views:

> It appears to me that New South Wales and Victoria are like the two Powers on the European Continent—viz., Austria and Prussia. Austria was a power in Germany before Prussia was heard of, but no sooner did Prussia become a power than Austria evinced jealousy and bitter feelings against her.[72]

The historic restrictions on occupation and land ownership of European Jewry resulted in different priorities to the dominant Anglo focus on land ownership and primary production. As a manufacturer, Steinfeld expressed this economic conflict in his arguments for free trade between the Australian colonies. 'Unfortunately the tendency amongst agriculturalists and pastoralists has been to decry all manufacturers and to confine attention to the acquirement of land.'[73] His rhetoric also recognised the diversity of the colonies as a characteristic that could foster unity:

We came to the Colonies long ago, and have done what we could to advance the interests of the land of our adoption, and have many of us now grown-up families, to whom we desire to hand over a heritage for which they will be grateful to us. But this inheritance will not be complete unless we hand over a united Australia ... Let us have in these broad lands no petty German States ideas. (Hear, hear.) We have been told that we are as yet too young to unite. I maintain that so far from that being an obstacle it is an advantage; and also that we can the better unite, because, whether we are English, Scotch, or German, we are still of one race ... I am an old Colonist, and my sympathies are all Australian. I am entirely an Australian. Every two or three years I visit the old world, and I am pleased to go, but far more pleased to come back ... Australia is my star, and to her I devote my whole existence! I hope to live for the good of my country.[74]

On the International Stage

Many of the international networks of the community were applied to colonial development, with the Jewish community prominent in the representation of foreign governments at an honorary consular level, whether from an individual's place of birth or another location. Jews represented Prussia, America, Denmark, Italy, the United States and Japan. Some, such as Jacob Cohn, representing Denmark, or Moritz Michaelis, acting consul for Prussia, held these posts with some connection to their place of birth, while others were appointed because of their international experience and networks. The irony for Michaelis was that in Prussia it would have been almost impossible for a Jew to have a diplomatic posting, while as an Australian Jew he could represent the kingdom.[75]

The international networks of the community were applied in other areas of colonial development. The somewhat peripatetic early life of New York–born Alexander Marks perhaps prepared him for his life as a trader in Asia and as the long-standing consul to Japan. His entrepreneurial father, Casper Marks, was born in Pest, and migrated to New York, where he married and began a family.

Leaving America, the family travelled to Manila before arriving in Sydney in 1842, where Casper began business as a dealer, selling clothing, tea, sugar, American pork and beef, but almost immediately he was declared insolvent and all his household furniture was sold.[76] He was charged with 'fraudulent insolvency' when it was discovered that he had concealed two

sovereigns prior to sailing to Bombay. The family then spent several years travelling between Sydney, Melbourne, Tasmania, Manila and California.

In 1851 Casper Marks's irregular business practices again caught up with
him in Honolulu, when he and his sons were charged in a case of conspiracy
over the alleged sale of gold dust, although Marks claimed that he was in
Sydney at the time.[77] By 1858 he was resident in St Kilda and in the 1860s he
was listed as the principal investor of the North Mount Useful Quartz Mining
Company at Donnelly's Creek, and could afford a £5 donation to the
Melbourne Hebrew Congregation.[78] During the 1860s the Marks's sons
moved to Yokohama, where they established Messrs Marks Bros, traded to
Guam and across the Pacific. They also provided Casper with stock for a new
business venture in Sydney, a shop in King Street specialising in Japanese
goods.

The retail side of this enterprise was not successful, and within months
the whole stock was auctioned. The sons' Japanese trading arm appears,
however, to have prospered, and was maintained until Alexander's death in
1919. International trade was not only financially hazardous, but could also be
personally perilous. Such was the case for the Marks family, when in 1871 two
of Casper Marks's sons, Henry and Lawrence, along with Samuel Benjamin,
were drowned on board the *Julia* in a typhoon off the cost of Guam while on
a business trip.[79]

In 1890 Alexander Marks's long-term connection to Japan resulted in his
appointment as the Japanese consul. Interviewed in 1902, he described having
spent forty years in the country and subsequently revisited it every eighteen
months to keep abreast of the current situation.[80] His experience trading and
representing Japanese interests gave him a political perspective that was at odds
with that of the establishment. Marks was strongly opposed to the White
Australia policy, and actively supported Japanese immigration and investment,
in particular, in a proposed agricultural investment in northern Australia.[81]

Along with his co-religionist and politician Ephraim Laman Zox,
Alexander Marks was appointed a commissioner for the 1880 Melbourne
International Exhibition and his connections to Japan facilitated participation
and a significant financial contribution from the Japanese Government for this
event.[82] His international perspective embraced issues of interest to the Jewish
community. After consultation with the Western Australian minister for lands
he promoted a proposal to purchase tracts of Western Australia for the settlement of Russian Jewish refugees.[83]

An international perspective could flow not only from the colonies but
also towards the metropole. This can be seen in the careers of members of the
Phillips family, who produced a generation of high-achieving cousins:
Constance Ellis, the first female Doctor of Medicine from the University of

Melbourne and a senior medical officer and pathologist at the Queen Victoria Hospital; Isabella Phillips, a surgeon at the Melbourne Hospital and the hospital's first female superintendent; the artist Emanuel Phillips Fox; and Marion Phillips, British social reformer and politician.

Marion's and Emanuel's influence was on the international stage, Emanuel as an artist in Paris and Marion as a politician in Britain. Marion was educated alongside her female cousins at the Presbyterian Ladies College and the University of Melbourne, and her intellectual and scholastic abilities were recognised: she won a Wyselaskie Scholarship in Political Economy, the Cobden Medal and a scholarship to complete a PhD at the London School of Economics. There she wrote a thesis entitled 'A Colonial Autocracy: New South Wales under Governor Macquarie 1810–1821', receiving another award, this time the Hutchinson Medal.[84]

Marion Phillips, Labour History Archive and Study Centre,
People's History Museum, Manchester

In 1906 she began her working life as a research assistant for Beatrice Webb on the Royal Commission of Enquiry into the Working of the Poor

Laws. The poverty she witnessed further galvanised her political views, resulting in a lifelong involvement in British Labour politics and social reform, particularly as it affected women and children. It has been argued that her greatest contribution to Labour policy was her attempt to correlate the needs of housewives and children to socialist philosophy. She was aware of the dichotomy in the fight for women's wage equality at a time when men were arguing for a living wage at a level that would support a wife and children at home. She perceived the need for family planning, a nutritional diet and labour-saving assistance. She believed they could be achieved through the provision of municipal laundries, restaurants and communal kitchens and by careful planning of housing designed to meet minimum standards.

Phillips's influence was wide and she took on many official responsibilities, including as secretary to the Women's Labour League. During the First World War she was a member of the War Workers' National Emergency Committee, secretary of the Joint Standing Committee of Industrial Women's Organisations, while her position as chief women's officer for the Labour Party gave her third place on the party's official letterhead. This political activity culminated in 1929, when she was elected Member for Sunderland.[85] Phillips became the first Australian woman to win a seat in a national parliament, and only one of two to have been elected to the House of Commons.

Until the graduation of Melbourne-born and -educated Felix Meyer in the 1880s, the limitations on Jews entering the major universities of England resulted in only two Jewish doctors in Melbourne: Jamaican-born and Glasgow-trained Solomon Iffla, an active member of Melbourne's scientific community, and German-born Bernard Lilienfeld. Lilienfeld was active in Jewish and wider German and medical areas, as honorary physician to both the Melbourne Hospital and the Eye and Ear Hospital, while also acting as the medical officer for the Hebrew Ladies Benevolent Society, secretary to the German Society and honorary secretary to the Medical Society of Victoria. Their younger colleague Louis Henry represents the shaping of Melbourne through his international connections. Henry, born in Melbourne to a German mother, was educated at Scotch College, but received his medical training in Heidelberg and his doctorate in Würzburg, followed by employment in hospitals in Berlin, Vienna, Dublin, Manchester and London.[86] On his return to Melbourne he applied to join the Medical Society of Victoria, the professional association for Victorian doctors, but was black-balled.

As the practice of medicine became more scientifically based, the medical community witnessed a period of turmoil and personal and professional rivalries.[87] This culminated in Henry's ostracism, which incensed his friend and colleague Dr James Neild, then honorary secretary of the society, lecturer in medicine and one of Melbourne's most eminent doctors. Together they decided to apply to London to establish a branch of the British Medical Association as an alternative representation for Victorian doctors.

Louis Henry sailed to England and secured authority for this venture. He returned in 1879 and established the Melbourne branch with Neild as president and Henry as its first secretary, before becoming president himself in 1886 (followed by Felix Meyer in 1894).[88] The association's aims were the advancement of medicine, ensuring best practice and the professional conduct of doctors as well as overseeing their appointments to public institutions, while the medical society saw its strength as enabling international communication for the medical profession.[89]

In promoting their cause, Henry argued that the British association was superior to its Victorian rival, as it provided a network of more than 9000 affiliates and 'in respect to social power, scientific progress, and moral advancement' it offered its members 'the advantage of mutual communication and support, through the columns of the British Medical Journal'.[90] Forging a link with the Royal Society, whose rooms were used for meetings, the association also took on a number of public causes, the first of which was the conditions at the Kew Lunatic Asylum. The two professional bodies operated in parallel until 1906, when they were amalgamated to form the British Medical Association, Victoria Branch.

Victoria's gold rush and the wealthy economy it produced brought many from across the globe. Although British laws were transferred to the Australian colonies, their adaptation by each colonial legislature reflected their respective and evolving place. The more welcoming attitudes of Melbourne enabled participation by a diverse citizenry in the city's economic and social development. The growth of the English-speaking diaspora extended their Judaism from its traditional European view to one that encompassed the Australian colonies. Isolated from large Jewish centres and distant from the authority of the chief rabbi, Melbourne Jewry evolved as a reconceptualisation of Anglo-Jewry in an Australian context, one that sought Jewish solutions to the realities of life in a new colony. As educated citizens they created a community reflective of their values, and participated in a society where their international and transnational experiences could be harnessed to assist in Melbourne's development and that of an environment far larger than the city itself. In this context and relative freedom, Jews endeavoured to embody both Jewish and colonial life, seeing little opposition between the two.

Notes

1   *Age*, 12 February 1875, 3.
2   Jacob Katz, *Exclusiveness and Tolerance: Studies in Jewish–Gentile Relations in Medieval and Modern Times* (Oxford University Press, Oxford, 1961), 11.

3   Cecil Roth, *A History of the Jews in England* (Clarendon Press, Oxford, 1964), 247.
4   New South Wales Parliament, 'An Act to Simplify the Oaths of Qualification for Office', 1857; Parliament of Victoria, 'An Act to Assimilate and Simplify the Oaths of Qualification for Office', 1858.
5   *Jewish Chronicle*, 16 March 1860, 7.
6   *Jewish Chronicle*, 31 January 1862, 6.
7   Weston Bate, *Victorian Gold Rushes* (McPhee Gribble, Fitzroy, 1988), 26–7.
8   Andrew Thompson, *The Empire Strikes Back? The Impact of Imperialism on Britain from the Mid-Nineteenth Century* (Pearson Longman, Harlow, 2005), 29.
9   Graeme Davison, 'Gold-Rush Melbourne', in Ian McCalman, Alexander Cook and Andrew Reeves (eds), *Gold: Forgotten Histories and Lost Objects of Australia* (Cambridge University Press, Cambridge, 2001), 56.
10   Roth, *A History of the Jews in England*, 252–3.
11   *Argus*, 11 January 1848, 4.
12   Geulah Solomon, 'Benjamin, Sir Benjamin (1834–1905)', *Australian Dictionary of Biography* (National Centre for Biography, Australian National University, Canberra, 1969), accessed 6 June 2013, <http://adb.anu.edu.au/biography/benjamin-sir-benjamin-2972>.
13   *Hebrew Standard of Australasia*, 17 February 1922, 11; *Prahran Telegraph*, 5 May 1917, 6; *Prahran Telegraph*, 2 September 1916, 4; *Argus*, 23 September 1933, 24.
14   Enid Campbell, 'Oaths and Affirmations of Public Office', *Monash University Law Review* 25, no. 1 (1999), 141.
15   Thomas A. Weber, 'The Origins of the Victorian Magistracy', *Australian New Zealand Journal of Criminology* 13, no. 2 (1980), 142.
16   William Irvine and David Wanliss, *Justices of the Peace* (Charles F. Maxwell, Melbourne, 1899), 4.
17   J. Lowndes, 'The Australian Magistracy: From Justices of the Peace to Judges and Beyond', *Australia Law Journal* 74, no. 9 (2000), 3.
18   Hilary Golder and Ian Pike, *High and Responsible Office: A History of the NSW Magistracy* (Sydney University Press, Sydney, 1991), 66.
19   *Jewish Herald*, 2 May 1884, 12.
20   ibid.
21   *Melbourne Times*, 4 December 1842, 3; *Melbourne Daily News*, 3 October 1850, 3; *Argus*, 31 August 1858, 3.
22   *Melbourne Daily News*, 24 August 1850, 3.
23   *Jewish Herald*, 2 May 1884, 12.
24   Victoria. Registrar-General's Office, *Statistics for the Colony of Victoria (Blue Book)* (John Ferres, Government Printer, Melbourne, 1887); Blue Books for the Colony of Victoria (John Ferres, Government Printer, Melbourne, 1868).
25   Todd M. Endelman, *The Jews of Britain, 1656 to 2000* (University of California Press, Berkeley, 2002), 248.
26   Michael Clark, 'Jewish Identity in British Politics: The Case of the First Jewish MPs, 1858–1887', *Jewish Social Studies* 13, no. 2 (2007), 96.
27   Edward Sweetman, Charles R. Long and John Smyth, *A History of State Education in Victoria* (published for Education Dept. of Victoria by Frank Critchley Parker, Melbourne, 1922), 1.
28   L.J. Blake, *Vision and Realisation, a Centenary History of State Education in Victoria* (Education Department of Victoria, Melbourne, 1973), 25.
29   Stuart Macintyre, *A Concise History of Australia,* (Cambridge University Press, Port Melbourne, 2004), 116.
30   *Jewish Chronicle*, 2 November 1855, 365.

31 As quoted in Joseph Aron and Judy Arndt, *The Enduring Remnant:The First 150 Years of the Melbourne Hebrew Congregation 1841–1991* (Melbourne University Press, Carlton, 1992), 282.

32 *Sydney Morning Herald*, 4 September 1847, 1; *Sydney Morning Herald*, 7 September 1847, 1.

33 *Sydney Morning Herald*, 25 March 1848, 2.

34 *Cornwall Chronicle*, 17 May 1848, 3.

35 *Peoples Advocate and New South Wales Vindicator*, 30 June 1849, 11; *Launceston Examiner*, 8 May 1850, 6.

36 *Argus*, 24 July 1855, 5.

37 Geulah Solomon, 'Minority Education in a Free Society: A Community History of Jewish Education in New South Wales and Victoria, 1788–1920', (PhD thesis, Faculty of Education, Monash University, 1972), 404.

38 *Australian Israelite*, 6 June 1873, 4.

39 *Australian Israelite*, 22 November 1872, 2; *Australian Israelite*, 20 December 1872, 7.

40 *Advertiser*, 17 April 1893, 7.

41 Old Bailey trials online, trial of Henry Cohen, 1833, <t18330516-131>.

42 *Australasian Israelite*, 29 December 1871, 4.

43 Alan Barcan, *A History of Australian Education* (Oxford University Press, Melbourne, 1980), 130–1.

44 Parliament of Victoria, Legislative Assembly, Debates, 2 October 1872, 1628.

45 Parliament of Victoria, 'Report of the Royal Commission appointed by His Excellency to Enquire into and Report upon the operation of the system of Public Education together with minutes of evidence and Appendices, Presented to both Houses of Parliament by his Excellency on Command', 1867, 13.

46 ibid., 235.

47 Parliament of Victoria, Legislative Assembly, Debates, 3 October 1872, 1673.

48 ibid., 1673-1674.

49 *Australian Israelite*, 7 March 1873, 7.

50 *Australian Israelite*, 7 March 1873.

51 *Australian Israelite*, 17 October 1873, 66.

52 *Jewish Chronicle*, 28 November 1873, 583.

53 *Argus*, 29 December 1873, 4.

54 Airlie Worrall, 'Single Tax and Free Trade:Victoria, 1890–1900', (Honours thesis, School of Historical and Philosophical Studies, University of Melbourne, 1975), 9.

55 Fredman, Lionel E, 'Some Jewish Politicians', *Australian Jewish Historical Society, Journal and Proceedings* IV, no. III (1955), 97–115.

56 Free Trade, Platform adopted at the General Conference of delegates held in Melbourne on 28 August 1894, in the *Beacon* (no date), but appendixed to Worrell, 'Single Tax and Free Trade'.

57 Craufurd D.W. Goodwin, *Economic Enquiry in Australia* (Duke University Commonwealth Studies Center by Duke University Press, Durham, 1966), 59.

58 Bruce Scates, *A New Australia: Citizenship, Radicalism and the First Republic* (Cambridge University Press, Cambridge, 1997), 17; *Argus*, 5 March 1909, 4.

59 Max Hirsch, *Democracy Versus Socialism, a Critical Examination of Socialism as a Remedy for Social Injustice and an Exposition of the Single Tax Doctrine* (Macmillan, New York, 1901), 398–411.

60 Hirsch, *Protection in Victoria: An Inquiry into the Influence of Protection on the Social & Economic Condition of the People* (Echo Publishing, Melbourne, 1891), 5, 21, 27.

61 ibid., 29.

62 Goodwin, *Economic Enquiry in Australia*, 119.

63   *Argus*, 5 March 1909, 4.
64   *Wodonga and Towong Sentinel*, 1 February 1895, 2–3.
65   Hilary L. Rubinstein, *The Jews in Australia: A Thematic History* (William Heinemann Australia, Port Melbourne, 1991), 391.
66   *Beacon* II, no. 6, October 1894.
67   Scates, *A New Australia*, 23.
68   *Ballarat Courier*, 29 October 1872, 3.
69   *Ballarat Star*, 2 November 1872, 2.
70   *Ballarat Star*, 23 September 1873, 3; *Argus*, 24 September 1873, 1.
71   *Ballarat Star*, 13 January 1872, 3.
72   Australasian Commercial Congress, *Report of Proceedings of the Congress of the Chambers of Commerce of the Australasian Colonies, Held in Melbourne on the 31st October, 1st and 2nd November, 1888* (Melbourne, 1889), xxxi.
73   Intercolonial Free Trade Conference, *Report of the Proceedings at the Intercolonial Free Trade Conference of Delegates from the Chambers of Manufactures in the Various Australian Colonies Held at Adelaide, South Australia, 5th to 7th October, 1887*, 63.
74   ibid., 92.
75   Peter Pulzer, *Jews and the German State: The Political History of a Minority, 1848–1933* (Blackwell, Oxford, 1992), 19.
76   *Sydney Morning Herald*, 22 July 1842, 4.
77   *Launceston Examiner*, 23 July 1851, 474; *Sydney Morning Herald*, 1 July 1851, 3.
78   *Gippsland Times*, 11 October 1865, 4; *Argus*, 18 June 1866, 3.
79   *Australian Israelite*, 1 September 1871, 4–5.
80   *Table Talk*, 13 March 1902, 12.
81   *Richmond River Express and Casino Kyogle Advertiser*, 30 May 1905, 4.
82   *Australasian*, 17 January 1880, 21.
83   *South-Western News*, 26 April 1907, 2.
84   Marian Groronwy-Roberts, *A Woman of Vision, a Life of Marion Phillips, MP* (Bridge Books, Wrexham, 2000), 19, 23.
85   Beverley Kingston, 'Yours very Truly, Marion Phillips', in Ann Curthoys, Susan Eade and Peter Spearritt (eds), *Women at Work* (Australian Society for the Study of Labour History, Canberra, 1975), 129.
86   *Table Talk*, 30 June 1904, 13.
87   For a detailed discussion see Harold Love, *James Edward Neild: Victorian Virtuoso* (Melbourne University Press, Carlton, 1989).
88   Gerald Segal, 'Request for a Grant for the Erection of a Monument and Restoration of the Grave of Dr James Neild', *Argus*, 1 September 1937, 14.
89   *Argus*, 26 September 1879, 7.
90   Australian Medical Association, 'In the Beginning: Victoria', <https://ama.com.au/article/beginning-victoria>.

Glossary

Agunah	A wife deserted by her husband
Ashkenazi	Literally the Jews from Germany, but referring to Jews from central and eastern Europe
Ba'al Kore	The individual in synagogue who chants Torah from the scroll
Bar mitzvah	A ceremony for boys at the age of thirteen, at which time they are considered responsible for their actions
Beth Din	Jewish court of law, consisting of three rabbis
Brit / brit Milah	A circumcision
Chazan	The vocalist in the synagogue who leads the congregation in prayer
Cheder (plural *Chederim*)	Traditional Jewish school teaching Hebrew and religious subjects
Chuppah	A canopy under which a Jewish marriage ceremony is performed
Conversos	Those who converted to Catholicism during the Inquisition (or their descendants)
Crypto Jews	Those who converted to Catholicism, but secretly continued to practise Judaism
Dhimmi	A non-Muslim living in a Islamic state as a protected person
Eruv	The rabbinic provision that permits the alteration of certain Sabbath restrictions
Get	Formal document of divorce
Guersits	Convert
Halachah	Jewish law
Haskalah	The Jewish enlightenment, initiated in Germany

Kehillah	Community, semi-autonomous communal structure
Kest	Room and board provided to a newly married couple
Ketubah	Marriage contract
Kosher / Kashrut	Jewish dietary rules and regulations
Magen David	Star of David, regarded as the primary symbol of Judaism
Matzah	Unleavened bread eaten at Passover
Mellah	A walled Jewish quarter in a Moroccan city
Mikvah	Bath used for ritual immersion
Mishna	The first interpretation of the Jewish oral tradition, a collection of Jewish laws and ethics that forms the basis of the Talmud
Minhag	Custom or rite used for synagogue liturgy
Minyan	Quorum of ten adult males required for communal prayer (and women in reform congregations)
Mishibirach	A public prayer or blessing for an individual or group in need of healing. Traditionally a pledge of charity was made in response to this blessing.
Mishpacha	Extended family by blood or marriage
Mitzvah (plural *Mitzvot*)	Commandments by God, a good deed
Mohel	The person who performs circumcisions
Sefer Torah	Scrolls containing the five books of Moses
Sephardi	Literally Spanish, referring to Jews from Spain and Portugal
Shoah	Hebrew term for 'calamity', used to denote the catastrophic destruction of European Jewry by Nazi Germany.
Shochet	Ritual slaughter of meat, according to Jewish law
Shtetl	A small town in Central and Eastern Europe, with a large Jewish population.
Shul	Yiddish for synagogue
Sukkah	A temporary dwelling constructed during the festival of Sukkot
Talmud	The collection of ancient Jewish writing, commentary and laws
Talmud Torah	School for children of modest means, teaching elementary Hebrew and religious studies
Tikun Olam	Acts of kindness to repair the world
Tsedakah	Charity, one of the tenants of Judaism

Bibliography

Primary Sources

Australia

Australia, Birth Indexes 1788–1922
Australia, Marriage Indexes, 1788–1950
Australia, Death Indexes 1787–1985
Australia, Electoral Roll, 1903–1980

New South Wales

State Records Authority of New South Wales, 'New South Wales, Australia Historical
Electoral Rolls 1842–1864'.

Victoria

Victorian Electoral Roll 1856

Australian Jewish Historical Society

Lifecycle records, correspondence and minutes for the Adelaide Hebrew Congregation;
East Melbourne Hebrew Congregation; and St Kilda Hebrew Congregation.
Minute Books of the Melbourne Jewish Philanthropic Society
Minutes Books of the Hebrew Ladies Benevolent Society

Melbourne Hebrew Congregation

Lifecycle records, minutes and correspondence

Rates Books

City of Melbourne
Fitzroy City Council

Public Record Office Victoria

Colonial Secretaries' Files
Divorce Case Files
Index to Assisted Inward Passenger Lists to Victoria 1839–1871

Index to Unassisted Inward Passenger Lists to Victoria 1852–1923
Index to Wills, Probate and Administration Records 1841–2009

United Kingdom
Census for England, 1841–1911
England and Wales Births, 1837–1915
England and Wales Deaths, 1837–1915
England and Wales Marriages, 1837–1915
England and Wales, National Probate Calendar, 1858–1966

United States of America
United States Federal Census 1810–1910
United States Naturalization Records, 1840–1957

Databases and websites
Australian Medical Association, 'In the Beginning: Victoria', <https://ama.com.au/article/beginning-victoria>.
Berger, Solly, 'The Pre-History of the Great Synagogue, the Cape Town Hebrew Congregation, 1841–1905', <http://www.gardensshul.org/attachments/article/20/Early%20History%20by%20Solly%20Berger.pdf>.
Department of History, University College London, 'Legacies of British Slave-Ownership,' University College London', 2015, <https://www.ucl.ac.uk/lbs/search/>.
Founders and Survivors, 'Australian Life Courses in Historical Context 1803–1920', <http://www.foundersandsurvivors.org/>.
Jewish Gen, <http://www.jewishgen.org/>.
Jewish Women's Archives, 'Hebrew Sunday School, Rebecca Gratz, 1781–1869', <http://jwa.org/womenofvalor/gratz/hebrew-sunday-school>.
Lewis, Miles 'Melbourne Mansions', Miles Lewis, <http://www.mileslewis.net/melbourne-mansions.html>.
Linc Tasmania, <https://linctas.ent.sirsidynix.net.au/client/en_AU/names/>.
Museum Victoria, 'S. Schlank & Co., Adelaide, South Australia', <http://museumvictoria.com.au/collections/themes/2437/s-schlank-co-adelaide-south-australia>.
New Zealand Government, 'Birth, Death and Marriage Historical Records', <http://www.dia.govt.nz/Births-deaths-and-marriages>.
Old Bailey Online: The Proceedings of the Old Bailey, London's Central Criminal Court, 1674 to 1913, <https://www.oldbaileyonline.org/>.
Parliament of Victoria, Synagogue Scribes, Marriage Registers, <www. http://synagoguescribes.com>.
Tasmanian Archives, <https://linctas.ent.sirsidynix.net.au/client/en_AU/names/>.
Victorian Heritage Register, <https://www.parliament.vic.gov.au>.

Directories
Burr, J., *Port Phillip Separation Merchants' and Settlers' Almanac, Diary and Melbourne Directory*, 1844, Herald Office, Melbourne, 1845.
Butterfield, James, The Commercial, Squatters and Official Directory for 1854, James Blundell & Co, Melbourne, 1854.
Kerr, William, Kerr's Melbourne Almanac and Port Phillip Directory, 1841–1842, Kerr & Holmes, Melbourne, 1841.
Mouritz, J.J., Port Phillip Almanac and Directory for 1847, Herald Office, Melbourne, 1847.

Needham, John, *Melbourne Commercial, Professional and Legal Directory, 1856*, James J.
Blundell, Melbourne, c. 1855.
—— Melbourne, *Commercial, Professional and Legal Directory*, James Blundell & Co,
Melbourne, 1856.
Pierce, P W., Melbourne Commercial Directory including Collingwood and Richmond,
and Almanac for the Year 1853, James Shanley, Melbourne, 1853.
Raymond, James, New South Wales and Port Phillip General Post Office Directory for
1839, James Maclehose, Sydney, 1839.
Sands and McDougall Directories, Sands and McDougall, Melbourne, 1857–1910.
Squatters' directory, containing a list of all the occupants of Crown lands in the
intermediate and unsettled districts of Port Phillip, 1849, Edward Wilson, Melbourne,
1849.

Government Publications
Parliament of Victoria, 'Papers Presented to Both Houses of Parliament by Command of
His Excellency the Governor.', Part VI, Census of Victoria, Birthplace of the People,
Victorian Government Printer, Melbourne, 1857.
—— 'Presented to both Houses of Parliament by His Excellency's Command, Census for
Victoria 1861', John Ferres Victorian Government Printer, Melbourne, 1861.
—— 'Report of the Royal Commission appointment by his Excellency to Enquire into
and Report upon the operation of the system of Public Education together with
minutes of evidence and Appendices, Presented to both Houses of Parliament by his
Excellency on Command.' 1867
—— Parliamentary Debates, Legislative Council and Legislative Assembly, vol. 15, John
Ferres Government Printer, Melbourne, 1872
Victoria, Register-General's Office, Blue Books for the Colony of Victoria, John Ferres,
Government Printer, Melbourne, 1868.
—— Statistics for the Colony of Victoria (Blue Book), John Ferres, Government Printer,
Melbourne, 1869–1887.

Newspapers and Journals
Adelaide Observer
Advertiser
Age
Argus
Ashburton Guardian
Auckland Star
Australasian
Australian Israelite
Australian Leather Journal
Ballarat Star
Beacon
Brisbane Courier
Capricornian
Courier
Daily Standard
Geelong Advertiser
Geelong Advertiser and Squatters' Advocate
Gippsland Times
Goulburn Evening Penny Post

Hay Standard and Journal of Water Consumption
Hebrew Standard of Australasia
Illustrated Australian News for Home Readers
Jewish Chronicle
Jewish Chronicle and Hebrew Observer
Jewish Herald
Launceston Examiner
Leader
London Gazette
Mail
Maitland Mercury and Hunter River General Advertiser
Maitland Weekly Mercury
Melbourne Punch
Mount Alexander Mail
Newcastle Morning Herald and Miners Advocate
Otago Daily Times
Port Phillip Gazette
Port Phillip Patriot and Melbourne Advertiser
Prahran Telegraph
Richmond River Express and Casino Kyogle Advertiser
Riverina Times
Riverine Herald
Rockhampton Bulletin
Shepparton Advertiser
South Australian Advertiser
South Australian Register
South Bourke Standard
Southern Australian
South-Western News
Star
Sydney Gazette and New South Wales Advertiser
Sydney Monitor
Sydney Morning Herald
Table Talk
Telegraph, St Kilda, Prahran and South Yarra Guardian
The Times
Voice of Jacob
Wagga Wagga Advertiser
Wallaroo Times and Mining Journal
Wanganui Chronicle
West Australian
Wodonga and Towong Sentinel

Private Letters
Joan Flight, Correspondence, private collection
Levinson Family Correspondence, private collection
Steinfeld Family Correspondence, private collection
Isaac Gross Correspondence, private collection

Published Reports

Fitzroy City Council. 'Glass Terrace, 64–78 Gertrude Street, Fitzroy, Victoria, 3065, A Report on Its Architectural Significance and Historic Merit. Fitzroy', The Sub-Committee of the Fitzroy City Council, 1977.

Jacobs Lewis Vines Architects, Miles Lewis and Fitzroy Urban Planning Office, 'South Fitzroy Conservation Study. Fitzroy', Fitzroy City Council and the Historic Buildings Preservation Council, 1979.

Willingham, Allan, 'The Mansion Formally 'Clarence', the Residence of Lawrence and Clara Benjamin, 83 Queens Road St Kilda 3183', Assessment of Cultural Significance. Interprop Investments, 1998.

Unpublished Manuscripts and Theses

Ellis, A.S, 'The Cousins, Descendants of Solomon and Caroline Phillips', 1990.

Freeze, ChaRan Y., 'Making and Unmaking the Jewish Family, Marriage and Divorce in Imperial Russia 1850–1914', PhD thesis, Brandeis University, 1997.

Jacobs, Philip Acland, 'The Family Tree', n.d.

Kaye, Geoffrey, 'Alfred Kaye: A Study in Adaptation'. 1932–35, revised 1969.

McConville, Chris, 'Emigrant Irish and Suburban Catholics: Faith and Nation in Melbourne and Sydney 1851–1933', PhD thesis, University of Melbourne, 1984.

Nussbaum, Daniel, 'Social Justice and Social Policy in the Jewish Tradition: The Satisfaction of Basic Human Needs in Pozan in the 17th and 18th Centuries', PhD thesis, Brandeis University, 1977.

Raggatt, Howard, 'A Study of the Development of St. Kilda from Its Beginning till 1873', undergraduate thesis, University of Melbourne, 1978.

Segal, Gerald, 'Request for a Grant for the Erection of a Monument and Restoration of the Grave of Dr James Neild', 2015.

Solomon, Geulah, 'Minority Education in a Free Society: A Community History of Jewish Education in New South Wales and Victoria, 1788–1920', Phd thesis, Monash University, 1972.

Worrall, Airlie, 'Single Tax and Free Trade: Victoria, 1890–1900', Honours thesis, School of Historical and Philosophical Studies, University of Melbourne, 1975.

Books and Articles

Primary Sources

Booth, Charles, *Life and Labour of the People in London Vol. 4: The Trades of East London Connected with Poverty*, Augustus M. Kelley, New York, 1969.

—— *Life and Labour of the People in London, Third Series: Religious Influences, Vol. 2*, Macmillan, London, 1902.

Colquhoun, Patrick, *A treatise on the commerce and police of the River Thames: Containing an historical view of the trade of the Port of London, and suggesting means for preventing the depredations thereon, by a legislative system of river police: With an account of the functions of the various magistrates and corporations exercising jurisdiction on the river, and a general view of the penal and remedial statutes connected with the subject*, Printed for J. Mawman, London, 1800.

—— *A Treatise on the police and crimes of the metropolis: … Also an account of the courts of justice and prisons of London: And an inquiry into the causes of the increase of crime; the tendency of the debtor laws: And into the present state of the licensed victuallers' trade: with suggestions for the improvement of the protective instructions of the metropolis and the prevention of offences*, Longman, Rees, Orme, Brown and Green, London, 1829.

Hirsch, Max, *Democracy Versus Socialism, a Critical Examination of Socialism as a Remedy for Social Injustice and an Exposition of the Single Tax Doctrine*, Macmillan, New York, 1901.

—— *Protection in Victoria: An Inquiry into the Influence of Protection on the Social & Economic Condition of the People*, Echo, Melbourne, 1891.

Jacobs, Isaac, *Conservative Reform in Jewish Observance*, Alex McKinley & Co, Melbourne, 1910.

Jacobs, Joseph, *Studies in Jewish Statistics, Social Vital and Anthropometric*, D. Nutt, London, 1891.

Mayhew, Henry, *London Labour and the London Poor*, 4 vols, Dover Publications, New York, 1968.

Michaelis, Moritz, *Chapters from the Story of My Life*, Norman Brothers, Melbourne, 1899.

Russell, C., and H.S. Lewis, *The Jew in London: A Study of Racial Character and Present-Day Conditions*, T.Y. Crowell & Co., New York, 1901.

Secondary Sources

Aaron, Aaron, 'The Sephardi Presence in Australia', http://jewishhistoryaustralia.net/sephardim/Sephardi_Australia.pdf.

—— *The Sephardim of Australia and New Zealand*, Aaron Aaron, Australia, 1979.

Abramitzky Ran, Leah Platt Boustan and Katherine Eriksson, 'Europe's Tired, Poor, Huddled Masses: Self-Selection and Economic Outcomes in the Age of Mass Migration', *American Economic Review* 102, no. 5 (2012), 1832–56.

Abu-Lughod, Janet L., 'The Islamic City-Historic Myth, Islamic Essence, and Contemporary Relevance', *International Journal of Middle East Studies* 19, no. 2 (1987), 155–76.

Alderman, Geoffrey, *Modern British Jewry*, Oxford University Press, Oxford, 1992.

Anchel, Robert, 'The Early History of the Jewish Quarters in Paris', *Jewish Social Studies* 2, no. 1 (1940), 45–60.

Anderson, Benedict R. O'G., *Imagined Communities: Reflections on the Origin and Spread of Nationalism*, Verso, London, 1983.

Andrade, Jacob A. P. M., and Basil Oscar Parks, *A Record of the Jews in Jamaica from the English Conquest to the Present Times*, Jamaica Times Ltd., Kingston, 1941.

Appelbaum, Diana Muir, 'Jewish Identity and Egyptian Revival Architecture', *Journal of Jewish Identities* 5, no. 2 (2012), 1–25.

Aron, Joseph, and Judy Arndt, *The Enduring Remnant: The First 150 Years of the Melbourne Hebrew Congregation 1841–1991*, Melbourne University Press, Carlton, 1992.

August, Thomas G., 'Family Structure and Jewish Continuity in Jamaica since 1655', *American Jewish Archives* XLI no. 1 (1989), 27–42.

—— 'An Historical Profile of the Jewish Community of Jamaica', *Jewish Social Studies* 49, nos 3–4 (1987), 303–16.

—— 'Jewish Assimilation and the Plural Society in Jamaica', *Social and Economic Studies* 36, no. 2 (1987), 109–22.

Austin, Albert Gordon, *Australian Education, 1788–1900: Church, State, and Public Education in Colonial Australia*, Greenwood Press, Westport, 1976.

—— *Select Documents in Australian Education, 1788–1900*, Pitman Pacific Books. Carlton, 1972.

Baader, Benjamin Maria, *Gender, Judaism, and Bourgeois Culture in Germany, 1800–1870: The Modern Jewish Experience*, Indiana University Press, Bloomington, 2006.

Baile, David, 'Childhood, Marriage and the Family in the Eastern European Jewish Enlightenment', in Steven M. Cohen and Paula E. Hyman (eds), *The Jewish Family: Myths and Reality*, Holmes & Meier, New York, 1986.

Ballantyne, Tony, 'Putting the Nation in Its Place?: World History and C.A. Bayly's the Birth of the Modern World', in Ann Curthoys and Marilyn Lake (eds), *Connected Worlds: History in Transnational Perspective*, ANU Press, Canberra, 2006.

—— *Webs of Empire: Locating New Zealand's Colonial Past*, University of British Columbia Press, Vancouver, 2014.

Ballantyne, Tony, and Antoinette Burton, *Moving Subjects: Gender, Mobility and Intimacy in an Age of Global Empire*, University of Illinois Press, Urbana, 2009.

Bar-Itzhak, Haya, 'A Materialized Settlement and a Metaphysical Landscape in Legends of Origin of Polish Jews', in Julia Brauch, Anna Lipphardt and Alexander Nocke (eds), *Jewish Topographies: Visions of Space, Traditions of Place, Heritage, Culture and Identity* Ashgate Publishing, Aldershot, 2008.

Barcan, Alan, *A History of Australian Education*, Oxford University Press, Melbourne, 1980.

Barnavi, Eli, *A Historical Atlas of the Jewish People, from the Time of the Patriarchs to the Present*, trans. Miriam Eliav-Feldon, Hachette Litteratures, Paris, 2002.

Barrett, Bernard, *The Inner Suburbs: The Evolution of an Industrial Area*, Melbourne University Press, Carlton, 1971.

Barth, Gunther Paul, *Instant Cities: Urbanization and the Rise of San Francisco and Denver*, University of New Mexico Press, Albuquerque, 1988.

Baskin, Judith R., *Jewish Women in Historical Perspective*, Wayne State University Press, Detroit, 1998.

Bate, Weston, *Victorian Gold Rushes*, McPhee Gribble/Penguin, Fitzroy, 1988.

Belich, James, *Replenishing the Earth: The Settler Revolution and the Rise of the Anglo-World, 1783–1939*, Oxford University Press, Oxford, 2008.

Benjamin, Rodney, *A Serious Influx of Jews: A History of Jewish Welfare in Victoria*, Allen & Unwin, St Leonards, 1998.

Berkovitz, Jay R., 'Acculturation and Integration in Eighteenth-Century Metz', *Jewish History* 24, nos 3–4 (2010), 271–94.

Biale, Rachel, *Women and Jewish Law: An Exploration of Women's Issues in Halakhic Sources*, Schocken Books, New York, 1984.

Bickers, Robert A., *Settlers and Expatriates: Britons over the Seas,* The Oxford History of the British Empire Companion Series. Oxford University Press, Oxford, 2010.

Birch, Tony, 'Fitzroy', in *The Encyclopaedia of Melbourne*, edited by Andrew Brown-May and Shurlee Swain, Cambridge University Press, Melbourne, 2005.

Black, Eugene Charlton, *The Social Politics of Anglo-Jewry, 1880–1920*, B. Blackwell, Oxford, 1988.

Bonfil, Robert, 'Memories, Identities, Histories', *Jewish Quarterly Review* 100, no. 4 (Fall 2010), 744–57.

Brasch, Charles, and C.R Nicholson, *Hallensteins—the First Century 1873–1973*, Hallenstein Bros Ltd, Dunedin, 1973.

Brauch, Julia, Anna Lipphardt, and Alexander Nocke (eds), *Jewish Topographies: Visions of Space, Traditions of Place, Heritage, Culture, and Identity*, Ashgate Publishing, Aldershot, 2008.

Bridge, Carl, and Kent Fedorowich, 'Mapping the British World', *Journal of Imperial and Commonwealth History* 31, no. 2 (2010), 1–15.

Briggs, Asa, *Victorian Cities*, Penguin, Ringwood, 1971.

Brinkman, Tobias, '"German Jews?', Reassessing the History of Nineteenth-Century Jewish Immigrants in the United States', in Ava F. Kahn and Adam Mendelsohn (eds), *Transnational Traditions, New Perspectives on American Jewish History*, Wayne State University, Detroit, 2014.

Brown-May, Andrew, *The Itinerary of Our Days: The Historical Experience of the Street in Melbourne, 1837–1923*, Australian Scholarly Publishing, North Melbourne, 1993.

Brown, Callum G., 'The Mechanisms of Religious Growth in Urban Societies', in Hugh McLeod (ed.), *European Religion in the Age of the Great Cities 1830–1930*, Routledge, London, 1995.

Burchett, Winston H., *East Melbourne, 1837–1977: People, Places, Problems*, Craftsman Press, Hawthorn, 1978.

Burnard, Trevor, 'European Migration to Jamaica, 1655–1780', *The William and Mary Quarterly* 53, no. 4 (1996), 769–96.

Butlin, N. G., *Investment in Australian Economic Development, 1861–1900*, Dept. of Economic History, Research School of Social Sciences, Australian National University, Canberra, 1976.

Campbell, Enid, 'Oaths and Affirmations of Public Office', *Monash University Law Review* 25, no. 1 (1999), 132–65.

Cannadine, David, 'Victorian Cities: How Different?' *Social History* 2, no. 4 (1977), 457–82.

Cannon, Michael, 'Brodzky, Maurice (1847–1919)', in *Australian Dictionary of Biography*, National Centre of Biography, Australian National University, Canberra, 1979, <http://adb.anu.edu.au/biography/brodzky-maurice-5365>.

—— 'Fink, Benjamin Josman (1847–1909)', in *Australian Dictionary of Biography*, National Centre of Biography, Australian National University, Canberra, 1972, <http://adb.anu.edu.au/biography/fink-benjamin-josman-3516>.

—— *The Land Boomers, the Complete Illustrated History*, Heritage Publications, Melbourne, 1972.

Cannon, Michael, and Ian MacFarlane, *Historical Records of Victoria. Foundation Series*, Victoria. Public Record Office, Victorian Government Printing Office, Melbourne, 1984.

Carter, Paul, *Road to Botany Bay: An Exploration of Landscape and History*, University of Minnesota Press, Minneapolis, 2010.

Casey, Maie, Joan Lindsay, D.A. Casey, John R. Freeman, Tom D. Freeman and Allan R. Henderson, *Early Melbourne Architecture 1840 to 1888*, Oxford University Press, Melbourne, 1966.

Cesarani, David, *The Jewish Chronicle and Anglo-Jewry, 1841–1991*, Cambridge University Press, Cambridge, 1994.

—— *The Making of Modern Anglo-Jewry*, Basil Blackwell, Oxford, 1990.

—— *Port Jews: Jewish Communities in Cosmopolitan Maritime Trading Centres, 1550–1950*, Parkes-Wiener Series on Jewish Studies, Frank Cass, London, 2002.

Cesarani, David, and Mary Fulbrook, *Citizenship, Nationality, and Migration in Europe*, Routledge, London, 1996.

Chadwick, Owen, *The Secularization of the European Mind in the Nineteenth Century*, Cambridge University Press, Cambridge, 1977.

Cherlin, Andrew, and Carin Celebuski, 'Are Jewish Families Different? Some Evidence from the General Social Survey', *Journal of Marriage and Family* 45, no. 4 (1983), 903–10.

Cheyette, Bryan, 'Jewish Stereotyping and English Literature, 1875–1920', in Anthony Kushner and Kenneth Lunn (eds), *Traditions of Intolerance: Historical Perspectives on Fascism and Race Discourse in Britain*, Manchester University Press, Manchester, 1989.

Chilton, Lisa, 'A New Class of Women for the Colonies: The Imperial Colonist and the Construction of Empire', *Journal of Imperial and Commonwealth History* 31, no. 2 (2003), 36–56.

Clark, Michael, *Albion and Jerusalem: The Anglo-Jewish Community in the Post-Emancipation Era*, Oxford University Press, Oxford, 2009.

—— 'Jewish Identity in British Politics: The Case of the First Jewish MPs, 1858–87', *Jewish Social Studies* 13, no. 2 (2007), 93–126.

Cleall, Esme, Laura Ishiguro and Emily J. Mantelow, 'Imperial Relations: Histories of Family in the British Empire', *Journal of Colonialism and Colonial History* 14, no. 1 (2013), n.p.

Clifford, James, 'Diasporas', *Cultural Anthropology* 9, no. 3 (1994), 302–38.

Coben, Lawrence A., 'A Note on Shtetl Definitions and the Dating of the First Shtetl', *East European Jewish Affairs* 41, no. 3 (2011), 203–6.

Cohen, Gary B., 'Jews among Vienna's Educated Middle Class Elements at the Turn of the Nineteenth Century', in Yehudah Don and Victor Karady (eds), *A Social and Economic History of Central European Jewry*, Transaction Publishers, New Brunswick, 1990.

Cohen, Mark, 'Islam and the Jews: Myth, Counter-Myth, History ', in Shlomo Deshen and Walter P. Zenner (eds), *Jews among Muslims: Communities in the Precolonial Middle East*, Palgrave Macmillan, London, 1996.

Cohen, Robert, 'Early Caribbean Jewry: A Demographic Perspective', *Jewish Social Studies* 45, no. 2 (1983), 123–34.

Connell, John, 'The Jewish Ghetto in Nineteenth Century Leeds: A Case of Urban Involution', *Urban Anthropology* 10, no. 1 (1981), 1–26.

Constantine, Stephen, 'British Emigration to the Empire-Commonwealth since 1800: From Overseas Settlement to Diaspora?', *Journal of Imperial and Commonwealth History* 31, no. 2 (2003), 16–35.

Cooper, Davina, 'Talmudic Territory? Space, Law, and Modernist Discourse', *Journal of Law and Society* 23, no. 4 (1996), 529–48.

Cousineau, Jennifer, 'Rabbinic Urbanism in London: Rituals and the Material Culture of the Sabbath', *Jewish Social Studies* 11, no. 3 (2005), 36–57.

Crown, Alan David, 'The Jewish Press, Community and Jewish Publishing in Australia', in David Kessler and Alan David Crown (eds), *Noblesse Oblige: Essays in Honour of David Kessler Obe*, Vallentine Mitchell, London, 1998.

Darragh, Thomas A., and Robert N. Wuchatsch, *From Hamburg to Hobson's Bay, German Emigration to Port Phillip (Australia Felix) 1848–1851*, Wendish Heritage Society of Australia, Melbourne, 1999.

Dash Moore, Deborah, *At Home in America: Second Generation New York Jews*, Columbia University Press, New York, 1981.

Davenport-Hines, R.P.T., and Judy Slinn, *Glaxo: A History to 1962*, Cambridge University Press, Cambridge, 1992.

Davidoff, Leonore, and Catherine Hall, *Family Fortunes: Men and Women of the English Middle Class, 1780–1850*, Hutchinson, London, 1987.

Davison, Graeme, 'Australia: The First Suburban Nation?', *Journal of Urban History* 22, no. 1 (November, 1995), 40–74.

—— 'Colonial Origin of the Australian Home', in Patrick Troy (ed.), *A History of European Housing in Australia*, Cambridge University Press, Melbourne, 2000.

—— 'Gold-Rush Melbourne', in Ian McCalman, Alexander Cook and Andrew Reeves (eds), *Gold: Forgotten Histories and Lost Objects of Australia*, Cambridge University Press, Cambridge, 2001.

—— *The Rise and Fall of Marvellous Melbourne*, Melbourne University Press, Carlton, 1981.

de Serville, Paul, *Athenaeum Club: A New History of the Early Years 1868–1918*, Athenaeum Club, Melbourne, 2013.

Debenedetti-Stow, Sandra, 'The Etymology of "Ghetto": New Evidence from Rome', *Jewish History* 6, nos 1–2 (1992), 79–85.

Delevante, Marilyn, and Anthony Alberga, *The Island of One People: An Account of the History of the Jews of Jamaica*, Ian Randle, Kingston, 2006.

Demsky, Aaron, *Pleasant Are Their Names: Jewish Names in the Sephardi Diaspora*, University Press of Maryland, Bethesda, 2010.

Deshen, Shlomo A., and Walter P. Zenner, *Jews among Muslims: Communities in the Precolonial Middle East*, Palgrave Macmillan, London, 1996.

Dick, Malcolm, 'Birmingham Anglo-Jewry c. 1780 to c. 1880: Origins, Experiences and Representations', *Midland History* 36, no. 2 (2011), 195–214.

Driver, Felix, and Raphael Samuel, 'Rethinking the Idea of Place', *History Workshop Journal* 39, Spring (1995), v–vii.

Dubin, Lois, 'Introduction: Port Jews in the Atlantic World', *Jewish History* 20, no. 2 (2006), 117–127.

—— 'Jewish Women, Marriage Law and Emancipation: A Civil Divorce in Late-Eighteenth-Century Trieste', *Jewish Social Studies, New Series* 13, no. 2 (2007), 65–92.

—— *The Port Jews of Habsburg Trieste: Absolutist Politics and Enlightenment Culture,* Stanford Studies in Jewish History and Culture, Stanford University Press, Stanford, 1999.

Dwyer, Ruth, 'A Jewellery Manufactory in Melbourne: Rosenthal, Aronson and Company', *The Journal of the Public Record Office Victoria* 7 (2008), <https://prov.vic.gov.au/publications/provenance/provenance2008/jewellery-manufactory>.

Dwyer-Ryan, Meaghan, Susan L. Porter and Lisa Fagin Davis, *Becoming American Jews: Temple Israel of Boston,* Brandeis Series in American Jewish History, Culture, and Life, Brandeis University Press, Waltham, Mass., 2009.

Eisenbach, Artur, *The Emancipation of the Jews in Poland, 1780–1870,* Basil Blackwell in association with the Institute for Polish-Jewish Studies, Oxford, 1991.

Endelman, Todd M., 'Secularization and the Origins of Jewish Modernity-on the Impact of Urbanization and Social Transformation', *Simon-Dubnow Institute Year Book* VI (2007), 155–68.

—— 'German Jews in Victorian England: A Study in Drift and Defection', in Jonathan Frankel and Steven J. Zipperstein (eds), *Assimilation and Community, the Jews in Nineteenth Century Europe,* Cambridge University Press, Cambridge, 1992.

—— 'Communal Solidarity among the Jewish Elite of Victorian London', *Victorian Studies* 28, no. 3 (1985), 491–526.

—— *Comparing Jewish Societies,* University of Michigan Press, Ann Arbor, 1997.

—— 'English Jewish History', *Modern Judaism* 11, no. 1 (1991), 91–109.

—— *The Jews of Britain, 1656 to 2000,* University of California Press, Berkeley, 2002.

—— *The Jews of Georgian England, 1714–1830: Tradition and Change in a Liberal Society* University of Michigan Press, Michigan, 1999.

—— 'The Legitimization of the Diaspora Experience in Recent Jewish Historiography', *Modern Judaism* 11, no. 2 (1991), 195–209.

—— *Radical Assimilation in English Jewish History, 1656–1945, The Modern Jewish Experience,* Indiana University Press, Bloomington, 1990.

Etkes, Immanuel, 'Marriage and Torah Study among the 'Lomdim' in Lithuania in the Nineteenth Century', in David Kraemer (ed.), *The Jewish Family: Metaphor and Memory,* Oxford University Press, Oxford, 1989.

Etzioni, Amitai, 'The Ghetto—a Re-evaluation', *Social Forces* 37, no. 3 (1959), 255–62.

Faber, Eli, *Jews, Slaves and the Slave Trade: Setting the Record Straight,* New York University Press, New York, 1998.

Faerber, Ruth, 'Eliezer Levi Montefiore', *Australian Jewish Historical Society* 8, no. 4 (1977), 185–95.

Falk, Barbara, *No Other Home: An Anglo-Jewish Story 1833–1987,* Penguin, Ringwood, 1988.

Farrer, Keith, *To Feed a Nation: A History of Australian Food Science and Technology,* CSIRO Publishing, Melbourne, 2005.

Fedorowich, Kent, and Andrew S. Thompson, *Empire, Migration and Identity in the British World,* Studies in Imperialism, Manchester University Press, Manchester, 2013.

Feiner, Shmuel, *The Origins of Jewish Secularization in Eighteenth-Century Europe,* trans. Chaya Naor, University of Pennsylvania Press, Philadelphia, 2010.

—— 'The Pseudo-Enlightenment and the Question of Jewish Modernization', *Jewish Social Studies* 3, no. 1 (1996), 62–88.

Feldman, David, *Englishman and Jews, Social Relations and Political Culture 1840–1914,* Yale University Press, New Haven, 1994.

—— 'Jews and the British Empire c. 1900', *History Workshop Journal* 63, Spring (2007), 70–89.

Ferris, William R., Deborah Dash Moore, John Shelton Reed, Theodore Rosengarten and George J. Sanchez, 'Regionalism: The Significance of Place in American Jewish Life', *American Jewish History* 93, no. 2 (2007), 113–27.

Finestein, Israel, 'Jewish Emancipation in Victorian England: Self Imposed Limits on Assimilation', in Jonathan Frankel and Steven J. Zipperstein (eds), *Assimilation and Community: The Jews in Nineteenth Century Europe*, Cambridge University Press, Cambridge, 1992.

—— *Jewish Society in Victorian England: Collected Essays*, Vallentine Mitchell, London, 1993.

Finlay, Henry, *To Have but Not to Hold: A History of Attitudes to Marriage and Divorce in Australia 1858–1975,* Federation Press, Sydney, 2005.

Fishman, Robert, *Bourgeois Utopias: The Rise And Fall Of Suburbia*, Basic Books, New York, 1996.

Fishman, Talya, 'Forging Jewish Memory, Besamin Rosh and the Invention of Pre-emancipation Culture', in Carlebach Elisheva, John M. Efron and David N. Myers (eds), *Jewish History and Jewish Memory*, Brandeis University Press, Hanover, 1998.

Fletcher, Frank, 'The Victorian Jewish Community 1891–1901: Its Relationship with the Majority Gentile Society', *Australian Jewish Historical Society* 8, no. 5 (1978), 221–71.

Fonrobert, Charlotte Elisheva, and Vered Shemtov, 'Introduction: Jewish Conceptions and Practices of Space', *Jewish Social Studies* 11, no. 3 (2005), 1–8.

Fox, Len, *E. Phillips Fox and His Family*, Len Fox, Sydney, 1985.

Fredman, L.E., 'Nathaniel Levi', *Australian Dictionary of Biography*, in *Australian Dictionary of Biography*, National Centre of Biography, Australian National University, Canberra 1974, <http://abdn.edu.au/biography/levi-nathaniel-4015>.

Fredman, Lionel E., 'Some Jewish Politicians', *Australian Jewish Historical Society, Journal and Proceedings* IV, no. III (1955), 97–115.

Friedlander, Evelyn, and Helen Fry, *The Jews of Devon and Cornwall, Essays and Exhibition Catalogue*, The Hidden Legacy Foundation, Bristol, 2000.

Frost, Lionel, 'The Urban History Literature of Australia and New Zealand', *Journal of Urban History* 22, no. 1 (November 1995), 141–53.

Funkenstein, Amos, 'Collective Memory and Historical Consciousness', *History and Memory* 1 (1989), 5–26.

Gafni, Isaiah M., 'The Institution of Marriage in Rabbinic Times', in David Kraemer (ed.), *The Jewish Family: Metaphor and Memory*, Oxford University Press, Oxford, 1989.

Gantner, Eszter Brigitta, and Matyas Kovacs, 'Altering Alternatives, Mapping Jewish Subcultures in Budapest', in Julia Brauch, Anna Lipphardt and Alexander Nocke (eds), *Jewish Topographies. Visions of Space, Traditions of Place, Heritage, Culture and Identity*, Ashgate Publishing, Aldershot, 2008.

Gartner, Lloyd P., *History of the Jews in Modern Times*, Oxford University Press, Oxford 2001.

Gay, Ruth, 'Inventing the Shtetl', *American Scholar* 53, no. 3 (Summer 1984), 329.

Gentry, Kynan, *History, Heritage and Colonialism: Historical Consciousness, Britishness and Cultural Identity in New Zealand 1870–1940,* Studies in Imperialism, Manchester University Press, Manchester, 2015.

Getzler, Israel, 'Montefiore, Joseph Barrow (1803–1893)', *Australian Dictionary of Biography*, National Centre of Biography Canberra: Australian National University, 1967, <http://adb.anu.edu.au/biography/montefiore-joseph-barrow-2472>.

—— *Neither Toleration nor Favour; the Australian Chapter of Jewish Emancipation*, Melbourne University Press, Carlton, 1970.

Gillerman, Sharon, 'Rainer Liedtke, Jewish Welfare in Hamburg and Manchester, c. 1850–1914', *Journal of Modern History* 73, no. 3 (2001), 659–60.

Gilman, Abraham, *The Emancipation of the Jews in England 1830–1860*, Garland Publishing, New York, 1982.

Gilman, Sander L. and Milton Shain, *Jewries at the Frontier: Accommodation, Identity, Conflict*, University of Illinois Press, Urbana, 1999.

Glanz, Rudolf, 'Jewish Names in America', *Jewish Social Studies* 23, no. 3 (1961), 143–169.

Goad, Philip, and Julie Willis, *The Encyclopedia of Australian Architecture*, Cambridge University Press, Melbourne, 2012.

Golder, Hilary, and Ian Pike, *High and Responsible Office: A History of the NSW Magistracy*, Sydney University Press, Sydney, 1991.

Goldfarb, Michael, *Emancipation: How Liberating Europe's Jews from the Ghetto Led to Revolution and Renaissance*, Simon & Schuster, New York, 2009.

Goldman, L., 'The History of the Hobart Hebrew Congregation Part 1', in Peter Elias and Ann Elias (eds), *A Few from Afar: Jewish Lives in Tasmania from 1804*, Hobart Hebrew Congregation, Hobart, 2003.

Goldman, Lazarus M, *The Jews in Victoria in the Nineteenth Century*, self-published, Melbourne, 1954.

Goodwin, Craufurd D. W., *Economic Enquiry in Australia*, Duke University Commonwealth Studies Centre, Duke University Press, Durham, 1966.

Gothard, Jan, *Blue China: Single Female Migration to Colonial Australia*, Melbourne University Press, Carlton, 2001.

—— '"Pity the Poor Immigrant": Assisted Single Female Migration to Colonial Australia', in Eric Richards (ed.), *Poor Australian Immigrants in the Nineteenth Century: Visible Immigrants: Two*, Division of Historical Studies and Centre for Immigration and Multicultural Studies, Research School of Social Sciences, Australian National University, Canberra, 1991.

Gottreich, Emily, 'Historicizing the Concept of Arab Jews in the Maghrib', *Jewish Quarterly Review* 98, no. 4 (2008), 433–51.

—— 'On the Origins of the Mellah of Marrakesh', *International Journal of Middle East Studies* 35, no. 2 (2003), 287–305.

—— 'Rethinking the "Islamic City" from the Perspective of Jewish Space', *Jewish Social Studies* 11, no. 1 (2004), 118–46.

Graetz, Michael, 'From Corporate Community to Ethnic Religious Minority, 1750–1830', *Leo Baeck Institute Year Book* XXXVII (1992), 71–82.

Graff, Werner, Malcom J. Turnbull, and Eliot J. Baskin, *A Time to Keep, the Story of Temple Beth Israel 1930–2005*, Hybrid Publishers, Melbourne, 2005.

Green, Geoffrey, 'Anglo- Jewish Trading Connections with Officers and Seamen of the Royal Navy 1740–1820', *Jewish Historical Studies* 29 (1982–1986), 97–133.

—— *The Royal Navy and Anglo-Jewry, 1740–1820: Traders and Those who Served*, G.L. Green, London, 1989.

Green, Nancy L., 'The Comparative Method and Poststructural Structuralism—New Perspective for Migration Studies', *Journal of American Ethnic History* 13, no. 4 (Summer 1994), 3.

—— 'Immigrant Jews in Paris, London and New York: A Comparative Approach', *Judaism* 49, no. 3 (2000), 280–91.

Grimshaw, Patricia, and Graham Willett, 'Women's History and Family History: An Exploration of Colonial Family Structure', in Norma Grieve and Patricia Grimshaw (eds), *Australian Women: Feminist Perspectives*, Oxford University Press, Melbourne, 1981.

Groronwy-Roberts, Marian, *A Women of Vision, a Life of Marion Phillips, MP*, Bridge Books, England, 2000.

Halbwachs, Maurice, *The Collective Memory*, Harper & Row, New York, 1950.

Hall, Catherine, *Civilising Subjects: Metropole and Colony in the English Imagination, 1830–1867*, Polity, Cambridge, 2002.

Hamburger, Ernest, 'One Hundred Years of Emancipation', *Leo Baeck Institute Year Book* XIV (1969), 3–66.

Hamer, D.A., *New Towns in the New World: Images and Perceptions of the Nineteenth-Century Urban Frontier,* Columbia University Press, New York, 1990.

Hammer, Gael R., *Phillip Blashki, a Victorian Patriarch, Melbourne,* P. Blashki and Sons, Melbourne, 1986.

Hammerton, A. James, *Emigrant Gentlewomen: Genteel Poverty and Female Emigration 1830–1914,* ANU Press, Canberra, 1979.

Hareven, Tamara K., 'The Home and Family in Historical Perspective', *Social Research* 58, no. 1 (1991), 253–285.

Harland-Jacobs, Jessica, *Builders of Empire: Freemasons and British Imperialism, 1717–1927,* University of North Carolina Press, Chapel Hill, 2007.

Harper, Marjory, and Stephen Constantine, *Migration and Empire,* the Oxford History of the British Empire Companion Series, Oxford University Press, Oxford, 2010.

Hassam, Andrew, *Sailing to Australia: Shipboard Diaries by Nineteenth-Century British Emigrants,* Manchester University Press, Manchester, 1994.

Haut, Irwin H., *Divorce in Jewish Law and Life,* Studies in Jewish Jurisprudence, Sepher-Hermon Press, New York, 1983.

Heilman, Samuel C., 'Orthodox Jews, the City and the Suburbs', in Ezra Mendelsohn (ed.), *People of the City: Jews and the Urban Challenge,* Oxford University Press, Oxford, 1999.

Henriques, H.S.Q., *Jewish Marriage and English Law,* Jewish Historical Society of England, Oxford, 1909.

Herz, Manuel, '"Eruv" Urbanism, towards an Alternative 'Jewish Architecture' in Julia Brauch, Anna Lipphardt and Alexander Nocke (eds), *Jewish Topographies: Visions of Space, Traditions of Place, Heritage, Culture and Identity,* Ashgate Publishing Ltd., Aldershot, 2008.

Hitzer, Bettina, and Joachim Schlor, 'Introduction to God in the City: Religious Topographies in the Age of Urbanization', *Journal of Urban History* 37, no. 6 (2011), 819–27.

Hobsbawm, E. J., *Nations and Nationalism since 1780: Programme, Myth, Reality,* Wiles Lectures, Cambridge University Press, Cambridge, 1990.

—— *The Age of Empire 1875–1914,* Weidenfeld & Nicolson, London, 1987.

Hoffman, Christhard, 'From Heinrich Heine to Isidor Kracauer: The Frankfurt Ghetto in German-Jewish Historical Culture and Geography', *Jewish Culture and History* 10, nos 2–3 (2008), 45–64.

—— 'Constructing Jewish Modernity: Mendelssohn Jubilee Celebrations within German Jewry 1829–1929', in Rainer Liedtke and David Rechter (eds), *Towards Normality? Acculturation and Modern German Jewry,* Mohr Siebeck, Tübingen, 2003.

Hölscher, Lucian, 'Secularisation and urbanisation in the nineteenth century: An interpretive model', in Hugh McLeod (ed.), *European Religion in the Age of Great Cities, 1830–1930,* Routledge, London, 1995.

Hone, J Ann, 'Moritz Michaelis (1820–1902)' in *Australian Dictionary of Biography,* National Centre for Biography, Australian National University, 1974, <http://adb.anu.edu.au/biography/michaelis-moritz-4194>.

Hull, Isabel V., *Sexuality, State, and Civil Society in Germany, 1700–1815,* Cornell University Press, Ithaca, N.Y., 1996.

Humphreys, H. Morin, *Men of the Time in Australia: Victorian Series,* McCarron Bird & Co, Melbourne, 1882.

Hundert, Gershon David, 'Jewish Children and Childhood in Early Modern East Central Europe', in David Kraemer (ed.), *The Jewish Family: Metaphor and Memory,* Oxford University Press, Oxford, 1989.

—— *Jews in Poland-Lithuania in the Eighteenth Century,* University of California Press, Berkeley, 2004.

Hyman, Paula E., *The Emancipation of the Jews of Alsace, Acculturation and Tradition in the Nineteenth Century.* Yale University Press, New Haven, 1984.

—— 'Introduction: Perspectives on the Evolving Jewish Family', in Steven M Cohen and Paula E. Hyman (eds), *The Jewish Family, Myths and Reality,* Holmes & Meier, New York, 1986.

—— 'The Modern Jewish Family: Image and Reality', in *The Jewish Family: Metaphor and Memory,* edited by David Kraemer, Oxford University Press, Oxford, 1989.

Irvine, William, and David Wanliss, *Justices of the Peace,* Charles F. Maxwell, Melbourne, 1899.

Israel, Jonathan I., *European Jewry in the Age of Mercantilism, 1550–1750,* Clarendon Press, Oxford, 1985.

Jacob, Margaret C., *The Origins of Freemasonry: Facts & Fictions,* University of Pennsylvania Press, Philadelphia, 2006.

James, Margaret, 'Not Bread but a Stone: Women and Divorce in Colonial Victoria', in Patricia Grimshaw, Chris McConville and Ellen McEwen (eds), *Families in Colonial Australia,* George Allen & Unwin, Sydney, 1985.

Jamilly, Edward, 'Patrons, Clients, Designers and Developers: The Jewish Contribution to Secular Building in England', *Jewish Historical Studies* 38 (2003).

Jehle, Manfred, '"Relocations" in South Prussia and New East Prussia: Prussia's Demographic Policy Towards the Jews in Occupied Poland 1772–1806', *Leo Baeck Institute Year Book* 52 (2007), 23–47.

Jephcott, Sir Henry, *The First Fifty Years: An Account of the Early Life of Joseph Edward Nathan and the First Fifty Years of His Merchandise Business that Became Glaxo,* W.S. Cowell, Ipswich, 1969.

Joseph, Anthony P, 'Patterns of Migration 1850–1914', paper presented at the *International Academic Conference of the Jewish Historical Society of England and the Institute of Jewish Studies,* University College London, London, 1996.

Kadish, Sharman, 'Constructing Identity: Anglo Jewry and Synagogue Architecture', *Architectural History* 45 (2002), 386–408.

Kaganoff, Benzion C., *A Dictionary of Jewish Names and Their History,* Schocken Books, New York, 1977.

Kahn, Ava F, and Adam Mendelsohn, *Transnational Traditions, New Perspectives on American Jewish History,* Wayne State University, Detroit, 2014.

Kalmar, Ivan Davidson, 'Moorish Style: Orientalism, the Jews and Synagogue Architecture', *Jewish Social Studies* 7, no. 3 (2001), 68–100.

Kalra, Virinder S., Raminder Kaur, and John Hutnyk, *Diaspora & Hybridity, Theory, Culture & Society,* Sage Publications, London, 2005.

Kaplan, Debra, 'Woman and Worth: Female Access to Property in Early Modern Urban Communities', *Leo Baeck Institute Year Book* 55 (2010), 93–113.

Kaplan, Justin, and Anne Bernays, *The Language of Names,* Simon & Schuster, New York, 1997.

Kaplan, Marion A., 'For Love or Money: The Marriage Strategies of Jews in Imperial Germany', in Marion A. Kaplan (ed.), *The Marriage Bargain: Women and Dowries in European History,* Hanworth Press, Philadelphia, 1985.

—— 'Friendship on the Margins: Jewish Social Relations in Imperial Germany', *Central European History* 34, no. 4 (2001), 471–501.

—— *Jewish Daily Life in Germany, 1618–1945,* Oxford University Press, Oxford, 2005.

—— *The Making of the Jewish Middle Class: Women, Family, and Identity in Imperial Germany, Studies in Jewish History,* Oxford University Press, New York, 1991.

Kaplan, Zvi Jonathan, 'A Marital Dilemma: French Courts, Foreign Jews and the Secularization of Marriage', *Journal of Jewish Studies* 64, no. 2 (2013), 365–82.

—— 'The Thorny Area of Marriage: Rabbinic Efforts to Harmonize Jewish and French Law in Nineteenth-Century France', *Jewish Social Studies* 13, no. 3 (2007), 59–72.

Katburg, Nathaniel, 'Central European Jewry between East and West', in *A Social and Economic History of Central European Jewry,* edited by Yehudah Don and Victor Karady, Transaction Publishers, New Brunswick, 1990.

Katz, David S., *The Jews in the History of England, 1485–1850*, Oxford University Press, Oxford, 1994.

Katz, Jacob, *Exclusiveness and Tolerance: Studies in Jewish-Gentile Relations in Medieval and Modern Times,* Oxford University Press, Oxford, 1961.

—— 'German Culture and Jews', in Jehuda Reinharz and Walter Schatzberg (eds), *The Jewish Response to German Culture, from the Enlightenment to the Second World War*, Clark University by University Press of New England, Hanover, 1985.

—— *Jews and Freemasons in Europe 1723–1939*, Harvard University Press, Cambridge, 1970.

—— *Out of the Ghetto; the Social Background of Jewish Emancipation, 1770–1870*, Harvard University Press, Cambridge, 1973.

Kiddle, Margaret, *Men of Yesterday: A Social History of the Western District of Victoria, 1834–1890*, Melbourne University Press, Melbourne, 1962.

Kieval, Hillel J., 'Neighbours, Strangers, Readers: The Village and the City in the Jewish-Gentile Conflict at the Turn of the Nineteenth Century', *Jewish Studies Quarterly* 12 (2005), 69–75.

Kingston, Beverley, 'Phillips, Marion (1881–1932)', *Australian Dictionary of Biography*, National Centre of Biography, Australian National University, Canberra, 1988, <http,// adb.anu.edu.au/biography/phillips-marion-8036/text14011>.

—— 'Yours Very Truly, Marion Phillips', in Ann Curthoys, Susan Eade and Peter Spearritt (eds), *Women at Work,* Australian Society for the Study of Labour History, Canberra, 1975.

Kingston, Ralph, 'Mind over Matter? History and the Spatial Turn', *Cultural and Social History* 7, no 1 (2010).

Kippen, Rebecca, 'The Church, Conscience and the Colonies, Marriage with a Deceased Wife's Sister in Britain and British Australia', in A. Fauve-Chamoux and I. Bolovan (eds), *Families in Europe between the Nineteenth and Twenty-First Centuries: From the Traditional Model to Contemporary PACS*, Presa Universitară Clujeană, Cluj-Napoca, 2009.

Kiron, Arthur, 'An Atlantic Jewish Republic of Letters?', *Jewish History* 20, no. 2 (2006), 171–211.

Klooster, Wim, 'Communities of Port Jews and Their Contacts in the Dutch Atlantic World', *Jewish History* 20, no. 2 (2006), 129–45.

Kobrin, Francis E., 'Out-Migrations and Ethnic Communities', *International Migration Review* 17, no. 3 (1983), 425–444.

Kraemer, David, *The Jewish Family: Metaphor and Memory*, Oxford University Press, Oxford, 1989.

Kranidis, Rita S., *The Victorian Spinster and Colonial Emigration: Contested Subjects*, St. Martin's Press, New York, 1999.

Krinsky, Carol Herselle, *Synagogues of Europe: Architecture, History Meaning,* The Architectural History Foundation, New York, 1985.

Kvidera, Peter, 'Rewriting the Ghetto: Cultural Production in the Labor Narratives of Rose Schneiderman and Theresa Malkiel', *American Quarterly* 57, no. 4 (2005), 1131–54.

Lambert, David, and Alan Lester, *Colonial Lives across the British Empire: Imperial Careering in the Long Nineteenth Century*, Cambridge University Press, Cambridge, 2006.

Lavander, A.D., 'United States Ethnic Group in 1790: Given Names as Suggestions of Ethnic Identity', *Journal of American Ethnic History* 19, no. 1 (1989), 36–66.

Leavitt, Thad. W.H., *Australian Representative Men,* Wells & Leavitt, Melbourne, 1887.

Lees, Andrew, *Cities Perceived, Urban Society in European and American Thought, 1820–1940,* Manchester University Press, Manchester, 1985.

Leff, Lisa Moses, 'Jewish Solidarity in Nineteenth-Century France: The Evolution of a Concept', *Journal of Modern History* 74, no. 1 (2002), 33–61.

Lerner, L. Scott, 'The Narrating Architecture of Emancipation', *Jewish Social Studies* 6, no. 3 (2000), 1–30.

—— 'Narrating over the Ghetto of Rome', *Jewish Social Studies* 8, nos 2–3 (2002), 1–38.

Lester, Alan, *Imperial Networks: Creating Identities in Nineteenth Century South Africa and Britain,* Routledge, London, 2001.

Levene, Mark, 'Port Jewry of Salonika: Between Neo-Colonialism and Nation-State', in David Cesarani (ed.), *Port Jews: Jewish Communities in Cosmopolitan Maritime Trading Centres 1550–1950,* Frank Cass, London, 2002.

Levenson, Alan, 'The Posen Factor', *Shofar: An Interdisciplinary Journal of Jewish Studies* 17, no. 1 (1998), 72–80.

Levi, John S., *Rabbi Jacob Danglow: The Uncrowned Monarch of Australian Jews,* Melbourne University Press, Carlton, 1995.

—— *These Are the Names: Jewish Lives in Australia, 1788–1850,* Miegunyah Press, Melbourne University Publishing, Carlton, 2006.

Levi, John S., and G. F. J. Bergman, *Australian Genesis: Jewish Convicts and Settlers, 1788–1860,* Melbourne University Press, Carlton, 2002.

Levine, Philippa, *Gender and Empire,* the Oxford History of the British Empire Companion Series, Oxford University Press, Oxford, 2004.

Lewis, Miles, *Melbourne: The City's History and Development,* City of Melbourne, Melbourne, 1995.

—— 'Terrace Houses and Gothic Splendour: The Architecture', in Peter Yule (ed.), *Carlton, a History,* Carlton Residence Association, Carlton, 2004.

Lieberson, Stanley, and Eleanor O. Bell, 'Children's Names: An Empirical Study of Social Taste', *American Journal of Sociology* 98, no. 3 (1992), 511–554.

Liedtke, Rainer, *Jewish Welfare in Hamburg and Manchester, c. 1850–1914,* Oxford University Press, Oxford, 1998.

Liley, Keith '"One Immense Gold Field!" British Imaginings of the Australian Gold Rush 1851–1859', *Landscape Research* 27, no. 1 (2010), 67–80.

Lipis, Miriam, 'A Hybrid Place of Belonging, Constructing and Siting the Sukkah', in Julia Brauch, Anna Lipphardt and Alexander Nocke (eds), *Jewish Topographies: Visions of Space, Traditions of Place Heritage, Culture and Identity,* Ashgate Publishing, Aldershot, 2008.

Lipman, Vivian D., 'The Anglo-Jewish Community in Victorian Society', in Dov Noy and Issachar Ben- Ami (eds), *Studies in the Cultural Life of the Jews in England,* Magnes Press, Hebrew University, Jerusalem, 1975.

—— 'Jewish Settlement in the East End 1840–1940', in Aubrey Newman (ed.), *East End 1840–1940, Proceedings of the Conference Held on 22 October 1980 Jointly by the Jewish Historical Society of England and the Jewish East End Project of the Association of Jewish Youth,* Jewish Historical Society of England, London, 1981.

—— *Social History of the Jews in England 1850–1950,* Watts & Co., London, 1954.

—— 'The Structure of London Jewry in the Mid-Nineteenth Century', in H.J. Zimmels, J. Rabbinowitz and I Finestein (eds), *Essays Presented to Chief Rabbi Israel Brodie on the Occasion of His Seventieth Birthday,* Jews College Publications, London, 1967.

—— 'Trends in Anglo-Jewish Occupations', *Journal of Jewish Sociology* II, no. 2 (1960), 202–18.

Litwak, Eugene, 'Geographic Mobility and Extended Family Cohesion', *American Sociological Review* 25, no. 3 (1960), 385–94.

—— 'Occupational Mobility and Extended Family Cohesion', *American Sociological Review* 25, no. 1 (1960), 9–21.

Loeb, Laurence D., 'Dhimmi Status and Jewish Roles', in Shlomo Deshen and Walter P. Zenner (eds), *Jews among Muslims, Communities in the Precolonial Middle East*, Palgrave Macmillan, London, 1996.

Love, Harold, *James Edward Neild: Victorian Virtuoso*, Melbourne University Press, Carlton, 1989.

Lowenstein, Steven M., 'Ashkenazic Jewry and the European Marriage Pattern: A Preliminary Survey of Jewish Marriage Age', *Jewish History* 8, nos 1–2 (1994), 155–75.

—— 'The Beginning of Integration 1780–1870', in Marion A. Kaplan (ed.), *Jewish Daily Life in Germany 1618–1945*, Oxford University Press, Oxford, 2005.

—— 'Was Urbanization Harmful to Jewish Tradition and Identify in Germany?', in Ezra Mendelsohn (ed.), *People of the City: Jews and the Urban Challenge*, Oxford University Press, Oxford, 1999.

Lowndes, J., 'The Australian Magistracy: From Justices of the Peace to Judges and Beyond', *Australia Law Journal* 74, no. 9 (2000), 592–612.

Luft, Edward David, *The Naturalized Jews of the Grand Duchy of Posen in 1834 and 1835*, Scholars Press, Atlanta, 1987.

Magee, Gary B., and Andrew S. Thompson, '"Migrapounds": Remittance Flows within the British World, c. 1875–1913', in Kate Darian-Smith, Patricia Grimshaw and Stuart McIntyre (eds), *Britishness Abroad: Transnational Movements and Imperial Cultures*, Melbourne University Press, Melbourne, 2007.

Magee, Gary Bryan, and Andrew S. Thompson, *Empire and Globalisation: Networks of People, Goods and Capital in the British World, c. 1850–1914*, Cambridge University Press, Cambridge, 2010.

Magnus, Shulamit S., *Jewish Emancipation in a German City: Cologne, 1798–1871*, Stanford University Press, Stanford, 1997.

Mandelbaum, David G., 'Change and Continuity in Jewish Life', in Marshall Sklare (ed.), *The Jews Social Patterns of an American Group*, Free Press, Glencoe, 1960.

Mann, Barbara, 'Literary Mappings of the Jewish City: Other Languages, Other Terrains', *Prooftexts* 26, nos 1–2 (2006), 1–5.

—— *Space and Place in Jewish Studies*, Rutgers University Press, New Brunswick, 2012.

Marcus, Ivan G., *The Jewish Life Cycle: Rites of Passage from Biblical to Modern Times*, the Samuel & Althea Stroum Lectures in Jewish Studies, University of Washington Press, Seattle, 2004.

Markreich, Max, 'Notes on the Transformation of Place Names by European Jews', *Jewish Social Sciences* 23, no. 4 (1961), 265–84.

Massey, Doreen, 'Places and Their Pasts', *History Workshop Journal* 39 (1995), 182–92.

Massey, Doreen, and Pat Jess, *A Place in the World? Places, Cultures and Globalization*, Open University, Oxford, 1995.

Massey, Douglas, 'The Social and Economic Origins of Immigration', *Annals of the American Academy of Political and Social Science* 510 (1990), 60–72.

Maxwell-Stewart, Hamish, 'Land of Sorrow, Land of Honey; Aspects of the Life of Judah Solomon (c. 1777–1856).' in Peter Elias and Ann Elias (eds), *A Few from Afar: Jewish Lives in Tasmania from 1804*, Hobart Hebrew Congregation, Hobart, 2003.

McDonald, Peter F., *Marriage in Australia; Age at First Marriage and Proportions Marrying, 1860–1971*, Australian Family Formation Project Monograph, Dept. of Demography, Institute of Advanced Studies, Australian National University, Canberra, 1974.

McIntyre, Perry, *Free Passage: The Reunion of Irish Convicts and Their Families in Australia, 1788–1852*, the Irish Abroad, Irish Academic Press, Dublin, 2011.

McLean, Ian W., *Why Australia Prospered: The Shifting Sources of Economic Growth*, Princeton University Press, Princeton, 2013.

McLeod, Hugh, *European Religion in the Age of Great Cities, 1830–1930*, Routledge, London, 1995.
—— *Secularisation in Western Europe, 1848–1914*, St. Martin's Press, New York, 2000.
Mendelsohn, Adam 'Tongue Ties: The Emergence of the Anglophone Jewish Diaspora in the Mid-Nineteenth Century', *American Jewish History* 93, no. 2 (2007), 177–209.
Merrett, David, 'Paying for It All', in Patrick Troy (ed.), *A History of European Housing in Australia*, Cambridge University Press, Cambridge, 2000.
Merrill, Gordon, 'The Role of Sephardic Jews in the British Caribbean Area during the Seventeenth Century', *Caribbean Studies* 4, no. 3 (1964), 32–49.
Metzler, Tobias, 'Secularization and Pluralism: Urban Jewish Culture in Early Twentieth-Century Berlin', *Journal of Urban History* 37, no. 6 (November 2011), 871–96.
Meyer, Michael A., *Jewish Identity in the Modern World,* University of Washington Press, Seattle, 1990.
—— 'Normality and Assimilation', in *Towards Normality? Acculturation and Modern German Jewry*, edited by Rainer Liedtke and David Rechter, Mohr Siebeck, Tubingen, 2003.
Meyer, Michael A., Michael Brenner, Mordechai Breuer and Michael Graetz, *German-Jewish History in Modern Times*, Columbia University Press, New York, 1996.
Miles, Andrew, *Social Mobility in Nineteenth- and Early Twentieth-Century England*, St. Martin's Press, New York, 1999.
Miller, Michael L., and Scott Ury, *Cosmopolitanism, Nationalism and the Jews of East Central Europe*, Routledge, Oxford, 2015.
Miller, O. Alexander, 'Colonial Capital: Advances in Understanding Caribbean Migration Experiences', *Social and Economic Studies* 57, nos 3–4 (2008), 157–80.
Miller, Susan Gilson, 'The Mellah of Fez, Reflections on the Spatial Turn in Moroccan Jewish History', in Julia Brauch, Anna Lipphardt and Alexander Nocke (eds), *Jewish Topographies: Visions of Space, Traditions of Place Heritage, Culture and Identity*, Ashgate Publishing, Aldershot, 2008.
Miller, Susan Gilson, Attilio Petruccioli, and Mauro Bertagnin, 'Inscribing Minority Space in the Islamic City: The Jewish Quarter of Fez (1438–1912)', *Journal of the Society of Architectural Historians* 60, no. 3 (2001), 310–27.
Molho, Anthony, 'The Jewish Community of Salonika: The End of a Long History', *Diaspora: A Journal of Transnational Studies* 1, no. 1 (1991).
Monaco, C. S., 'Port Jews or a People of the Diaspora? A Critique of the Port Jew Concept', *Jewish Social Studies* 15, no. 2 (2009), 137–66.
Mosse, Werner E., *Jews in the German Economy: The German-Jewish Economic Elite 1820–1935*, Clarendon Press, Oxford, 1989.
—— 'Judaism, Jews and Capitalism Weber, Sombart and Beyond', *Leo Baeck Institute Year Book* 24, no. 1 (January 1979), 3–15.
Naimark-Goldberg, Natalie, 'Health, Leisure and Sociability at the Turn of the Nineteenth Century: Jewish Women and German Spas', *Leo Baeck Institute Year Book* 55 (2010), 63–91.
Nathan, Howard T., 'The Benefits of a Conviction', *Australian Jewish Historical Society* XIII, no. 1 (1995), 5–14.
—— 'Rosetta Joseph: The Bell, Her Husband and His Money', *Australian Jewish Historical Society* XVII, no. 1 (2003), 5–18.
Newman, David, 'Integration and Ethnic Spatial Concentration: The Changing Distribution of the Anglo-Jewish Community', *Transactions of the Institute of British Geographers* 10, no. 3 (1985), 360–76.
Nora, Pierre, 'Between Memory and History: Les Lieux de Memoire', *Representations 26*, Spring (1989), 7–24.

Parks, Richard, 'The Jewish Quarters of Interwar Paris and Tunis: Destruction, Creation, and French Urban Design', *Jewish Social Studies* 17, no. 1 (2010), 67–87.

Penslar, Derek Jonathan, *Shylock's Children: Economics and Jewish Identity in Modern Europe*, University of California Press, Berkeley, 2001.

Pfeffer, Jeremy I., *'From One End of the Earth to the Other': The London Bet Din, 1805–1855, and the Jewish Convicts Transported to Australia*, Sussex Academic Press, Brighton, 2008.

Pickus, Keith H., *Constructing Modern Identities: Jewish University Students in Germany, 1815–1914*, Wayne State University Press, Detroit, 1999.

Pollins, Harold, *Economic History of the Jews in England*, Fairleigh Dickinson University Press, Rutherford, 1982.

Praszałowicz, Dorota, 'Overseas Migration from Partitioned Poland: Poznania and Eastern Galicia as Case Studies', *Polish American Studies* 60, no. 2 (2003), 59–81.

Proudfoot, L. J. and Dianne Hall, *Imperial Spaces: Placing the Irish and Scots in Colonial Australia*, Studies in Imperialism, Manchester University Press, Manchester, 2011.

Pulzer, Peter, *Jews and the German State: The Political History of a Minority, 1848–1933*, Blackwell, Oxford, 1992.

Rand, Anne, 'Temple House and the Judah Solomon Family', in Peter Elias and Ann Elias (eds), *A Few from Afar: Jewish Lives in Tasmania from 1804*, Hobart Hebrew Congregation, Hobart, 2003.

Ranston, Jackie, *The Lindo Legacy*, Toucan Books, London, 2000.

Ravenstein, E.G., 'The Laws of Migration', *Journal of the Royal Statistical Society* 52, no. 2 (1889), 241–305.

Ravid, Benjamin, 'All Ghettos Were Jewish Quarters but not All Jewish Quarters Were Ghettos', *Jewish Culture and History* 10, nos 2–3 (2008), 5–24.

Raz-Krakotzkin, Amnon, 'Jewish Memory between Exile and History', *Jewish Quarterly Review* 97, no. 4 (2007), 530–43.

Reinharz, Jehuda, and Walter Schatzberg, *The Jewish Response to German Culture: From the Enlightenment to the Second World War*, Published for Clark University by University Press of New England, Hanover, 1985.

Richards, Eric, *Britannia's Children: Emigration from England, Scotland, Wales and Ireland since 1600,* Hambledon & London, London, 2004.

—— *Poor Australian Immigrants in the Nineteenth Century: Visible Immigrants: Two*, Division of Historical Studies and Centre for Immigration and Multicultural Studies, Research School of Social Sciences, Australian National University, Canberra, 1991.

Richarz, Monika, Stella P. Rosenfeld and Sidney Rosenfeld, *Jewish Life in Germany: Memoirs from Three Centuries*, Indiana University Press, Bloomington, 1991.

Roberts, Giselle, 'A Grand Vision: Henry Philip Harris and the History of Burlington Terrace', *Australian Jewish Historical Society Journal* XV, no. 1 (1999), 60–8.

Roitman, Jessica Vance, 'Sephardic Journeys: Travel, Place and Conception of Identity', *Jewish Culture and History* 11, nos 1–2 (2009), 209–28.

Rosenbaum, Fred, *Cosmopolitans: A Social and Cultural History of the Jews of the San Francisco Bay Area,* University of California Press, Berkeley, 2011.

—— *Jewish Voices of the California Gold Rush: A Documentary History, 1849–1880*, Wayne State University, Detroit, 2002.

Rosenthal, Newman H., *Formula for Survival: The Saga of the Ballarat Hebrew Congregation.* Hawthorn Press, Melbourne, 1979.

—— *Look Back with Pride: The St. Kilda Hebrew Congregation's First Century*, T. Nelson, Melbourne, 1971.

Roth, Cecil, *A History of the Jews in England*, Clarendon Press, Oxford, 1964.

—— 'The Rise of Provincial Jewry', *JCR-UK Jewish Communities and Records*: The Susser Archive, 1950, <http://www.jewishgen.org/jcr-uk/susser/provincialjewry/index.htm>.

Rubinstein, Hilary L., *The Jews in Australia: A Thematic History,* William Heinemann Australia, Port Melbourne, 1991.
—— *The Jews in Victoria 1835–1985,* George Allen & Unwin, Sydney, 1986.
Rubinstein, W. D., *A History of the Jews in the English-Speaking World: Great Britain,* Macmillan, Basingstoke, 1996.
—— *Jews in the Sixth Continent,* Allen & Unwin, Sydney, 1987.
Ruderman, David B., *Connecting the Covenants, Judaism and the Search for Christian Identity on Eighteenth Century England,* University of Pennsylvania Press, Philadelphia, 2007.
—— *Jewish Enlightenment in an English Key: Anglo-Jewry's Construction of Modern Jewish Thought,* Princeton University Press, Princeton, 2000.
Rürup, Reinhard, 'Jewish Emancipation and Bourgeois Society', *Leo Baeck Institute Year Book* XIV (1969), 67–91.
—— 'A Success Story and Its Limits: European Jewish Social History in the Nineteenth and Early Twentieth Centuries', *Jewish Social Studies* 11, no. 1 (2004), 3–15.
—— 'The Tortuous and Thorny Path to Legal Equality, "Jew Laws" and Emancipatory Legislation in Germany from the Late Eighteenth Century', *Leo Baeck Institute Year Book* 14 (1986), 3–33.
Rutland, Suzanne D., *Edge of the Diaspora; Two Centuries of Jewish Settlement in Australia,* Brandl & Schlesinger, Sydney, 1997.
Salbstein, M.C.N., *The Emancipation of the Jews in Britain: The Question of the Admission of the Jews to Parliament, 1828–1860,* The Littman Library of Jewish Civilization, Fairleigh Dickinson University Press, Rutherford, 1982.
Sariel, Eliezer, '"In the East Lie My Roots; My Branches in the West". The Distinctiveness of the Jews of Posen in the First Half of the Nineteenth Century', *Leo Baeck Institute Year Book* 58 (2013), 175–92.
Sarna, Jonathan D., 'The Jews in British America', in Paolo Bernardini and Norman Fiering (eds), *The Jews and the Expansion of Europe to the West 1450–1800,* 519–31, Berghahn Books, New York, 2001.
—— 'Port Jews in the Atlantic: Further Thoughts', *Jewish History* 20, no. 2 (2006), 213–19.
Scates, Bruce, *A New Australia: Citizenship, Radicalism and the First Republic,* Cambridge University Press, Cambridge, 1997.
Schiller, Nina Glick, 'Transnationality, Migrants and Cities: A Comparative Approach', in Anna Amelina, Devrimsel D. Nergiz, Thomas Faist and Nina Glick Schiller (eds), *Beyond Methodological Nationalism: Research Methodologies for Cross-Border Studies,* Routledge, London, 2012.
—— 'From Immigrant to Transmigrant: Theorizing Transnational Migration', *Anthropological Quarterly* 68, no. 1 (1995), 45–63.
Schlor, Joachim, 'Jews and the Big City, Explorations on an Urban State of Mind', in Julia Brauch, Anna Lipphardt and Alexander Nocke (eds), *Jewish Topographies: Visions of Space, Traditions of Place, Heritage, Cultrure and Identity,* Ashgate Publishing, Aldershot, 2008.
Schroeter, Daniel J., 'The Jewish Quarter and the Moroccan City', in Yedida K. Stillman and George K. Zucker (eds), *New Horizons in Sephardic Studies,* State University of New York Press, New York, 1993.
—— 'The Shifting Boundaries of Moroccan Jewish Identities', *Jewish Social Studies: History, Culture, Society* 15, no. 1 (2008), 145–64.
Schroeter, Daniel J., and Joseph Chetrit, 'Emancipation and Its Discontents: Jews at the Formative Period of Colonial Rule in Morocco', *Jewish Social Studies* 13, no. 1 (2006), 170–206.
Schwartz, Bill, '"Shivering in the Noonday Sun": The British World and the Dynamics of "Nativisation"', in Kate Darian-Smith, Patricia Grimshaw and Stuart McIntyre (eds), *Britishness Abroad: Transnational Movements and Imperial Cultures,* Melbourne University Press, Melbourne, 2007.

Sen, Arijit, and Lisa Silverman, *Making Place: Space and Embodiment in the City*, Indiana University Press, Bloomington, 2014.

Serle, Geoffrey, *The Golden Age: A History of the Colony of Victoria, 1851–1861*, Melbourne University Press, Melbourne, 1963.

—— *John Monash: A Biography*, Melbourne University Press in association with Monash University, Carlton, 1982.

Sharot, Stephen, 'Jewish Acculturation in Premodern Societies', in Shlomo Deshen and Walter P. Zenner (eds), *Jews among Muslims: Communities in the Precolonial Middle East*, Palgrave Macmillan, London, 1996.

Shokeid, Moshe, 'Jewish Existence in a Berber Environment', in Shlomo Deshen and Walter P. Zenner (eds), *Jews among Muslims: Communities in the Precolonial Middle East*, Palgrave Macmillan, London, 1996.

Silberberg, Sue, 'Middle-Class Mobility. Jewish Convicts in Australia', *History Australia*, 15, no. 2 (2018).

Silverman, Lisa, 'Jewish Memory: Jewish Geography', in Arijit Sen and Lisa Silverman (eds), *Making Place: Space and Embodiment in the City*, Indiana University Press, Bloomington, 2014.

Singer, Steven, 'The Anglo-Jewish Ministry in Early Victorian London', *Modern Judaism* 5, no. 3 (1985), 279–99.

—— 'Jewish Education in the Mid-Nineteenth Century: A Study of the Early Victorian London Community', *Jewish Quarterly Review* 77, nos 2–3 (1986), 163–78.

—— 'Jewish Religious Thought in Early Victorian London', *Association for Jewish Studies Review* 10, no. 2 (1985), 181–210.

Snyder, Holly, 'English Markets, Jewish Merchants and Atlantic Endeavors: Jews and the Making of British Transatlantic Commercial Culture 1650–1800', in Richard L. Kagan and Philip D. Morgan (eds), *Atlantic Diasporas, Jews, Conversos and Crypto-Jews in the Age of Mercantilism, 1500–1800*, Johns Hopkins University Press, Baltimore, 2009.

—— 'Rules, Rights and Redemption: The Negotiation of Jewish Status in British Atlantic Port Towns, 1740–1831', *Jewish History* 20, no. 2 (2006), 147–70.

Snyder, Saskia Coenen, *Building a Public Judaism: Synagogues and Jewish Identity in Nineteenth-Century Europe*, Harvard University Press, Cambridge, 2013.

—— 'A Narrative of Absence: Monumental Synagogue Architecture in Late Nineteenth-Century Amsterdam', *Jewish History* 25 (2010), 43–67.

Sokolova, Alla, 'House-Building Tradition of the Shtetl in Memorials and Memories (Based on Materials of Field Studies in Podolia', *East European Jewish Affairs* 41, no. 3 (2011), 111–35.

Solomon, David F., 'From Convict to Colonist—Joseph Solomon of Evandale (c. 1780–1851)', in Peter Elias and Ann Elias (eds), *A Few from Afar: Jewish Lives in Tasmania from 1804*, Hobart Hebrew Congregation, Hobart, 2003.

Solomon, Geulah, 'Benjamin, Sir Benjamin (1834–1905)', *Australian Dictionary of Biography* (1969), <http://adb.anu.edu.au/biography/benjamin-sir-benjamin-2972>.

Sorkin, David, 'The Port Jew: Notes Towards a Social Type', *Journal of Jewish Studies* 1, no. 1 (1999), 87–97.

Sorkin, David Jan, *The Transformation of German Jewry, 1780–1840*, Oxford, Oxford University Press, 1987.

Stein, Sarah Abrevaya, *Plumes: Ostrich Feathers, Jews, and a Lost World of Global Commerce*, Yale University Press, New Haven, 2008.

Steinhoff Anthony, 'Nineteenth-Century Urbanisation as Sacred Process: Insights from German Strasbourg', *Journal of Urban History* 37, no. 6 (2011), 828–41.

Stone, Lawrence, *Broken Lives: Separation and Divorce in England, 1660–1857*, Oxford University Press, Oxford, 1993.

—— 'Family History in the 1980s, Past Achievement and Future Trends', *Journal of Interdisciplinary History* 12, no. 1 (1981), 51–87.

—— *The Family, Sex and Marriage in England, 1500–1800*, Harper & Row, New York, 1977.

—— *Road to Divorce: England 1530–1987*, Oxford University Press, Oxford, 1990.

Susser, Bernard, *The Jews of South-West England: The Rise and Decline of Their Medieval and Modern Communities*, University of Exeter Press, Exeter, 1993.

—— 'Social Acclimatisation of Jews in 18th and 19th Century Devon', *Exeter Papers in Economic History* 3, no. Industry and Society in the South West (1970), <http://www.jewishgen.org/jcr-uk/susser/acclimatisation.htm>.

Sutcliffe, Adam, 'Jewish History in the Age of Atlanticism', in Richard L. Kagan and Philip D. Morgan (eds), *Atlantic Diaspora's, Jews, Conversos and Crypto-Jews in the Age of Mercantilism, 1500–1800*, Johns Hopkins University Press, Baltimore, 2009.

—— 'The Origins of Jewish Secularization in 18th Century Europe', *Journal of Modern Jewish Studies* 10, no. 2 (2011), 307–10.

Thompson, Andrew, *The Empire Strikes Back? The Impact of Imperialism on Britain from the Mid-Nineteenth Century*, Pearson Longman, Harlow, 2005.

Tilly, Louise A., and Joan W. Scott, *Women, Work, and Family*, Holt, Rinehart & Winston, New York, 1978.

Upton, Dell, 'The Art and Mystery of Historical Archaeology', in Anne E. Yentsch and Mary Carolyn Beaudry (eds), *The Art and Mystery of Historical Archaeology: Essays in Honor of James Deetz*, CRC Press, Boca Raton, 1992.

Valins, Oliver, 'Institutionalised Religion: Sacred Texts and Jewish Spatial Practice', *Geoforum* 31, no. 4 (2000), 575–86.

Vaughan, Laura, and Alan Penn, 'Jewish Immigrant Settlement Patterns in Manchester and Leeds 1881', *Urban Studies* 43, no. 3 (2006), 653–71.

Vincent, Peter, and Barney Warf, 'Eruvim: Talmudic Places in a Postmodern World', *Transactions of the Institute of British Geographers* 27, no. 1 (2002), 30–51.

Watkins, Susan Cotts, and Andrew S. London, 'Personal Names an Cultural Change: A Study of the Naming Patterns of Italians and Jews in the United States in 1910', *Social Science History* 18, no. 2 (1994), 169–209.

Weber, Thomas A., 'The Origins of the Victorian Magistracy', *Australian New Zealand Journal of Criminology* 13, no. 2 (1980), 142–150.

Wegge, Simone A., 'Chain Migration and Information Networks: Evidence from Nineteenth Century Hesse-Cassel', *Journal of Economic History* 58, no. 4 (1998), 957–86.

Weinberg, David, 'Jews and the Urban Experience', *Judaism: A Quarterly Journal of Jewish Life and Thought* 49, no. 3 (2000), 278–9.

Weinryb, Bernard D., 'Jewish Immigration and Accommodation to America', in Marshall Sklare (ed.), *The Jews, Social Patterns of an American Group*, Free Press, Glencoe, 1960.

Weissbach, Lee Shai, *Jewish Life in Small-Town America: A History*, Yale University Press, New Haven, 2005.

Wigoder, Geoffrey, *The Story of the Synagogue: A Diaspora Museum Book*, Weidenfeld & Nicolson, London, 1986.

Williams, Bill, '"East and West": Class and Community in Manchester Jewry 1850–1914', in David Cesarani (ed.), *The Making of Modern Anglo-Jewry*, Basil Blackwell, Oxford, 1990.

—— *Jewish Manchester: An Illustrated History*, Breedon Books, Derby, 2008.

—— *The Making of Manchester Jewry, 1740–1875*, Manchester University Press, Manchester, 1976.

Wirth, Louis, 'The Ghetto', *American Journal of Sociology* 33, no. 1 (1927), 57–71.

Wirth, Louis and Reiss, Albert (ed.), *Louis Wirth on Cities and Social Life; Selected Papers,* University of Chicago Press, Chicago, 1964.

Woollacott, Angela, *Gender and Empire,* Palgrave, New York, 2006.

Wrigley, E.A., *English Population History from Family Reconstitution, 1580–1837,* Cambridge Studies in Population, Economy, and Society in Past Time, Cambridge University Press, Cambridge, 1997.

Wrigley, E.A., and R.S. Schofield, *The Population History of England, 1541–1871, A Reconstruction,* Edward Arnold for the Cambridge Group for the History of Population and Social Structure, London, 1981.

Yerushalmi, Yosef Hayim, 'Exile and Expulsion in Jewish History', in Benjamin R. Gampel (ed.), *Crisis and Creativity in the Sephardic World 1391–1648,* Columbia University Press, New York, 1997.

—— *Zakhor, Jewish History and Jewish Memory, The Samuel and Althea Stroum Lectures in Jewish Studies,* University of Washington Press, Seattle 1982.

Yogev, Gedalia, *Diamonds and Coral: Anglo-Dutch Jews and Eighteenth-Century Trade,* Leicester University Press, New York, 1978.

Zafrani, Haim, 'Mallāḥ', in *Encyclopedia of Islam,* 2nd edn, Brill Online, 2012, <https://referenceworks.brillonline.com/entries/encyclopaedia-of-islam-2/mallah-SIM_4881>.

Zenner, Walter P., 'Syrian Jews and Their Non-Jewish Neighbors', in Shlomo Deshen and Walter P. Zenner (eds), *Jews among Muslims: Communities in the Precolonial Middle East,* Palgrave Macmillan, London, 1996.

Zinger, Nimrod, 'Away from Home: Travelling and Leisure Activities among German Jews in the Seventeenth and Eighteen Centuries', *Leo Baeck Institute Year Book* 56 (2011), 53–78.

Zipperstein, Steven J., 'Jewish Historiography and the Modern City: Recent Writing on European Jewry', *Jewish History* 2, no. 1 (1987), 73–88.

Index

properties 148
Henry, Louis 200–1
Henry Marks & Co. 134
Herald and Weekly Times group 161, 162
Herman, Isaac 118
Herman, Marks 154
Herman, Rabbi Samuel 55
Herschell, Chief Rabbi Solomon 51
Heynemann, Herman 94
Hirsch, Max *191*, 192, 193–4
  Max Hirsch Commemoration Essay
    prize 194
  parliamentarian 192, 194
  Protection in Victoria (1891) 193
  taxation reform 193–4
Hoddle, Robert 141
Holland 13, 16, 24, 25, 90, 94
Holocaust xi, 4, 5, 20
Horwitz, Anna 100
Horwitz, Henry 148
Horwitz, Louis 173
Howell, Elizabeth 42, 98, 156
Howell, Hannah 41
Hyman, Ludwig 80, 90, 100
Hyman, Paula 39, 77

identity x, xi, xii, 3, 4, 5, 6, 13, 37–74, 81,
  94, 139, 167
  Ashkenazi *see* Ashkenazi communities
  communal structure 40–52
  conversion *see* conversion
  diaspora xi, xii, 2, 9, 10, 24, 81, 91, 108,
    109, 121, 201
  European perspective 38–40
  family *see* family identity
  kosher food *see* *kosher* food
  language *see* language
  marriage *see* marriage
  personal/family names 59–62
  philanthropy *see* philanthropy
  press *see* press (Jewish)
  public manifestation 62–4
  Sabbath *see* Sabbath
  Sephardi *see* Sephardi communities
  urbanism *see* urbanism/urbanisation
  wills 58–9
  Yiddish 6, 7, 13, 14, 22, 108
Iffla, Solomon 27–8, *28*, 72, 116, 181, 186,
  200
Illustrated Australian News for Home Readers
  70, 71, 183

Inter-Colonial Exhibition (1875) 144
international business 126–32
  Asher, Edward 132
  Benjamin, Leopold Emanuel 132
  Hallenstein family 108, 129–30
  Joseph, Jacob 128–9
  Joseph, Moses 127–8, 131
  Marks, Alexander 197, 198
  Marks, Gabriel Jacob *see* Marks, Gabriel
    Jacob
  Marks, Henry *see* Marks, Henry
  Montefiore family 24
  Nathan family 126–8, 129
  Tallerman brothers 131
investors ix, 141, 143, 149, 161, 162–5
  Benjamin, David *see* Benjamin, David
  Benjamin, Lawrence *see* Benjamin,
    Lawrence
  Benjamin, Moses *see* Benjamin, Moses
  Benjamin, Samuel 143, 144
  Benjamin, Solomon *see* Benjamin,
    Solomon
  Henriques family 115, 116, 148
  Isaacs, Barnett *see* Isaacs, Barnett
  Marks, Bernard 163
  Montefiore, Joseph Barrow *see*
    Montefiore, Joseph Barrow
  Moses, Elias 143, 144
  Moss, Mark 153
  Moss, Morton *See* Moss, Morton
  see also developers; financiers
Isaac Hallenstein & Co 129–30
Isaacs, Abraham Benjamin 62
Isaacs, Barnett 116, 117, 123
  Melbourne, development of 147, 148,
    149, 153
Isaacs, Benjamin 62
Isaacs, Caroline 116–17
Isaacs, Clara 116
Isaacs, Jacob Andrade 116
Isaacs, Joseph 163
Isaacs, Julia 156
Isaacs, Rev. D.M. 123
Isaacs, Sir Isaac ix
Isaacs, Solomon 142
Isaacs, Woolf Barnett 116

Jacob Montefiore & Co. 144
Jacob Joseph & Co 129
Jacobs, Augusta 118
Jacobs, Elias Rypinski 86, 117–18